Acclaim for Terry Temp...

"Truly astounding. . . . [Williams] has somehow managed to turn her encounter with the Bosch masterpiece in Spain into an intense and profound meditation on faith and belief."
—*Seattle Post-Intelligencer*

"Brilliantly constructed and deeply moving, the writing catapults us out of the static role as reader into a direct experience of the revelations of a trembling open eye. *Leap* awakens a fresh way of seeing our lives, art, religion, and nature in the present." —*Parabola*

"Williams has crafted something special . . . a search for the entwined roots of faith, wisdom and creativity that are wrought in the landscape of the imagination." —*The Denver Post*

"In a language that is deeply lyrical and critically intelligent. . . . *Leap* is a remarkable and wondrous book written by a writer at the height of her considerable power."
—*The Rain Taxi Review of Books*

"*Leap* is an intimate and revealing story. It solidifies Williams' position at the forefront of writers dedicated to passionate exploration of the intersection of landscape and community."
—*The Seattle Times*

"Turns an ardent study of *The Garden of Earthly Delights* . . . into a meditation on her Mormon heritage and an arresting and creative inquiry into our relationship with nature, the divide between religion and spirituality, and the significance of art and wilderness." —*Booklist* Editors Choice, 2000

"*Leap* is a devotional and a chronicle, an optics for the mind and spirit." —*The Bloomsbury Review*

TERRY TEMPEST WILLIAMS

LEAP

Terry Tempest Williams is the author of *Refuge, An Unspoken Hunger, Desert Quartet,* and *Red.* The recipient of a Lannan Literary Fellowship and a Guggenheim Fellowship, she lives with her husband, Brooke Williams, in the redrock desert of southern Utah.

LEAP

TERRY TEMPEST WILLIAMS

VINTAGE BOOKS

A Division of Random House, Inc.

New York

FIRST VINTAGE BOOKS EDITION, SEPTEMBER 2001

Portions of this work appeared, in different form, in *The Nation, Western Humanities
Review,* and *Parabola,* and in *Waste Land: Meditations on a Ravaged Landscape* by
David T. Hanson et al. (New York: Aperture, 1997).

The Garden of Delights by Hieronymus Bosch, which follows the last page of this book,
is reproduced by kind permission of the Prado Museum in Madrid. © Museo Nacional
del Prado, Madrid. All rights reserved.

Permissions acknowledgments appear on page 339.

The Library of Congress has cataloged the Pantheon edition as follows:
Williams, Terry Tempest.
Leap / Terry Tempest Williams.
p. cm.
Includes bibliographical references (p.).
ISBN 0-679-43292-2
1. Williams, Terry Tempest—Religion.   2. Spiritual life—Church of Jesus Christ of
Latter-Day Saints.   3. Bosch, Hieronymus, d. 1516. Garden of delights.   4. Bosch,
Hieronymus, d. 1516—Criticism and interpretation.   I. Title.
BX8695.W547 A3 2000
289.3'092—dc21
[B]   99-057914

Vintage ISBN: 0-679-75257-9

Author photograph © Arturo Patten

www.vintagebooks.com

Printed in the United States of America
10 9 8 7 6 5 4 3 2 1

For the men in my family:

John Henry Tempest III

Stephen Dixon Tempest

Daniel Dixon Tempest

William Henry Tempest

and, especially,

Brooke Williams

mi guía y amor para siempre

"Otro día veremos la resurrección de las mariposas disecadas."

We must follow the vein of our blood.

—Federico García Lorca, *Blood Wedding*

CONTENTS

I

PARADISE

1

II

HELL

43

III

EARTHLY DELIGHTS

127

IV

RESTORATION

235

Contents

NOTES

267

BIBLIOGRAPHY

317

ACKNOWLEDGMENTS

331

PERMISSIONS

339

Hieronymus Bosch's Garden of Delights
*appears on the gatefold following the
last page of this book.*

I

PARADISE

The new can bear fruit only when it grows
from the seeds implanted in tradition.

—Paul Tillich, *The Dogma of the Trinity*

I once lived near the shores of Great Salt Lake with no outlet to the sea.

I once lived in a fault-block basin where mountains made of granite surrounded me. These mountains in time were hollowed to house the genealogy of my people, Mormons. Our names, the dates of our births and deaths, are safe. We have records hidden in stone.

I once lived in a landscape where my ancestors sacrificed everything in the name of belief and they passed their belief on to me, a belief that we can be the creators of our own worlds.

I once lived in the City of Latter-day Saints.

I have moved.

I have moved because of a painting.

Over the course of seven years, I have been traveling in the landscape of Hieronymus Bosch. A secret I did not tell for fear of seeming mad. Let these pages be my interrogation of faith. My roots have been pleached with the wings of a medieval triptych, my soul intertwined with an artist's vision.

This painting lives in Spain. It resides in the Prado Museum. The Prado Museum is found in the heart of Old Madrid. I will tell you the name of the painting I love. Its name is *El jardín de las delicias.*

The doors to the triptych are closed. Now it opens like a great medieval butterfly flapping its wings through the centuries.

Open and close. Open and close. Open. Hieronymus Bosch has painted, as wings, Paradise and Hell. The body is a portrait of Earthly Delights. The wings close again. Open, now slowly, with each viewer's breath the butterfly quivers, Heaven and Hell quiver, the wings are wet and fragile, only the body remains stable. The legs hidden, six. The antennae, two. The eyes, infinite. The artist's brush with life, mysterious. Close the triptych. The outside colors are drab. Black, grey, olive blue. The organism is not dead. Hear its heart beating. After five hundred years, the heart is still beating inside the triptych. The wings open.

I step back.

Red. Blue. Yellow. Green. Black. Pink. Orange. White. Gold.

Paradise.   Hell.   Earthly Delights.

As a child, I grew up with Hieronymus Bosch hanging over my head. My grandmother had thumbtacked the wings of Paradise and Hell to the bulletin board above the bed where I slept. The prints were, in fact, part of the Metropolitan Museum of Art's series of discussions designed for home education. The Garden of Eden to the left with Christ taking Eve's pulse as Adam looks on—opposite—Hell, the bone-white face of a man looking over the shoulder of his eggshell body as the world burns: these were the images that framed the "oughts and shoulds" and "if you don'ts" of my religious upbringing.

Whenever my siblings and I stayed overnight, we fell asleep in "the grandchildren's room" beneath Truth and Evil.

Standing before *El jardín de las delicias* in the Prado Museum in Spain, now as a woman, I see the complete triptych for the first time. I am stunned. The center panel. The Garden of Earthly Delights. So little is hidden in the center panel, why was it hidden from me?

The body.

The body of the triptych.

My body.

The bodies of the center panel, this panel of play and discovery, of joyful curiosities cavorting with Eros, is not only a surprise to me, but a great mystery.

I stare at the painting. My eyes do not blink. They focus on the blue pool of bathers standing thigh-high in the middle of the triptych.

Bareback riders circle the black and white women bathing in the water, the black and white women who are balancing black and white birds on top of their heads. Cherries, too. Faster and faster, the bareback riders gallop their horses and goats and griffins; bareback riders, naked men, riding bulls, bears, lions, camels, deer, and pigs, faster and faster, circling the women.

The triptych begins to blur. My eyes begin to blur. I resist. Focus. I rein my eyes in from the pull of the bodies, the body of the triptych, the bodies bare, bareback on animals, circling, circling, circling them, circling me, black and white bodies, my body stands stoically inside the Prado determined to resist the galloping of my blood.

I feel faint. I turn from the painting and see a wooden chair shaped like a crescent leaning against the wall. The wall is white. I sit down, stare at the floor, the granite floor, and get my bearings.

I begin counting cherries in Bosch's Garden. I lose track, they are in such abundance. I stop at sixty. Cherries are flying in the air, dangling from poles, being passed from one person to the next, dropped into the mouths of lovers by birds, worn on women's heads as hats, and balanced on the feet as balls.

In Utah, my home, cherries are a love crop. They are also our state fruit. They grow in well-tended orchards along the Wasatch Front. Cherry picking was a large part of our childhood. Our parents, aunts, and uncles would load up their station wagons with kids and drop us off in one of the orchards alongside Great Salt Lake with empty buckets in hand. Sometimes we were paid by the pail or given bags to take home for our families. Once we were up in the trees, out of view, we could eat as many as we wanted.

One day, my great-uncle was standing on a ladder picking cherries with my cousin and me. We were perched on sturdy branches above him, ten-year-old girls unafraid of heights.

"What principle of the Gospel of Jesus Christ means the most to you?" he asked, filling his bucket.

Mormon children are used to these kinds of questions practiced on them by their elders, who consider this part of their religious training.

"Obedience," my cousin replied, pulling a cherry off its stem.

"Free agency," I answered, eating one.

It is early morning on my way to the Prado. Pink camellia petals cover the path inside the Real Jardín Botánico adjacent to the museum. I love coming here first before watching the painting. Flocks of white butterflies appear to have lit on bare branches. Up close, I recognize them as magnolia trees in bloom.

It is difficult not to touch everything. Blue hyacinths line the walks. Daffodils and narcissus tower above them. Red and yellow striated tulips are now cups holding last night's rain.

The gardener's hand is evident. There is an overall narrative to be followed, nothing is random. Each hedgerow, each bed now flowering was an idea before it took root in the land. The leaves of each plant express themselves rhythmically. Iambic pentameter. Blank verse. A sonnet. The arrangement of leaves can be read as poetry.

The miniature rock garden stops me. Sage grows next to verbena. I bend down and rub its blue-grey leaves between my fingers and smell the Great Basin of home.

Paradise.

The Tree of Life stands behind Adam. Vines of raspberries wrap around its trunk. Christ, who appears to be staring outside Eden, is dressed in a pink robe. He holds Eve's wrist. Eve kneels. Adam sits. Neither is clothed.

Focus on Eden. Remain in Eden. Today it is Christ's hand on Eve's that holds my attention. Eve's head is bowed. Her eyes are closed. Her knees are tight against each other. Eve's obeisance becomes my own baptism and confirmation.

I am dressed in white and descend into the warm waters of the baptismal font accompanied by my father, also dressed in white. We stand in the center of the pool and face family witnesses. My father raises his right hand to the square, fingers pointing toward heaven. He delivers a prayer, then holds my wrist as I hold my nose and with bended knees, I am leaned back into the holy waters. With one quick swoosh through the process of immersion, I am happily declared a Mormon.

I am eight years old.

The following Sunday, I wished I had not worn the white headband to keep my bangs out of my eyes. Even before the confirmation began, the weight of the men's hands on top of my head was forcing the plastic teeth to bite into my scalp. I opened my eyes seconds before the blessing to see the varied shoes pointing toward me around the circle: wing tips, Hush Puppies, and boots. I recognized the black polished cowboy boots as my father's, the wing tips belonged to the bishop, the slip-ons were his counselor's shoes. I couldn't wrap my eyes around far enough behind my ears to see what shoes my uncle or the remaining priesthood bearers were wearing.

The pressure of the warm hands on my head increased. I quickly closed my eyes. My father began, "Our beloved daughter of Zion, by the authority vested in me . . ."

And then the words "Receive the Holy Ghost."

The hands lifted. My eyes opened. I stood up and faced the congregation as the bishop congratulated me on becoming a member of the Church of Jesus Christ of Latter-day Saints. All the men in the circle shook my hand. My father put his arm around me as we walked back to where my mother and her mother and her mother's mother were sitting.

I sat down on the pew. My grandmother took my hand and patted it.

"I am possessed," I thought. "I am possessed by the Holy Spirit and protected from evil. I am a clean slate. There are no sins on my record before God."

The Paradise of childhood.

"Bosch is rubbish," I hear a British guide say to her group. She is wearing a brown wool suit just below her knees. "He ate rye bread that was rotten, which most certainly brought on the cruelest of hallucinations."

My view of Paradise is often blocked by other visitors. I have no choice but to watch them interact with the painting.

"What we have here, ladies and gentlemen, is a massive orgy. It is rumored Hieronymus Bosch belonged to a religious sect that believed in purification through gratification."

Some of the visitors cluck their tongues.

"Notice the preponderance of strawberries and other fleshy fruits, symbols of lust. It is true God said, 'Go forth and multiply,' but we are not supposed to enjoy it like we see here. Bosch presents a perversion, ladies and gentlemen. I ask you to note the clear references to bestiality as men and animals prance around the pool in a state of arousal."

The guide points to the naked women cavorting in the pool that the cavalcade circles.

"And here, please witness Chaucer's 'Wife of Bath' who, as you recall, possessed a libido much too strong for her own good. *'A likerous mouth moste han a likerous tayl. In wommen vinolent is no defence, This knownen lecchours by experience.'* "

As the matron of arts begins to lose herself in Chaucer's tale, her group are showing their own signs of arousal. Suddenly aware of her own titillating vocabulary, she quickly shifts her analysis to Hell.

"I must say, I find great comfort in Bosch's depiction of Hell. We will pay for our bloody sins if we cannot control our bodily obsessions. Here we see the lovely, dreadful sophistications of the Middle Ages. Each sin has its appropriate payback. Rightfully so; if you are gluttonous, you will be eaten gluttonously."

A man who seemed to be preoccupied with one section of Hell in particular raises his hand and points to the panel. "Might these be vats of semen?"

She lifts her arm high over her head. "Follow me, please."

. . .

My view of Paradise returns. Why has Bosch's panel of Paradise evoked the religious teachings of my childhood? Eve kneels before Christ with her eyes closed. Meanwhile, a world of exotic flora and fauna surrounds her. White-robed salamanders evolve on shore.

Minerals. Gemstones. Jewels. I stand up and walk past my own species toward the fertile mound that supports a tall pink fountain where water cascades into a clear pool. I wade in, dig my hands into the rich black soil and bring up emeralds, sapphires, rubies, and bloodstones, my body sinking under the weight of what I have found.

I leave the Prado. I am surprised to see it has been raining. Clouds seem to be traveling quickly down Calle Alcalá. The gold-winged messenger on top of the Metrópolis building is flying. Madrid is glistening. Blue skies are breaking. Elongated shadows walk down the sidewalks and appear more real than the silhouettes of pedestrians caught in the glare of the sun as it sets over the Puerta del Sol.

The clarity of light, the perfection of this moment, this very moment, seems to be winter passing its mantle to spring. What is the date? I've forgotten the date. The month, I know, is March. I squint. The sun is directly in my eyes about to disappear behind the skyline of black iron crosses and red-tiled roofs. I wrap my black shawl tight around me as I pick up my pace and turn left.

Before going to sleep, I open *The Waves* by Virginia Woolf:

I hold a stalk in my hand. I am the stalk. My roots go down to the depths of the world, through earth dry with brick, and damp earth, through veins of lead and silver. I am all fibre. All tremors shake me, and the weight of the earth is pressed to my ribs.

I cannot stop reading. It stays my hunger for words, for my own language.

Let us now crawl . . . under the canopy of the currant leaves, and tell stories. Let us inhabit the underworld. Let us take possession of our secret territory, which is lit by pendant currants like candelabra, shining red on one side, black on the other.

Did Virginia Woolf visit the Prado? The old ones who remember her at the Hotel Inglés say they have never met anyone so enthralled with Madrid. They say she was a woman who made people tired. I wonder if she ever stood before *El jardín de las delicias?*

This is our world, lit with crescents and stars of light; and great petals half transparent block the openings like purple windows. Everything is strange. Things are huge and very small. The stalks of flowers thick as oak trees. Leaves are high as the domes of vast cathedrals. We are giants here, who can make forests quiver.

It is Monday. The Prado is closed. An old woman dressed in a turquoise sweater and a black skirt with black stockings and shoes is breaking bread for the pigeons. There must be fifty pigeons cooing and circling around her. I see her every morning. She finishes her sacrament for the birds and always leaves with a couple of loaves under her arms.

I watch her walk away, legs bowed, toward the Plaza de la Cibeles, Madrid's great fountain named after Cybele, the goddess of caverns, who stands in the center of the city on a lion-drawn chariot. A fast-moving river of traffic flows around her. They say that during the Spanish Civil War, citizens risked their lives protecting her, sandbagging the monument while General Franco's army bombed Madrid.

Ten pigeons pick up the remaining crumbs left by their patron. A sudden flap of wings, they rise, bank, and return.

> *While of these emblems we partake,*
> *In Jesus' name and for his sake,*
> *Let us remember and be sure*
> *Our hearts and hands are clean and pure.*

> *For us the blood of Christ was shed;*
> *For us on Calvary's cross he bled*
> *And thus dispelled the awful gloom*
> *That else were this creation's doom.*

I think of all the years I have taken the formal sacrament in my church and the beautiful hymns sung with solemnity prior to the blessing given on the bread and water; the communal silence that permeated the chapel as silver trays were passed; the silence I loved and how I was taught to use this time each week to honor the broken body of Christ and His spilled blood. *Oh God, the Eternal Father, we ask thee in the name of thy Son, Jesus Christ, to bless and sanctify this bread to the souls of all those who partake of it, that they may eat in remembrance of the body of thy Son . . . that they do always remember him, that they may have His spirit to be with them. Amen.* I hold these moments of reflection dear, and I wonder how I too have come to a sacrament of birds.

And then I remember standing on the edge of Great Salt

Lake as a young girl, watching hundreds and thousands of birds fly over me, feeling the wind of wings, the songs of a world in motion.

Yes.

Yes, I would partake and participate.

Yes, I would break bread for the birds and say a prayer for safe travel, each one a cross against the sky.

On this particular day in the Prado, I begin my observation of the triptych with binoculars. I want to see what birds inhabit the Paradise of Bosch.

The cradle chair in the corner of the gallery is empty. I sit down and begin bird-watching.

A mute swan floats gracefully in the pond behind Eve. It has an orange bill with a black knob. The knob is greatly enlarged in the male in the spring. This bird would have been familiar to Bosch in the Low Countries. This swan is not mute but makes a formidable hissing sound. In its wild state, it frequents remote wetlands. Why not Eden?

Mallards and shovelers float nearby as three white egrets stand in shallow water perfectly still, eyes intent on fish. Their long, sinuous necks and spearlike bills are mirrored in the pool alongside a unicorn bending down to drink. Their feathers form an elegant cloak easily unraveled by the wind.

Close to them is a spoonbill. I walk slowly toward this long-legged bird, a standing grace in the water. It swings its peculiar beak side to side in the white marl for crustaceans. The quivering nerve endings that line the interior of its mouth are feeling for clues and will send messages of what is below. Adam and Eve would do well to pay attention. Life is to be touched. The bill snaps shut, a crayfish struggles. It is decided: the crayfish becomes the spoonbill, who continues walking in Eden, seen or unseen, it does not matter.

North of the wading birds, flocks of swifts are swirling like smoke through a furnace-like mountain, transforming themselves from black to red to white, the colors of alchemy.

I sit down on the grassy hillside near the congregation of birds below the stone furnace. Wild geese fly in the formation of an arrow. If we follow their migrations will we better understand our own spiritual genesis?

As a child I remember believing that if I could ride on the backs of Canada geese they would deliver me to the future because they had arrived from the past. When I would bear my testimony before members of my own congregation, I would say I believed in God not because of what I had learned in church but because of the geese I watched each spring and fall, the fact that they knew their way, that they always returned. My parents said it was a sweet analogy. Not knowing what that word meant, I said, "No, they are not my analogy, they are my truth."

Rooks. Ravens. Crows. True conspirators. They converse in pairs while sitting on the rims of Bosch's canyons. One by one, they drop like stones only to recover in a joyous upswing. Back on the rim, they sit as bards disguised as birds and listen to everything being said. At night, they will enter Adam and Eve's dreams as subversive thoughts.

In Eden, I continue my search for birds.

Below Eve, there is a kingfisher with red legs, two toes forward, two toes back, syndactyl, speaking to a three-headed phoenix while a grey bee-eater fans its short broad wings and bows. Pheasants in courtship strut on the bottom margins of Paradise, a female opens herself to the approaching male, the spurs on her tarsi are exposed should she need to defend herself.

I turn around.

There, inside the eye of the pink fountain, sits a yellow-eyed owl, possibly Tengmalm's owl, distinguished by its round head, deep facial disks, and chocolate plumage. It nests in the cavities of trees. I kneel behind the thicket and watch. I have never seen this bird before. It scarcely moves. Were Hieronymus Bosch's acute skills as a naturalist appreciated? Were there medieval ornithologists who caught the painter's sardonic humor in Paradise, knowing this particular owl's call is a rapid, musical phrasing of *poo-poo-poo*?

I take down my binoculars and let them dangle around my neck. The guards are staring. I open my notebook and make a checklist of all the birds seen so far in *El jardín de las delicias*.

Swifts
Scarlet Ibis
Great White Egret
Little Egret
Wagtail
Blue Rock Thrush
Cuckoo
Spoonbill
White Pelican
Night Heron
Blue Heron
Stork
White Ibis
Jackdaw
Stonechat

Redstart

Rook

Brambling

Pheasant

Jay

Mallard

Gadwall

Hoopoe

Green Woodpecker

Kingfisher

Robin

Magpie

Goldfinch

Great Tit

Long-eared Owl

Tengmalm's Owl

Tawny Owl

Pygmy Owl

Little Owl

Widgeon

I look up. The guard nods. The Prado is closing. Who knows how much time has passed in the country of Bosch? I tuck my binoculars into my bag with my notebook and leave.

Walking up toward the Parque del Retiro, I hear the tapping of typewriter keys. There is a window open on the ground floor of an apartment building. I stop and stand quietly to the side of the open French doors. Looking in, I can see only a woman's hands. No jewelry. Rounded, short red nails. A wall of books from floor to ceiling ascends behind her. White woodwork, white walls, wood floors. I suspect a Persian carpet comforts the writer's feet.

The woman takes a break, her right hand reaches for a cigarette. She strikes a match with her left, lights it. The smoke curls around her hands, shaping words, crafting sentences. I covet this stable desk where a black leather container holds the blood instruments of pens and pencils.

A large door, very tall, is ajar to another room. I stretch to see. The woman's dog, a schnauzer, gives me away, yet the writer is so deep in trance she is oblivious to another writer imagining her life outside.

On the corner of Calle de Ruíz de Alarcón and Calle de Felipe IV there is a flower vender. He tries to sell me a bouquet of tulips. I would have loved to have left them on the steps of the writing woman with words from Virginia Woolf, "Some people go to priests; others to poetry; I to my friends, I to my own heart," but I do not have enough money in my leather pouch to buy them. I savor their extravagant beauty without ownership, an interlude of color, simply that. The tulips will move and arrange themselves in someone else's arms, in someone else's vase.

I am simply a traveler, a voyeur who casts no shadow.

There is a Japanese woman who is painting *El jardín de las delicias*. Her name is Mariko Umeoka Taki. She has been working on her reproduction for four years. Placing the triptych on an imaginary grid, she has divided it into eight squares, each one three feet by three and a half feet, two canvases for each of the wings and six canvases for the center panel. She has her easel set up to the side of the triptych and is working on the bottom center quadrant of the Garden of Delights. A bluejay is perched on what looks like a red coral tepee, dropping berries into the mouths of the hungry.

I introduce myself to the painter. I ask her why she has chosen this particular painting to copy.

"Because I need it," she replies matter-of-factly. "I feel it from the inside." She searches for the correct words in English. "I was an attorney in Japan. I came to Spain on vacation and visited the Prado. I became obsessed with this triptych. I couldn't sleep. It took me over. I knew I had to paint it, to learn what it had to say."

And what do you think Bosch is trying to say?

"Now that I am here, I don't think about it. I just paint what he painted."

The artist steps out from behind her canvas. Both arms are in splints. Carpal tunnel syndrome. She looks at what she has done and shakes her head.

"For many years," she says, "I could not paint. Nothing came to me. I mean I could paint what people wanted me to paint—floral arrangements, still lifes—but nothing gave me pleasure. I gave up my art for a legitimate profession. El Bosco is teaching me how to paint again. I am learning to paint from the inside, from what I feel, not just from what I see."

She opens a tube of paint the color of flesh and squeezes a small dot on her wooden palette.

"I have so much left to do, each expression, each face, each set of eyes."

Returning the next morning, I expect to find the artist again; instead only her canvas remains. I look at what Mariko painted from the day before. Half a shell, that is all I see, a blue flame flickering on a tongue of mother-of-pearl. She has not added the bodies yet, nor closed the shell. I am allowed to peek inside. Blue, white, turquoise—colors as mesmerizing and hypnotic as the sea itself.

I check the colors and precision of image against El Bosco's mussel. The copy lacks the confidence of the original; the complexity of the psyche is missing, the depth of the painter's hand, but through its innocence and authentic intention, something else is translated through the copied fragment.

What is it? I am searching, searching for something and no one can tell me what it is or where to find it.

My eyes move back to Paradise and settle on the grove of trees that separate Adam, Christ, and Eve from the pool with the mound of gems and pink fountain.

Through the trees, I see a young man kneeling in the darkness of the woods. A shaft of light falls on his praying hands. His voice is audible. He is pleading God to deliver him from his questions, to tell him which of the churches are true. Suddenly, a blinding light unfolds from Heaven. God appears, accompanied by Jesus Christ. What the young man hears is that none of the churches are true, that he must reclaim the true and living faith to this Earth. In the sanctity of this sacred grove, he is given a vision of restoration.

On another occasion, he holds a green seer-stone to his eye; what he sees inside frightens him. He receives a second vision.

While I was thus in the act of calling upon God, I discovered a light appearing in my room, which continued to increase until the room was lighter than at noonday, when immediately a personage appeared at my bedside, standing in the air, for his feet did not touch the floor. . . .

He called me by name and said unto me that he was a messenger sent from the presence of God to me, and that his name was Moroni; that God had a work for me to do. . . . He said there was a book deposited, written upon gold plates, giving an account of the former inhabitants of this continent, and the source from whence they sprang. He also said that the fullness of the everlasting Gospel was contained in it, as delivered by the Savior to the ancient inhabitants; also, that there were two stones in silver bows—and these stones, fastened to a breastplate, constituted what is called the Urim and Thummim—deposited with the plates; and the possession and use of these stones were what constituted Seers in ancient or former times; and that God had prepared them for the purpose of translating the book.

There was another visitation. He was working in the field when a voice began speaking to him.

I looked up, and beheld the same messenger standing over my head, surrounded by light as before. He then again related unto me all that he had related to me the previous night. . . . I left the field, and went to the place where the messenger had told me the plates were deposited; and owning to the distinctness of the vision which I had had concerning it, I knew the place the instant that I arrived there. Convenient to the village of Manchester, Ontario County, New York, stands a hill of considerable size, and the most elevated of any in the neighborhood. On the west side of this hill, not far from the top, under a stone of considerable size, lay the plates, deposited in a stone box. . . .

Having removed the earth, I obtained a lever, which I got fixed under the edge of the stone, and with a little exertion raised it up. I looked in, and there indeed did I behold the plates, the Urim and Thummim, and the breastplate, as stated by the messenger.

I recognize the young man that I see in El Bosco's forest as Joseph Smith, the date, September 21, 1823, the place, Palmyra, New York. This is the genesis of my religion, a religion born out of questions in a post–Revolutionary War America, a religion that honored personal revelation, a religion whose sacred texts were housed and hidden in the earth.

The Book of Mormon was pulled out of the side of a mountain, golden plates sealed and buried by the prophet Moroni, who was entrusted with this record of ancient peoples of the Americas by his father, Mormon, who compiled these histories. Almost two thousand years later, these engraved plates were uncovered by Joseph Smith, a contemporary prophet, who copied, then translated them.

There is a promise in *The Book of Mormon* given by Moroni, the same prophet who visited Joseph Smith. It reads:

When ye shall receive these things, I would exhort you that ye would ask God, the Eternal Father, in the name of Christ, if these things are true; and if ye shall ask with a sincere heart, with real intent, having faith in Christ, he will manifest the truth of it unto you, by the power of the Holy Ghost.

Fresh out of high school, I was hired for the summer as a cabin maid at Elk Creek Ranch in Island Park, Idaho, on the periphery of Yellowstone National Park. Before entering college, I wanted to find out what I truly believed and so, each morning, I would rise early and read from *The Book of Mormon*. I would underline passages in red and ponder them.

Yea and are ye willing to mourn with those that mourn; yea and comfort those that stand in need of comfort, and to stand as witnesses of God at all times and in all things, and in all places that ye may be in, even until death, that ye may be redeemed of God....

These were beautiful passages, passages that stirred my soul within the language of my own sacred texts, yes, I could feel the presence of God *in all things* and *in all places* and then as the full, broad light of morning came forward, I would digress from *The Book of Mormon* and turn to the Psalms. I read these scriptures from the Old Testament not so much for theology as for the elegance of language, the beginning of poetry. Hours would pass. I would put away my books, realizing the work I had not yet done, then dash into the cabins and change beds. I would note the sheets with drops of matrimonial blood and look for the newly married.

During the afternoon, after my chores were complete, I would walk to the lake and fish. Worms, not flies, were my bait, pulled out of the rich soil where we worked. I kept them in wet thimbleberry leaves inside a little wicker basket on a leather strap draped over my chest. I was aware of the worm's sacrifice as I wound its long maroon body around the metal hook until it pierced its skin. I pinched small weights onto the line. With my finger on the reel's button, I would cast across the lake and wait for the worm to sink. The line, evident by a clear bubble half filled with water, would bob for what seemed like hours until a strong nod acknowledged that the worm had been taken by a trout. Reeling the fish in was always a surprise. More often than not, a rainbow appeared with pastel scales glistening on its side.

My father taught me what to do: reel the fish to shore, take it in my hand, cut the line with the other, then quickly hit its head with the bone handle of my knife. Next, turn it over on its back and slit its pearl-white belly from vent to gills, then slip my bloody fingers through its scarlet gills and rip the guts out, throwing them in the bushes for weasels or magpies to eat. Finally, I would run the nail of my thumb down the trout's spine to clean the fish thoroughly, which is exactly what I did.

Returning to the ranch for dinner, I would be shunned by the fly fishermen, who thought me less pure having caught my fish with a worm. I entered the kitchen, cooked the trout, and ate the sweet flesh by myself. I was healthy and strong and sun-tanned, so tan that when I bathed before bed and removed my silver bracelet, I wore another bracelet of white skin.

Toward the end of the summer, I made the decision that I would take Moroni up on his promise. I took time off from work and fasted for two days, drinking only water. I walked to a favorite place of mine, studied and prayed, felt the sun on my face, listened to Clark's nutcrackers calling each other from lodgepole pines, and watched an osprey fish, hovering high with a crook in each brown-and-white-checkered wing, eyes down, wings pulled back. The fish hawk dropped like a bullet, feet first, splashed, rose with a trout in the grip of her talons, then sailed across the lake to her perch, a dead snag, secured the fish, and flew to her nest.

I read more, returning to favorite passages.

Let the mountains shout for joy, and all ye valleys cry aloud; and all ye seas and dry lands tell the wonders of your Eternal King! And ye rivers and brooks, and rills, flow down with gladness. Let the woods and all the trees of the field praise the Lord; and ye solid rocks weep for joy! And let the eternal creations declare his name forever and ever!

I pressed petals of wildflowers between these pages, blue penstemon, scarlet gilia, and yarrow. The day was long and luxurious. I felt a humility rise out of my own hunger.

That night, in the solitude of my cabin in Idaho, I prayed. I prayed I might know of the truthfulness of the Gospel in my heart.

The words of Isaiah spoke to me:

In horror of my darkness
in terror of inhuman space
exposed to private death

totally vulnerable on the surface
of earth's
material matter . . .

Then one of the seraphim
flew toward me
a live coal in his hand

a fire from the interior
of the earth
the core of my being

it was a burning stone
under the fire
on the altar

With the priest's tongs
he reached in the holy altar
and took it

and touched my lips
with it
and he was saying

you are seeing
the purifying fire of creation
burn up your past

I lay in my bed trembling.

The next morning, I telephoned my mother and grand-mother to tell them I had had a vision. I told them a figure draped in a white robe of light had stood at the foot of my log bed. I was still shaking from the terror, the wonder, the awe, the fire in me still burning. Neither one of them said much, they listened. I hung up the receiver and walked back to the ranch house. By the time I had arrived in the kitchen to join the others for breakfast, my mother had called and left a message. "Kathryn and I are on our way up. Love you, Mother."

This was no small gesture. It was a six-hour drive from Salt Lake City. At four o'clock, they arrived at Elk Creek Ranch. I was leaning against the buck n' rail fence waiting for them. When I saw them coming down the dirt road, I began to cry. They both held me and one of them said, "Let's go."

We drove to Mesa Falls on a narrow, winding road through the lodgepole forest, parked the car, and walked to the over-look. The force and volume of the cascading water articulated my own spiritual free fall. I tried to follow single drops all the way down to the catch pool like a specific thought but failed; how does one speak coherently about a thundering in the heart?

The three of us watched in silence; a rainbow arched over the falls. We found a place to sit in the shade.

I told them my story all over again.

"I knelt down by the side of my bed and told my Heavenly Father that I had sincerely read and studied the scriptures, that

I had a deep desire to know if the Church was true. On my knees with clasped hands, I prayed and listened to the emptiness of my soul. After a fair amount of time, I got up and climbed into bed.

"Suddenly, a small, narrow figure, surrounded by light, as though it was being seen from a great distance, stood at the foot of my bed. It was—"

"What, dear?" my mother asked.

"It was—I don't know—I don't know if I was seeing things or if it was real. Something moved through my body like a current. Heat, warmth, I can't describe it. And then the figure disappeared. I couldn't stop shaking, I just lay in bed awake until dawn. Then I called you."

And then as a young woman of seventeen years still unable to trust what I had just shared, I asked the women in my life who mattered most if they believed me, if they thought this apparition meant the Church was true.

"Nobody can answer that for you. The question isn't really whether or not the Church is true—" my grandmother Mimi said, pausing.

My mother reminded me of the patriarchal blessing I had received from one of the Brethren shortly before I left home. She brought the typed copy with her and read a passage:

Live in tune with the Holy Spirit. Seek the truth always. Be not afraid to learn the truth of anything, for no truth will be revealed to you as such that will be in conflict with God's kingdom.

"It's all true," my grandmother said, looking out at the great expanse before us. "All of this—"

We sat on the edge of Mesa Falls in silence, mesmerized,

hypnotized by the rushing water, the seemingly endless water, and I wondered about the source from which this water falls.

The vision I had in Idaho after fasting and praying in the wilderness was the same vision I had of the osprey fishing at the lake—wings folded in a free fall—the surface of water breaks, holy food is within our grasp.

I emerge from El Bosco's woods exhausted and walk to the edge of the clear pond and splash my face and arms.

Back on the streets of Madrid, I cross the Paseo del Prado, walk past the Palace Hotel and up to Calle de Echegaray, where I am staying.

"Freedom," I whisper to myself as I make my way through a crowded sidewalk. "No one knows my history and I do not know theirs."

A man and woman arm in arm walk by. I am hungry and make a quick detour across Cedaceros down Alcalá and over to the Paseo Recoletos to the Café Gijón.

Once inside the smoky establishment, I stand at the entrance and wait for a table. In a few moments I am seated by the window and handed a menu. I read over the choices slowly. The waiter disappears.

The waiter returns.

"Merluza a la riojana, por favor," I say.

"Muy fresca," he responds.

He disappears again and I watch people as I break off a heel of bread. The café is full at four o'clock in the afternoon. Men are leaning over tables whispering to women. Women are talking loudly to each other. Round tables occupied by what look like regulars are engaged in lively discussions, with cigarettes being lit, waved, smoked, and scrunched over and over again. Limber conversation is the most bewitching of lures. Eyes held. Minds caught in the promise of new ideas. For that moment, those engaged in the aerial dance of words are held in the dazzling light of possibilities. Most *madrileños* are wearing black. No one is rushed. For as long as one chooses to sit, *esta es su mesa,* this is your table.

I clear my table of crumbs with the side of my hand and note the cold, smooth surface of marble.

Three elderly men are sitting near, huddled around each other. One begins to sing in a quivering voice, a melancholy voice, his left hand rising and falling with his voice. The other two men close their eyes, clapping their left hands into their right.

Their coffee comes. It does not interrupt them. The man continues to sing his *cantos* largely unnoticed by the crowd conversing around him in the Café Gijón.

My hake arrives covered in red chilies. It is so tender. If one can swoon over fish, I do. I am both a participant in my own meal and an observer of others.

The *cantador* stands up and turns his chair around so he can sit on it backwards, his arms resting on its back, legs spread. He continues to sing, his eyes focusing on the ceiling fans, his left hand accepting the lyricism of the right, where the second and third fingers are joined leaving space for the sound to travel. His eyes are yellow. Can a man's eyes be yellow? I look twice, he catches my stare. The singing ends.

He lights a cigarette and listens to his friends.

Profiteroles con chocolate. My tab keeps rising with the musicality of the collective voices. Two hours pass. I lean back against the window absorbed in the theater before me.

The three men stand up. They help each other put on their green wool jackets, touching each other's arms, patting one another's backs. Two leave. The singer moves to another table and taps his hand on the marble. He buttons the top button of his orange shirt and then holds his first two fingers with one hand as if to quiet his impulse.

"*¿Le ha gustado la comida, señora?*" the waiter asks.

"*Sí, la comida estuvo muy bien, gracias.*"

Today I decide to walk through the Bosch Room and pretend not to notice the triptych. But the painting is my lover's stare and I cannot resist. A side glance. My eyelids lower. I turn and walk briskly toward Dürer's *Adam*.

The return. Always the return. I am living inside my own triptych. Love is a triangle of desire, a movement of three: lover, beloved, and all that circulates through us, another person, another landscape, another home away from home. The geometric problem of Eros. Do I see Pythagoras in the corner of El Bosco's Garden?

Stay in Paradise.

For the first time in Paradise, I notice a white giraffe and an elephant posing in the background. A monkey sits on top of the elephant's back. A lion devours a deer. A boar chases a hyena. A porcupine turns with his quills exposed. And in the foreground of Eden, a cat carries a rat in its teeth.

What are we to make of death in Paradise? Does Hieronymus Bosch portend what is to come?

Have we never been comfortable with our place on Earth

because we have never been comfortable with death? Earth has never been the Christian's soulful inhabitation. Earth is to be endured. Hell is to be avoided. Heaven is what we seek.

El Bosco's Eden is the menagerie before the Flood.

With a map in hand, I find my way to the Museo Nacional de Ciencias Naturales. It takes several minutes for my eyes to adjust once inside the museum and when they do giant insects rule the dark interior. *Oruga de papilionido.* A caterpillar devouring a leaf. *Cucaracha.* Cockroach. *Escarabajo atlas.* Two rhinoceros beetles fighting on a log. They are the size of Volkswagens. *Saltamontes.* Grasshopper. *Hormiga.* Ant. *Mosca.* Fly. *Mariposa.* Butterfly. *Pulga.* Flea. *Langosta de desierto.* Lobster of the desert. We call them Jerusalem crickets at home. *Mantis oratorial.* Praying mantis.

I push a button that sets all the insects in motion, buzzing, hissing, biting, sucking, and flying.

Beyond the Hall of Insects, one moves through a long, shadowed corridor of heads, horns, and skulls, a death walk through Africa: six leopards, two rhinos, two crocodiles, two zebras, two warthogs. India: nine tigers. The Arctic: three walrus, four seals, a musk ox. And a pastiche of antlers: moose, elk, deer.

This trail of trophies leads to a room that contains the tools of a naturalist: a microscope, magnifying glasses, leather-bound books with engraved hand-watercolored plates of flora and fauna; jars, some empty, some filled with fetuses floating in formaldehyde. There are bird eggs blown dry; shells; black boxes with glass windows where the backs of beetles and butterflies are pinned to beds of cotton; and a myriad of natural curiosities: a rabbit with four arms, a frog with five legs, the spiraled horn of a narwhal, flying fish.

I look closely at these perversions of wonder. Hieronymus Bosch painted them. He created a world of hybrids and hypotheticals, alongside actual marvels of the natural world. Flying fish swim through his skies. Duck-billed seals read and moth-bodied, bird-headed humans climb ladders in Hell. Evolution in nature may simply be the evolution of an imagination.

Suddenly, I find myself staring at two human skeletons in a glass case. The sign reads, *Adán y Eva en el Jardín del Edén.*

Adán y Eva en el Jardín del Edén? Adam and Eve are standing in front of a potted ficus tree in a natural history museum in Madrid. Adam is looking directly at me with his jaw open. Eve, standing behind to his left, is watching him. Her bony right hand is open as she offers him an apple with a leaf still attached to its stem. They stand on a mound of dried moss. A red parrot is perched on Adam's shoulder like a pirate's. A barn owl presides in the tree, its braided trunk reminiscent of a serpent.

Behind Adam is a small table with two glass jars resting on top. One jar contains a coiled rattlesnake yellowed by formaldehyde. The other jar contains apples. These are not simply specimens, they are evidence that Eden was a place, the temptation of Eve was real.

Stalagmites and quartz crystals are embedded in the moss with a rat scurrying across. In El Bosco's Paradise, the rat has been stopped by the cat and is carried away.

A great horned owl stands directly behind Eve. A black and white sloth has climbed a stump and a pink flamingo in the corner stares at her. A scarlet ibis stands behind the Tree of Knowledge of Good and Evil. All are attendants to the Mother of Creation.

I walk around the case. At the rear of the Garden on a table by itself—one rib.

Hieronymus Bosch could not have done better if he had curated this biblical terrarium himself.

A sign reads (as far as I can translate correctly):

The Garden of Eden is for so many the place metaphorically where matter was named, and the unending process of identification and arrangement of the natural world began. This biblical event may be our first literal model of taxonomy.

What are the colors of Creation?

Vermilion, pink madder, raw sienna, yellow, Prussian blue, flesh red, white, green, blue, deep grey, blue violet, light chrome, Vandyke brown, vegetable green, buff, purple, new yellow, Indian red, yellow ochre, emerald green, orange, sap green, carmine, gamboge, rust brown, leaf green, Venetian red, Payne's grey, burnt sienna, new blue, rose, light red, Cassel earth, violet, moss green, neutral tint, cobalt blue, brown ochre, mauve, lemon yellow, Roman ochre, black, deep yellow, brown oxide, Antwerp blue, cream, burnt umber, purple brown, light green, yellow lake, pink, sea green, Chinese white, umber, Hooker's green, Naples yellow, Venetian green, light grey, cerulean blue, crimson lake, dark chrome, electric blue, red, dark ochre, brown pink, ultramarine, grey, turquoise blue, yellow oxide, primrose, ivory black, chocolate brown, natural sienna, maroon, red violet, green, acid green, red oxide, indigo.

What is the Tree of Knowledge?

Pinus pinea, Quercus robur, Acer pseudoplatanus, Pseudotsuga menziesii, Acer negundo, Trachycarpus fortunei, Platanus hispanica, Tilia platyphyllos, Ulmus minor, Taxus baccata, Acer campestre, Lager-

stroemia indica, Aesculus glabra, Prunus dulcis, Sophora japonica, Pinus wallichiana, Fraxinus ornus, Parrotia persica, Punica granatum, Celtis occidentalis, Wisteria sinensis, Prunus cerasus, Cupressus sempervirens, Aesculus hippocastanum Celtis australis, Diospyros virginiana, Gleditsia triacanthos, Gymnocladus dioicia, Maclura pomifera, Ailanthus altissima, Photinia serrulata, Cercis siliquastrum, Juglans nigra, Gleditsia sinensis, Dracaena draco.

Adam and Eve, the Truth, became Adam and Eve, the story, when I fell in love with biology. The study of evolution became my own. To evolve, to evolve from other forms of life—I saw the process of natural selection as an act of biotic faith, an organic definition, an extension, of what I understood the concept of eternal progression to be in Mormon theology, that of *advanced perfectionism.* If we believe that we too can become gods and goddesses, creators of our own worlds, what else is the attainment of godhood if not natural selection, "this gradually unfolding course of advancement and experience, a course that began in a past eternity and will continue in ages future."

A grand and almost untrodden field of inquiry will be opened, on the causes and laws of variation. . . . Our classifications will come to be, as far as they can be so made, genealogies; and will then truly give what may be called the plan of creation. . . . When I view all beings not as special creations, but as the lineal descendants of some few beings which lived long before the first bed of the Cambrian system was deposited, they seem to me to become ennobled. . . . And as natural selection works solely by and for the good of each being, all corporeal and mental endowments will tend to progress towards perfection. . . . There is grandeur in this view of life, with its several powers, having been originally breathed by the Creator into a few according to the fixed law of gravity; from so simple a beginning endless forms most beautiful and most wonderful have been, and are being evolved.

A baby gorilla with its arms around its mother is looking toward the Garden of Eden from the corner of the room. *Pithecia pithecia,* another primate ancestor, sits with his elbow on one of his knees, his middle finger raised from a clenched fish. Behind him are color plates of various species of monkeys with balls and chains around them.

The last object I see in the natural history museum is a magnifying glass left on a dusty shelf next to a large shell. I pick up the long wooden handle and examine through its cloudy lens the exposed chambers of a nautilus. This is the face of God, not a human face, but the profile of beauty, the elegance of form in the context of function.

Sitting in the cradle chair back in the Prado, I continue to watch *El jardín de las delicias.*

Below Adam, Eve, and Christ, there is a dark pool writhing. Inside, a black spoonbill with a mermaid's tail is sparring with a three-headed bird on shore, a platypus-seal is reading a book, a flying fish is swimming on its back.

I fall asleep on the banks of the pool in Paradise and dream of leviathans diving deep, then stalling to rise slowly, giant lungs expanding until they explode on the surface as rain and the great whales swim to shore, emerging on land, leg by leg, as elephants.

We have been everything before.

.   .   .

If I were to look into the eyes of Creation: insect, fish, spider, serpent, snail, hawk, fox, giraffe, and turtle, even bird by bird, what would I see? What do they know? Would we dare to take the evidence of our kinship seriously?

Adam is a man. Eve is a woman taken from the rib of man. All creatures great and small are under our domain. This is what I was taught.

I am Eve standing in the Temple of the Lord. Across from me is Adam, the man I am about to marry; his name is Brooke. We have been chosen as the Divine Couple to stand before our brothers and sisters in a reenactment of the Garden of Eden, a collective ceremony where a trilogy of questions will be answered.

Where did we come from?
Why are we here?
Where are we going?

We will receive earthly instructions on how to behave, how to endure, how to progress, all principles given and covenants made are to remain secret. Call it our endowment, our spiritual dowry. Our clothing is white with green aprons tied around our waists to represent the fig leaves that covered the First Couple after they were cast out of Paradise. Call it sacred.

As God now is, man will become. We can enter the covenant of eternal progression through the Plan of Salvation and become gods and goddesses creating and populating future worlds.

I am Eve holding the hand of Adam. We are in a holy room of mirrors, kneeling at the altar of marriage in the Salt Lake Temple. Our families are gathered around us. One of the Twelve Apostles, S. Dilworth Young, begins the ceremony. Brooke

and I look into each other's eyes with an endless image of ourselves and our posterity stretching in both directions. With our
fathers as our witnesses before God, we are pronounced husband and wife, not *until death do you part,* but *for time and all
eternity.*

I bow my head as a young woman of nineteen and feel the
sweet circle of platinum slide down my finger. My new husband raises my chin and kisses me.

A Spanish woman in a dark pageboy approaches *El jardín de las
delicias.*

"Are you a student of El Bosco?" she asks.

I tell her I am simply an American visitor intrigued by its
mystery.

She walks closer to the painting and curls her fingers to create a small circle around Paradise. "That first bubble of love—
eventually breaks." Her fingers release the illusion. "We think
everything comes from God. It comes from within. Our gift is
our liberty. This is what we have destroyed."

That night, I dream I am being chased by one of El Bosco's
monsters in Hell. The pink amphibious creature wearing a
monk's frock demands that the musical notes burned on the
buttocks of human beings be read. I do not know how to translate music into words. Suddenly, flaming rivers turn to ice.
Everything freezes. The triptych shatters into a thousand puzzle pieces on the granite floor of the Prado. I am on my knees
picking up the pieces, trying to put the painting back together
again.

Everything in the world is broken. Nothing but silence remains.

What are we told?
What do we fear as a result of what we have been told?
And what do we know within our own bodies?

The memory of creation, the pulse of love, love the impulse, recover the impulse, the burning impulse, in my body, the body of the universe, the coming together of steam, gas, water, and fire, elemental swirling, twirling, tumbling of imagination, the upheaval of chaos, the settling of matter, the cooling of matter, what is the matter with rock, land, the rupturing and tearing of continents, the filling and spilling of seas, spirals of cells organize, specialize, differentiate, mutate, bottom, middle, surface, breaths realized and held through the covenant of waves one after another delivering consciousness to shore: eyes, ears, nose, mouth, lungs, legs, feet, arms, hands reach.

> *Out of the river rides a naked girl, shoulders of her horse star-lathered . . .*

Close the triptych. Quiet the triptych. Hieronymus Bosch has painted the Earth round. In A.D. 1500, he has created the world in grisaille, tones of grey on two wooden panels, the two wooden panels closed. The Earth is a crystal ball to be seen from the outside in and so this transparent globe floats in space.

I recognize this image akin to one created by Joseph Smith when he delivered specific instructions to his congregation at Ramus, Illinois, on April 2, 1843, speaking of the time when Jesus Christ will reappear, how the Earth will be transformed to its glorified state: *The angels do not reside on a planet like this earth; but they reside in the presence of God, on a globe like a sea of glass . . .*

where all things for their glory are manifest, past, present, and future, and are continually before the Lord. . . . This earth, in its sanctified and immortal state, will be made like unto crystal. . . .

The medieval mind intersects with the modern mind.

The Earth—a vessel, a drop of magic enclosed in glass. We live inside this vessel that is constantly transforming us.

Bosch painted the Earth round with a floating disk inside, a flat world within a spherical one. It is a fluid topography with dry land emerging like blue crabs on shore abandoned by the sea. Where did El Bosco receive "his instructions"? And how does one's creativity inform and interpret any Truth? Certainly word of Columbus's voyage to the New World in 1492 had reached the Flemish painter even in his small village of Hertogenbosch. How might this have massaged his imagination? And with Copernicus's theory of the solar system to come fifty-one years later, followed by Magellan's circumnavigation of the world, completed by his crew in 1522, could Hieronymus Bosch have planted the seed of a circular Earth?

God presides in the upper-left-hand corner of the closed triptych in a cave of dark clouds. I move closer. From heaven, his finger points to an open book. The Latin words appear:

Ipse dixit et facta sunt. Ipse mandavit et creata sunt.
For he spake and it was done. He commanded and it was created.

A stream of light cascades from boiling clouds, falling on vegetal landforms below. Grey green. Olive green. Green black. Reflective waters. Call it the third day of Creation:

And God said, Let the waters under the heaven be gathered together unto one place, and let the dry land appear: and it was so.

And God called the dry land Earth; and the gathering together of the waters called he Seas: and God saw that it was good.

And God said, Let the earth bring forth grass, the herb yielding seed, and the fruit tree yielding fruit after his kind, whose seed is in itself, upon the earth: and it was so.

And the earth brought forth grass, and herb yielding seed after his kind, and the tree yielding fruit, whose seed was in itself, after his kind: and God saw that it was good.

And the evening and the morning were the third day.

Earth, an eye, a butterfly, opens to *El jardín de las delicias* once again.

I am back in my cradle chair. It is quiet. Early morning light illuminates Eden. On a rocky outcropping stands a palm with a serpent winding its way up the trunk.

I am Eve. I walk toward the Tree of Knowledge. I am hungry for knowledge. Where is knowledge? Blood drips from its bark when scratched. I hear the voice of the Father: "You shall not eat of the fruit of the tree that is in the middle of the Garden, nor shall you touch it, or you shall die."

The serpent, slowly wrapping herself around the Tree, says, "Taste the apple. Your eyes will be opened. You will become like God, knowing good and evil."

I am Eve. I pick the apple from the Tree of Knowledge and eat. I grow taller, my feet feel the ground and my forehead touches stars. I turn toward Adam and share the fruit.

I am Eve. With a green apron tied around my waist, I hold the hand of Adam. Together we walk out of Eden into the wilderness. To separate ourselves from the presence of God is to face the illusion of Paradise.

Can a painting be a prayer?
Can wilderness be a prayer?

I do not blame Eve for choosing to bite into the apple. I thank her. I thank her for opening our eyes.

The frame disappears from the painting.
The boundaries of wilderness blur.

I return to the Eden of Bosch and wander through his woods. Little light is allowed to pass through the density of branches. I walk into the clearing toward the fertile mound that supports the pink fountain where water cascades into another pool, this one clear. A tiny owl stands in the center of the round base of the fountain like the pupil of an eye.

I stare at the owl.

The owl stares back.

My vision blurs, eyes cross, two eyes slowly converge into one, darkness and light revolving, Earth evolving. I blink. The owl is still there, a burning glare behind the Savior, Jesus Christ. I fear His pink robes might suddenly ignite.

II

HELL

I am asking you to study the dark.

—Anne Carson, *Plainwater*

Open and close. Open and close. The wings of El Bosco's butterfly are fanning the fires, the fires of Hell. The flames blur, obscure, the view of Paradise.

Now I see El Bosco's masterpiece as a map of the human mind. On the left, the mind of the child, pure and innocent. We believe what we are told. We stay in Paradise as long as possible. On the right, the mind of the mad, dark and duplicitous. We are all manic-depressives with mood swings bashing against brass like the tongues of bells that erode our sense of equilibrium. Left hollow, our bodies are taken over by demons. My mind, out of my mind, I have abandoned Paradise.

El Bosco's mind is the flame I flutter around at night. Other winged beings congregate, leading me to Hell. They are not angels. Do I dare to extend my hands to that which will burn, I am burning, I sit at the feet of this altarpiece in the Prado, against the rules, until I am caught watching the painting, watching the mind, watching the pale figures crouch and cover themselves before they ascend, descend, the ladders, there are so many ladders, why all the ladders in El Bosco's Hell?

I count the rungs, every one, as I walk up the ladder to the Tree Man's body, his eggshell body, one, two, three, four, who is holding this ladder for me, don't look down, keep rising, keep counting, five, six, slowly to seven, there are no cherries in Hell, eight, nine, I must suffer this heat, steady my feet, and here I stand, I am standing inside the body of a hollow man, brittle and dry, dry heat, I look down as my hands blister at the thought of all that is burning. Is the Tree Man the Hollow Man, Hieronymus Bosch himself, looking over his shoulder at his creation, our creation now? Look at his eyes, his searing eyes, his mouth looks as though he has just pushed air through his lips. His eyes, his eyes, how could he paint his eyes if not from the inside out?

Once I held an eye in the palm of my hand. I held on to the optic nerve like an anchor so the eyeball would not slip away.

With scissors in hand, I cut into the eye, midpoint, halfway from the cornea to the optic nerve, then downward in a circle, turned the eye around and continued. The eye was tough, like cutting into canvas.

The vitreous humor, a gelatinous ball, oozed out intact. This holds the lens of the eye. By removing it, the beautiful retina, fanning out from the optic nerve is revealed, an outpost of the brain that translates sight.

I remember standing in awe of the pink slime, wiggling it with my probe, realizing when light strikes the retina tiny nerves send impulses, messages, through the optic nerve to the brain and, miraculously, we see.

"Cones and rods," a friend said when asked about her first-time perceptions of Utah's redrock desert. "Cones and rods—there's nothing mystical about it."

From the vantage point of the retina, the lens is held in place with what looks like a brown halo of mushroom gills. These tiny ciliary bodies or cables are attached to muscles. The back of the eye is turquoise.

I cut into the gelatinous ball, the lens popped out. The lens is hard, solid, and clear like a crystal. I held it between my thumb and forefinger and raised it against the palm of my other hand. It magnified lines and ridges, another topography.

This lens that bends the rays of light until they merge is a sublime invention, not without consequence. I felt as though I had discovered the secret of desire.

I placed the lens to the side and faced the aqueous humor, another gelatinous sac, liquid, that inflates the cornea, creating the bulge of the eye. The cornea is milky, transparent, so light can pass through. The iris, now visible from the inside out, protects the eye by controlling the amount of light that enters like the aperture of a camera.

In Hell, my eyes dilate. Even the Hollow Man's eyes are black.

Inside, a woman fills a jug with wine as three individuals, naked, are sitting on the backs of toads around a red table playing cards, I see their cards, they flash them toward me like a mirror, in the mirror I see a woman's back, she is looking out of the eggshell cavern, her hand barely holding up her head.

There are others climbing the ladder. I want out. I want down. I have to wait my turn. Turn. The millstone hat turns on the Hollow Man's head, it grinds and creaks. I am dizzy, dizzy in Hell. The noise. The crowds. The tightening of strings, in my head I feel a tightening of strings. There, a woman hangs from the strings of a harp like a crucifix. *Father forgive them for they know not what they do.* I don't know what to do. I back down, down each rung of the ladder, nine, eight, seven, six, five, four, almost there, three, two, one foot on land, I thought it was land, it is ice, I am skating on ice. It cracks. I fall. My hands try and brace my body on ice. The ice breaks, I flounder, I reach for the Hollow Man's shoes, two boats wavering in a frozen sea, my body burns, I look for the hand of someone to hold, but in this landscape of sin there is no one here to rescue me.

A crowd gathers in front of the triptych. I can barely see Bosch's Hell from the floor. People crowd around me, touch my shoulders, kick my feet, bump my knees, disturb my pen, do not disturb my pen, I must protect and preserve these images in my mind.

The music outside, inside, is too loud, the vibrations agitate, irritate, rotate my thoughts over and over, faster and faster just like the hurdy-gurdy the gentleman is playing in Hell. I find myself screwed in place

t i g h t e r

a n d

t i g h t e r

a n d

t i g h t

er

The column of voices rises, raises, razors, I am sick to my stomach, I try to steady my gaze, shadows bleed on the page, darken my words, all I can see are shoes, legs, voices, more voices. I want them gone, all of them gone, they are not looking at the painting, they are blocking the painting, they are standing in Hell, all of them in Hell, my mind is in Hell, they are tromping all over this landscape, go aware, go away, leave me in peace with my own imago, imagined Hell, images of Hell. I am comfortable in my own contemplations of the Dark. It is Hell to know the Devil is the intimate near faraway stranger, strangler, our own family, this is clear, this nausea I am feeling is the anxiety I embody when I cannot breathe, I cannot breathe in this endless crowd of too many feats, feet, these noxious smells must surely pass.

. . .

The brain between my ears has turned into a knife, El Bosco's knife is on a canon of ears, a knife that slices my reality in two—bipolar—we are all bipolar. North Pole. South Pole. Ice Caps. Brain caps. The hole in the ozone is the tear in my own psyche.

No one has any idea as I sit here quietly in the midst of the gathering, passing crowd in front of the triptych, that my calm is my cover. Once when someone asked if I knew anything about panic attacks, I said, "Yes." I told them I heard it was like having your blood replaced by ants. "Must be terrible," he said. "Must be," I replied, as the black-bodied, red-bodied army of ants marched through every vessel in my body.

The world is on fire. *What are we to do?* Hope flickers the flame inside this cave, this cavern of light and dark, can you see? I have seen the bulls who dance on the walls of Altamira, light and dark, they return to me here in the cavern, tavern, the bulls are standing upright, their cloven hooves paw my mind, sear my mind, their muscles are made of stone, my brothers and sisters can you see these drawings too, painted on the white walls of skulls, here in El Bosco's Hell, images that flicker and flare, flicker and flare, then fade? *What are we to do?* In times of trouble, I call on the painters ancient and new to draw our world together. It is the nightjar, the night ajar, the open door of doubt that allows demons to devour my mind, my conscious, unconscious mind, this delectable mind.

Flectere si nequeo Superos, Acherunta movebo.
If I cannot bend the higher powers, I will stir up the lower depths.

How can the man in El Bosco's Hell not hear the bickering of the triangle above his head? So his body is being carried away by ghouls, is he already numb to his fate? Are we? The man directly behind him has his ears covered as he grimaces in pain.

A woman in a shroud of white (could she be a nun?) peers out from inside the giant hurdy-gurdy, holds the triangle in one hand and strikes it with an iron rod in the other.

Clang de la clang de la clang de la clang!

This was our mother's instrument of choice when she called us home from the neighborhood for dinner.

Clang de la clang de la clang de la clang!

I once loved this sound. I now hate this sound. What once healed me, now hurts me.

In Bosch's Hell, few seem to be listening to anything but the voices of their own tortured souls.

And what about the man above the tinkering nun who is trying to balance an egg on his back? It is not the equinox. There is no equilibrium in Hell.

As I wander through this nightmare where the smell of sulphur chokes my throat, my compass has gone mad, spinning wildly without relief. There is no True North in Hell. All is relative. Is this the curse of modernity, to live in a world without judgment, without perspective, no context for understanding or distinguishing what is real and what is imagined, what is manipulated and what is by chance beautiful, what is shadow and what is flesh? There is little to orient me here. What I take to be stars in the midst of smoke are merely sparks that disappear.

I put my hands over my ears to stay the confusion. I turn my head and look into the eyes of a demon. A demon dog is clutching a woman's breast who sleeps with a toad on her chest. Upright ears, yellow eyes, tree branches for arms and hands.

Look.

Look away.

There is such a thing as evil.

I hide behind another human being. I can find no friends in Hell. I watch a game of solitaire where the last remaining cards are a two of hearts and a three of clubs.

Let the cards fall as they may, they say.

Must we?

Must we witness and watch and do nothing as roadcuts, clearcuts, the cut bodies of coyote, mountain lion, and deer are strung up by their hind legs as a warning to others that they are not welcome.

Must we witness and watch and do nothing as the peeled bodies of elders named Douglas Fir, Cedar, and Larch are chained to the flatbeds of trucks and hauled away on our highways, highways littered with roadkills, roadkills paving the way to dams, dammed rivers: the Colorado, the Columbia, the Snake and Mississippi; dammed canyons—Glen Canyon, Davis Gulch, Cathedral in the Desert—speak their names— remember their names—these places of beauty, these places of origin, toxic, toxic wastes, toxic deserts, bombed, battered, and betrayed in the name of national security—speak their names— remember their names—the Nevada Test Site in the Mojave, Hanford on the banks of the Columbia, Rocky Flats, Alamogordo, Dugway, the floodplains of eastern Idaho, the nuclear waste is simmering, shimmering, Coyote watches with burning eyes, burning eyes Bosch's owl with burning eyes in Paradise.

There is a war raging within our own nation and it is not civil. Speak their names. Remember their names. They are going, going, the salmon, grizzly, tortoise, tiger beetle, bobcat and lynx, marbled murrelet, red-spotted frog, they are disappearing before our eyes, our own eyes. Find their eyes. Burning eyes. We are slowly committing suicide.

This is *The Natural History of the Dead.*

The land is being stripped. Strip-mined. Strip-searched. Gold-blooded murderers. There was a World War I sergeant investigating the teeth of the dead. He opened their mouths, pried out fillings, always the gold fillings, with a trench knife. He picked up a piece of pipe and broke out the other filled teeth and put them inside a gas mask tin for later, *who knows how much gold may be extracted from them?*

Let the cards fall where they may, they say.

I run to the corner of Bosch's Hell and pick up the cards; they no longer bear the two of hearts, the three of clubs. I turn them over. The cards burst into flames. I throw them on the ground. White salamanders scurry behind the table and hiss.

I am convinced that the twenty-first century will be the century of Noahs, when human beings will feel compelled to save the ecosystems and species dying around us in biological arks, since it will no longer be possible to save everything. . . . The moral dilemma will reside in which and whom to choose, and on what knowledge, not to say wisdom, we should base our choice; and finally, who are we to decide on the right to exist of other life forms?

Novalis, in his "Legend of the Poet," evokes distant eras when there were poets who by making strange sounds on fantastical instruments, could awaken the secret life of forests and plants. I call on the women and men of science, on the environmentalists, and on the poets, so that together we can make it possible for the mythical Orpheus to sing again among us in the next millennium. Ecology, like poetry, should be practiced by everyone.

Bosch's fools shiver on the edge of the frozen lake with their arms crossed, their hands covering up their funny bones. They could not feel the heat in life and they cannot feel the heat in Hell.

And so they shiver.

Are they the *Passionless Ones* who commit to nothing? They have no opinions. They take no stands. Unmoved by life, they wait for life to move them.

These wretches, who ne'er lived,
Went on in nakedness, and sorely stung
By wasps and hornets, which bedew'd their cheeks
With blood, that, mix'd with tears, dropp'd to their feet,
And by disgustful worms was gather'd there.

Never shed for a cause in life, their blood now falls freely, drawing worms on the banks of the River of Sorrows. This river glows on the horizon of Hieronymus Bosch's Hell.

A raven flies.

Give me an aerial perspective. Give me an atmospheric perspective. Attribute this haze, this regional haze, this global haze, this psychic haze to bitumen, these fires burning on Earth as they are in Hell.

Anticipate the craquelure on the shrinking surface of *El jardín de las delicias,* the small seismic cracks that break open a painting.

· · ·

Art is not immune.

The body is not immune.

The greatest sin is the sin of indifference.

There is nothing we can do.

A singed book lies on top of a panther's head. I grab it as a man crosses his hands in front of his breasts. Prying the pages loose, I find stories.

KIDS' FITS CANCEL CARTOONS

TOKYO—A TV network canceled broadcasts of a popular action-packed cartoon show Wednesday and a rental chain yanked video versions from its shelves because of brilliantly flashing scenes blamed for causing convulsions, spasms, or nausea in hundreds of children.

Nearly 600 children were rushed to hospitals Tuesday night after watching the program "Pokémon." By Wednesday evening, the number of afflicted children climbed to more than 700 after others watched videotaped versions of the show.

"Kids don't watch this program the way most people watch TV," said Toshio Okada, a writer specializing in animation and comic books. "You can't take your eyes off it without missing crucial visual clues about the meaning of the action."

The fast-paced action of Japanese cartoons requires intense concentration to be understood, Okada said. And children watch it all on increasingly large TV screens from less than a yard away—typical viewing style in Japan's cramped homes.

TV Tokyo canceled the airing of "Pokémon" on 30 stations around Japan on Wednesday.

National broadcaster NHK said 729 people had been

taken to hospitals by late Wednesday; about 200 remained hospitalized.

Philip Sheridan, chief of the epilepsy branch of the National Institute of Neurological Disorders and Stroke in Bethesda, Maryland, said the children's reactions could have two quite different causes.

Some children may have started to hyperventilate from the excitement and the flashing lights, he said. That can cause dizziness, nausea, and fainting. This kind of problem often spreads in groups of children as they see each other having trouble, Sheridan said.

In other children, the flashing lights might have acted directly on the brain to cause seizures, he said. An affected child would momentarily stare and not respond even to shouting, or have a stiffening of the body with jerking arms and legs for up to a minute. That would happen if the flashing disrupted the natural pacemakers that regulate patterns of activity in the brain's circuits, he said.

MONKEYS PUT TO WORK IN COCONUT GROVES

A workforce of several thousand monkeys in southern Thailand help pick the country's crop of about 1.5 million tons of coconuts. Villages often have at least one monkey per household and the animal is rented out to a local plantation at a modest fee.

HEADLESS FROGS REIGNITE ROW OVER GENETICS

British scientists have created headless frogs in experiments aimed at mass-producing human organs. The frogs were created by Professor Jonathan Slack, after he and his colleagues altered genes that control the development of the embryo.

Such genes can be switched on or off using chemicals, and have led to the creation of mutant flies with legs in place of eyes.

HUMANS VOLUNTEER TO INGEST
PESTICIDES FOR MONEY

AMVAC Chemical Corporation, a California pesticide company, hired a lab in England to conduct three related feeding trials using people to test the toxicity of dichlorvos. Paid volunteer subjects also drank doses of the extremely toxic insecticide aldicarb in a 1992 study in Scotland commissioned by Rhone-Poulenc. . . . Spokesman Rick Rountree told *Pesticide & Toxic Chemical News,* "The protocol met with all the requirements established globally for such tests."

These tests were to confirm the NOEL (No Observable Effect Level) of the previous human study, done about twenty years ago.

FRANKENSTEIN FOODS

WASHINGTON—That's what Europeans are calling genetically modified crops that abound in America. . . . Companies such as Monsanto introduced herbicide-resistant soybeans and corn that makes its own insecticide. U.S. farmers loved the products; by 1998, 40 percent of America's corn crop and 45 percent of its soybeans were genetically modified. A Cornell University study published in the journal *Nature* in May found that half of a group of monarch butterfly caterpillars that ate the pollen of insecticide-producing Bt corn died after four days. What if the pollen spreads to the milkweed the monarchs lay their eggs in? "The arguments aren't enough to say we shouldn't have any biotechnology," says Rebecca Goldburg of the Environmental Defense Fund. "But they are enough to say we should be looking before we leap."

RADIOACTIVE MILL TAILINGS NEED
TO BE MOVED, OFFICIAL SAYS

WASHINGTON—A huge pile of uranium mill tailings near the Colorado River in Utah is a "radioactive time bomb" that must be moved to protect drinking water for Nevada, Arizona, and southern California, a water official told lawmakers Friday.

But the federal regulators said the 10.5 million tons of radioactive and toxic waste near Moab, Utah, don't pose a significant threat to the Colorado River drinking water used by about 25 million people.

The waste pile was left over from more than two decades of uranium processing, mostly by the now-bankrupt Atlas Corporation, which ended in 1984. The federal Nuclear Regulatory Commission has approved the company's plans to cover the pile with clay and rock, and is working on plans to treat contaminated underground water that flows from the waste 750 feet to the river.

MICE INJECTED WITH DNA FROM
FIREFLIES HAVE GLOWING EARS

WASHINGTON—Scientists have extracted DNA from fireflies and injected the luminescent chemical compound into laboratory mice. The result is as hoped, mice with glowing ears.

This is the first of many experiments in the genetic alteration of species where useful traits of one species can be biologically engineered into another.

WAR LEAVES POISON LEGACY

PANČEVO, YUGOSLAVIA—For the first time in memory, there are no mosquitoes, flies, or gnats here; they've mysteriously disappeared.

Something's also wrong with the soil and water; towns-people who drink the water often develop a rash, fever, or diarrhea. Doctors warn local residents of the likelihood a pregnancy will end in a miscarriage.

"Suddenly, it's become dangerous to live, even breathe, here," said Simon Bancov, the government's regional health inspector. "NATO has poisoned us all."

UN environmental experts arrive here today to begin investigating what local officials call the most toxic city in the Balkans.

NATO airstrikes destroyed the city's petrochemical plant, fertilizer factory, and oil refinery in mid-April, spewing thousands of tons of noxious chemicals into the air, water, and soil. A white cloud engulfed the city for days, causing many of the 120,000 residents here to become ill.

Officials said they were aware of the environmental dangers associated with hitting the site but felt its military risk outweighed the environmental concerns.

Now the city's clinic is packed with people vomiting in the waiting room, fighting to breathe, and covered in full body rashes.

Images of blank stares, monkeys leading humans by the hand, hybrid frogs, the shining ears of mice, poison cocktails and drinking water that glows, and refugees who cover their mouths with rags are just some current events. I close the book. Sins. Deadly sins. I can read no further.

In the right wing of Hell, a man is shitting gold coins as another is puking blood into a black pool where human faces look up in horror. Could it be Hieronymus Bosch was painting from the future?

. . .

The skull stares from the edges of Hell. Where to find my footing? The soles of my feet are burning. There is no solid ground, only ice. I touch the large white skull, a horse's skull. I suddenly panic. I place my hands on my face. My left eye is gone, the socket bare. The eyeball is resting on the melting ice. I pick it up and try to put it back where it belongs. To my horror, the detached eyeball can still see.

I crouch down close to the ice, which now acts as a mirror. My vision blurs as I watch my two eyes merge into a globe, Earth is rotating in the center of my forehead.

A SHARK IN THE MIND OF SOMEONE CONTEMPLATING WILDERNESS

A shark swims past me in a kelp forest that sways back and forth with the tide. It is deliberate and focused. I watch the shark's sleek body dart left and right as its caudal fin propels it forward. Its eyes seem to slice through the water in a blood-gaze as the gills open and close, open and close. Around and around, I watch the shark maneuver through schools of fish. It must not be hungry. The only thing separating me from the shark is a tall glass pane at the Monterey Sea Aquarium. Everything is in motion. I press my hands on the glass waiting for the shark to pass by again, and when it does I feel my own heart beating against the mind of this creature that kills.

In the enormous blue room of the American Museum of Natural History, I stare at the tiger shark mounted on the wall of the second floor. Its surface shines with the light of taxidermy, creating the illusion of its having just left the sea, now our own natural history trophy. I see how out of proportion its mouth is to the rest of its body and wonder how many teeth hung from its gums during its lifetime, the rows of teeth, five to twenty of them, biting and tearing, thrashing and chomping on flesh, the teeth constantly being replaced by something akin to a conveyer belt system. Somewhere in my mind I hold the fact that a shark may go through 20,000 teeth in a life span of ten years. I imagine this shark sensing the electrical field of a seal, swimming toward the diving black body now rising to the surface, delivering with great speed its deadly blow, the jaws that dislocate and protrude out of its mouth, the strong muscles that open then close the razor teeth that clamp down on the prey with such force that skin, flesh, cartilage, and bone are reduced to one clean, round bite, sustained over and over again. The blue water, now bloody, screams to the surface. Even in death, I see this shark in motion.

Sensation. I enter the Brooklyn Museum of Art to confront another tiger shark, this the most harrowing of all the requiem sharks I have encountered in a one-week period. Requiem sharks. They say the name is derived from the observation that once this large shark of the family Carcharhinidae attacks a victim, the only task remaining is to hold a requiem, a mass for the dead. *Galeocerdo cuvieri.* It is neither dead nor alive, but rather a body floating in space, a shark suspended in solution. Formaldehyde. To preserve. What do we choose to preserve? I note the worn, used appearance of its mouth, shriveled and receding, looking more man than fish. The side view creates a triptych of head, dorsal fin, and tail, through the three panels of glass in the frames of a white-painted steel box. I walk around the shark and feel the charge of the front view, a turquoise nightmare of terror that spills into daylight. *Sensation.* Damien Hirst is the creator of *The Physical Impossibility of Death in the Mind of Someone Living, 1991.*

I do not think about the shark.

I like the idea of a thing to describe a feeling. A shark is frighten-ing, bigger than you are, in an environment unknown to you. It looks alive when it's dead and dead when it's alive. And it can kill you and eat you, so there's a morbid curiosity in looking at them. I like ideas of trying to understand the world by taking things out of the world. You kill things to look at them. You have to preserve a shark in liquid, which looks very similar to its natural habitat. It has to be that size. You expect it to look back at you. I hope at first glance it will look alive. It could have to do with the obsession with trying to make the dead live or the living live forever.

As a naturalist who has worked in a museum of natural history for over fifteen years, how am I to think about a shark in the context of art, not science? How is my imagination so quickly rearranged to see the suspension of a shark pickled in formal-dehyde as the stopped power of motion in the jaws of death, an image of my own mortality?

My mind becomes wild in the presence of creation, the artist's creation. I learn that the box in which the shark floats was built by the same company that constructs the aquaria of Brighton Sea World. I think about the killer whales kept in tanks for the amusement of humans, the killer whales that jump through hoops, carry humans on their backs as they circle and circle and circle the tank, day after day after week after month, a g a i n a n d a g a i n a n d againandagainandagainand how they go mad, the sea of insanity c h u rn ing inside them, inside me as I feel my own captivity within my own culture, any culture that thwarts creativity, we are stopped cold, our spirits suspended, controlled, controlled sensation.

Tiger Shark, glass, steel, 5% formaldehyde solution.

Damien Hirst calls the shark suspended in formaldehyde a sculpture. If it were in a museum of natural history, it would be called an exhibit, an exhibit where the organism is featured as the animal it is. Call it art or call it biology, what is the true essence of shark?

How is the focus of our perceptions decided?

Art. Artifact. Art by designation.

The fact that we designate something as art means that it is art for us, but says nothing about what it is in itself or for other people. Once we realize that the quest for essences is an archaic religious quest, there is no reason why something should not be art for one person or culture and non-art for another.

Wild. Wilderness. Wilderness by designation.

What is the solution to preserving that which is wild?

I remember standing next to an old rancher in Escalante, Utah, during a contentious political debate over wilderness in the canyon country of southern Utah. He kicked the front tire of his pickup truck with his cowboy boot.

"What's this?" he asked me.

"A Chevy truck," I responded.

"Right, and everybody knows it."

He then took his hand and swept the horizon. "And what's all that?" he asked in the same matter-of-fact tone.

"Wilderness," he answered before I could speak. "And everybody knows it, so why the hell do you have to go have Congress tell us what it is?"

Damien Hirst's conceptual art, be it his shark in a box or his installation called *A Thousand Years, 1990* (where the eye of a severed cow's head looks upward as black flies crawl over it and lay eggs in the flesh that metamorphose into maggots that mature into flies that gather in the pool of blood to drink, leaving tiny red footprints on the glass installation, while some flies are destined to die as a life-stopping buzz in the electric fly-killing machine), all his conceptual pieces of art, his installations, make me think about the concept and designation of wilderness.

Why not designate wilderness as an installation of art? Conceptual art? A true sensation that moves and breathes and changes over time with a myriad of creatures that formulate an instinctual framework of interspecies dialogues, call them predator-prey relations or symbiotic relations, niches, and ecotones, never before seen as art as dance as a painting in motion, only imagined through the calculations of biologists, their facts now seen as designs, spontaneously choreographed moment to moment among the living, can we not watch the habits of animals, the adaptations of plants, and call it performance art within the conceptual framework of wilderness?

To those who offer the critique that wilderness is merely a received idea, one that might be "conceptually incoherent" and entranced by "the myth of the pristine," why not answer with a resounding yes, yes, wilderness is our received idea as artists, as human beings, a grand piece of performance art that can embody and inspire *The Physical Impossibility of Death in the Mind of Someone Living?*

Squint your eyes: *Imagine a world of spots.* Colored dots in the wilderness. *They're all connected.* Damien Hirst paints spots.

Art's about life and it can't really be about anything else. There isn't anything else.

Tell us again, Damien Hirst, with your cabinet of wonders, we are addicted to wonders, bottles of drugs lined up, shelf after shelf, waiting to be opened, minds opened, veins opened, nerves opened. Wilderness is a cabinet of pharmaceuticals waiting to be discovered.

Just as we designate art, we designate wilderness, large and small, as much as we can, hoping it begins a dialogue with our highest and basest selves, we are animals, in search of a home, in relationship to Other, an expanding community with a mosaic of habitats, domestic and wild, there is nothing precious or nostalgic about it. We designate wilderness as an installation of essences, open for individual interpretation, full of controversy and conversation.

I always believe in contradiction, compromise . . . it's unavoidable. In life it can be positive or negative, like saying "I can't live without you."

Damien Hirst speaks again.

I cannot live without art. I cannot live without wilderness. Call it *Brilliant Love, 1994–95.* Thank the imagination that some people are brave enough, sanely crazy enough, to designate both.

Art is dangerous because it doesn't have a definable function. I think that is what people are afraid of.

Yes, Damien, exactly, you bad boy of British art who dares to slice up the bodies of cows, from the head to the anus, and mix them all up to where nothing makes sense and allow us to walk through with no order in mind, twelve cross-sections of cow, so we have to take note of the meat that we eat without thinking about the topography of the body, the cow's body, our body; we confront the wonder of the organism as is, not as a continuum, but as a design, the sheer beauty and texture of functional design. We see the black and white hide, there is no place to hide inside the guts of a cow sliced and stretched through space like an accordion between your very large hands. You ask us to find *Some Comfort Gained from the Acceptance of the Inherent Lies in Everything, 1996.*

We have been trying to explain, justify, codify, give biological and ecological credence as to why we want to preserve what is wild, like art, much more than a specimen behind glass. But what if we were to say, "Sorry, you are right, wilderness has no definable function. But can we let it be, designate it as art, *art of the wild,* just in case one such definition should arise in the mind of one standing in the tallgrass prairies of middle America or the sliding slope of sandstone in the erosional landscape of Utah?"

Wilderness as an aesthetic.

Freeze. Damien Hirst brought together a community of artists and displayed their work in a warehouse in England, these Neo-Conceptualists, who set out to explore the big things like death and sex and the meaning of life. Wilderness designation is not so dissimilar. In your tracks, freeze, and watch the performance art of a grizzly walking through the gold meadows of the Hayden Valley in Yellowstone. In your tracks, freeze, a constellation of monarch butterflies has gathered in the mountains of Mexico. No definable function except to say, wildness exists like art, look for an idea with four legs, with six legs and wings that resemble fire, and recognize this feeling called survival, in this received idea of wilderness, our twentieth-century installation as Neo-Conservationists.

A shark in a box.

Wilderness as a box.

Wilderness as *A Thousand Years* with flies and maggots cele-
brating inside the corpses of things.

Q: What is in the boxes?

A: Maggots.

Q: So you're going to put maggots in the white boxes, and
    then they hatch and then they fly around—

A: And then they get killed by the fly-killer, and maybe lay
    eggs in the cow heads.

Q: It's a bit disgusting.

A: A bit. I don't think it is. I like it.

Q: Do you think anyone will buy it?

A: I hope so.

Do I think anyone will buy the concept of wilderness as
conceptual art? It is easier to create a sensation over art than a
sensation over the bald, greed-faced sale and development of
open lands, wildlands, in the United States of America.

I would like to bring Damien Hirst out to the American
West, let him bring along his chain saw, *Cutting Ahead, 1994,* only
to find out somebody has beat him to it, creating clear-cut
sculptures out of negative space, eroding space, topsoil running like blood down the mountainsides as mud. Mud as material. He would have plenty of material.

The art of the wild is flourishing.

How are we to see through the lens of our own creative
destruction?

A shark in a box.

Wilderness as an installation.

A human being suspended in formaldehyde.

. . .

When I leaned over the balcony of the great blue room in the American Museum of Natural History after visiting the tiger shark, I looked up at the body of the blue whale, the largest living mammal on Earth, suspended from the ceiling. I recalled being a docent, how we brought the schoolchildren to this room to lie on their backs, thrilled beyond words, as they looked up at this magnificent leviathan, who if alive with one quick swoosh of its tail would be halfway across Central Park.

I only then noticed that the open space below where the children used to lie on their backs in awe was now a food court filled with plastic tables and chairs. The tables were crowded with visitors chatting away, eating, drinking, oblivious to the creatures surrounding them. How had I missed the theater lights, newly installed on the balcony, pointing down to illuminate the refrigerators humming inside the showcases with a loud display of fast foods advertising yogurt, roast beef sandwiches, apples and oranges.

The blue whale, the tiger shark, the sunfish, tuna, eel, manta ray, the walrus, the elephant seal, the killer whale—call it *Orca,* with its head poking up through the diorama of ice in Antarctica—are no longer the natural histories of creatures associated with the sea, but simply decoration.

Everything feels upside down these days, created for our own entertainment. The natural world is becoming invisible, appearing only as a backdrop for our own human dramas and catastrophes: hurricanes, tornadoes, earthquakes, and floods. Perhaps if we bring art to the discussion of the wild, we can create a sensation where people will pay attention to the shock of what has always been here *Away from the Flock, 1994.*

Wild Beauty in the Minds of the Living.

. . .

I am numb wandering in Hell circling around and around the daily performance of reward and applause and nonverbal treats oh yes and what is Heaven if not expectation when will we get to Heaven and if we dwell on the pleasures of our own bodies and imagination oh no don't count on it count to seven instead the seven deadly sins avarice slothfulness gluttony pride lust envy anger again say them again right now before you forget avariceslothfulnessgluttonypridelustenvyanger oh no heaven forbids the earthly delights here and now now look to heaven above look to hell below but never look right here right now do not do not do not look to where we are standing oh beautiful for spacious skies oh no continue circling around and around the great expectations of performance and reward of doing what we are told who told us why and when how old were we when we lost the ability to say no and yes and ask over and over again why tell me why and then I will decide whether or not to believe you them they who says I have free agency because in my heart of soul I know *The Physical Impossibility of Death in the Mind of Someone Living.*

A shark in a box.
Wilderness with a fence around it.
Me with my lips sealed, arms folded and legs crossed.

Two women dressed in suits stand before the shark. "This is not art, this is pornography."

Two women dressed in suits stand before *El jardín de las delicias.* "This is not art, this is pornography."

I hear these words inside El Bosco's Hell and then hear the triangle ringing, the drums beating, the choir singing. Again, I join the others whose eardrums are bursting and put my hands over my ears and scream.

I sink into my seat on the airplane with a sigh of relief. I cannot believe my good fortune. Due to overbooking, at the last minute, I am upgraded to business class where a flight attendant hands me slippers and a sleeping mask. I am going home. The man seated next to me already has his eyes closed.

"Ladies and gentlemen, this is your pilot speaking; unfortunately, due to fog, it looks like there will be a significant delay on the tarmac. We are sorry to inconvenience you and will try to make this as comfortable for you as possible. Thank you for your patience. We will update you as we receive more information."

There is a general moan throughout the plane. The man seated next to me shares his frustration. I agree. We both put our seats back to a reclining position.

A video is shown, something about extreme sports. I close my eyes.

"Ladies and gentlemen, this is your pilot speaking again, we have just received word that the delay may be up to an hour and a half before we are allowed to take off . . ."

"Well, it looks like it's going to be a while," the man next to me says.

"I'm just going to pretend we are in the air," I reply.

We exchange names and shake hands. I note his British accent, the clarity of his eyes, and the meticulous nature of his clothes; blue shirt, red tie, khaki pants, leather loafers. Before he sat down he carefully folded his navy blazer in the storage compartment above. I judge him to be in his late fifties.

"Have you been in Spain long?" he asks.

"Two months," I say. "And you?"

"I work the Mediterranean region, just had to check in on some business in Madrid. I'm on my way to a company meeting in Cincinnati."

"What company do you work for?"

"Procter & Gamble. I've been with the company for over thirty years."

There is a pause.

"And what do you do?"

"I'm a writer."

"Oh really, what kind of writing do you do?"

"A little bit of everything," I say, "but my focus is on environmental issues."

He smiles. "So you're one of them?"

"An environmentalist?" I tease. "Yes and I suppose you're one of—"

"Those corporate pigs, yes, how interesting." He folds his arms and reclines his seat once again.

Another pause.

"So is it as bad as everyone says?" I ask.

"Is what as bad?"

"Is Procter & Gamble as powerful as they say?"

"Do you mean do we have direct access to the president of the United States? No. In America, we pretty much have to do business like everybody else. But in Third World countries, that's another story."

"How so?"

"Let's just say when we go into a small country and tell the government leaders we want to invest X amount of money into their local economy and it's more than their entire national budget, we can pretty much move in and get whatever we want."

"Like relaxed environmental standards?"

"You said that, I didn't." He turns his head. "But that's a possibility; it depends on what we need. For example, I helped open China in 1988, the largest consumer market in the world, and they were more than willing . . ."

"And what was that like?"

"They have no environmental standards for all intents and purposes. The air is appalling and the rivers are filthy. We're just giving the people what they deserve, what they need to elevate their lifestyle and create a higher quality of life, what you and I already have."

"And what exactly are you *giving* them?"

"You've got to be kidding? Name a product—anything—chances are it's ours."

I draw a blank.

"Come on—okay, what toothpaste do you use?"

"Crest."

"Procter & Gamble. What soap do you use?"

"Ivory."

"Procter & Gamble. You see, there's not a household in America that doesn't use our products: Tide, Top Job, Bold, Bounce, Cascade, Joy, Comet, Dawn, Downy, Mr. Clean, Spic & Span. Clean, clean, clean, that's what we do."

"Do you enjoy your work?" I ask.

"What do you mean?"

"I mean do you enjoy what you do?"

He was quiet for a moment. "You know, I've done it for so long, I don't really think about it. It's made me a good living, I mean a really nice living. I've lived all over the world. I like the people I work with. I can pretty much control what I do. It's as good as anything else one could do."

"Are you from England?"

"No," he says.

"But your English is impeccable."

"I was born in Germany but left for London when I was six years old, during World War II."

He went on to recount his story of leaving Germany with his grandmother because she did not like her husband's politics, and having to go to school in Essex where the Germans had heavily bombed the region.

"Can you imagine what it was like to have a German accent in England during those postwar years? You learned very quickly after a few fights in the schoolyard that your survival meant speaking like everyone else did."

"So where's home for you?"

"Home is Procter & Gamble. I've never lived anywhere long enough to vote."

"Does that bother you?" I ask.

"Not really, what difference does it make if I have a vote or not? You're not so naive to believe your vote makes a difference, are you?"

"I guess I'm too much of an American to not believe that my vote matters."

The flight attendant brings us some water.

"May I ask you another question?"

The executive is getting a bit edgy.

"What?"

"Do you have a vote in your company?"

"Look, Procter & Gamble is a global company. I make my home wherever I am, that's not so unusual. You adapt, you adjust. We're all becoming one world anyway, so what difference does it make? Take Spain, for example, when PG came into the Mediterranean, we knew we had to break down, contaminate, if you will, the "siesta culture." It was simple. Basically, we went in and provided great jobs and said, "Okay, we know you want to go home at one in the afternoon to have dinner with your families and then rest and come back at five for another go until eight. We'll make you a deal: Work for us from nine A.M. until two P.M. and we'll call it quits for the day. What we ask in return is that you give us Saturday. They were not happy about it, but they agreed. The next year, we said, "We need you to work until three in the afternoon plus Saturdays, it's just one more hour in the day. Again, they complied. And then, after the third year, when the employees had gotten used to their new standard of living and were significantly in debt, we said, "Hey, we've got good news for you—you can have your weekends free—we are standardizing the work week from nine A.M. to five P.M. There was a revolt, but what could they do? Quit? The siesta was over."

"And that doesn't bother you?"

"It's progress."

An uncomfortable silence was growing.

"Don't go feeling sorry for the Spaniards we gave jobs to, Christ, the unemployment rate is as low as any country in Europe. If they don't like the rules, they'll quit. For example, people in Europe are not as willing to move for 'the company' as they are in the States. You talk about living in one place, nobody in America knows where they're from; it's a known fact, the American workforce will work wherever you tell them to work. They'll move for a hundred-dollar raise. It's never about where one is from in the States, it's where one is going. Again, what can I say, it's progress."

"Talk to me about progress."

"Well, I'll be honest with you, I get rather tired of that word myself—especially in Procter & Gamble, everything is done in the name of 'innovation,' but I'll tell you something, I've been around long enough to know that some things don't need changing in the name of progress, but the younger executives don't listen to the older, more experienced men. And I deplore that every year another 'innovation' is implemented so somebody can elevate their status and show how bright they are."

"You mean the younger executives don't respect what you know."

"Hardly. It's bigger and better. More, more, more. You just have to keep up the pace or somebody else is going to run over you. I can tell you, age is not something that is favored."

"You must get tired of the pace, of moving so fast in the world."

"Tired? That doesn't even approximate what I feel, but what am I supposed to do? I've got three houses, my wife and kids have their needs."

"But it must be hard on them, too?"

"It cost me my first marriage and I don't even know my older children. I was gone all the time. I keep thinking it will get better, but it just gets more and more insane. All these gadgets in the name of efficiency are just making us all crazier, but I can't stop or I'll have the next guy's footprints on my back and he's right there, breathing down my neck. It's cutthroat."

He takes a drink of water and looks out the window. We haven't moved.

"I go to church with my family. We go to the beach, we've got a place in Marbella where we can relax, but I'm telling you, it's out of control. Moving all the time. More products. Bigger sales."

"I guess this is what I don't understand—if you feel this way and you are one of the top executives, why don't you slow it down?"

"It's out of our hands."

"What do you mean it's out of your hands? Your hands are the ones creating it, aren't they?"

"You don't understand, the corporation is its own entity. Nobody sitting around the boardroom believes any one of them can change things. Even we who run Procter & Gamble speak of 'it' as though it is something outside ourselves."

I am quiet.

He turns to me abruptly. "You are as much a part of the corporate family as I am. Your teeth are white, aren't they? How do I justify what I do? Look, I'm a good citizen. I make a lot of money, a hell of a lot of money, and I give a fair share away that contributes to the community. I mean, how many times have you gone out to people like me with your hand open to fund your causes?"

More times than I care to, I say under my breath.

"My wife supports the arts. I give to local charities. We're just trying to make the world a better place for people. Clean, clean, clean, that's what Procter & Gamble does."

I am the woman in Bosch's Hell who is balancing one die on top of her head. Where is the other die? Has it rolled beneath the table? What table? Has someone stolen it? If so, who? and is it hidden inside their pockets? Which pocket? Where is the die? I want the other die? Shake the dice. Roll the dice. I am gambling. What am I gambling? I am gambling that there is neither Heaven nor Hell, only this one beautiful Earth, this glorious sky, this lake, this river, this city, this town, this village, this farm, this wild open place. I am gambling on the surprise of turkey vultures hovering above our home in the mountains, circling, waiting, watching, indifferent to my fate, whose only interest is in the spoil of bones. This is what I am gambling on—the gospel of *one life at a time, please,* here, now, in all its power and mystery and suffering and joy, that we might find our own prophets in poetry and paintings who are not afraid of the questions that plague us.

I will balance this die on my head and say to the inquisitors, yes, there are times I inhabit Hell right here on Earth and yes, there are times I dwell in Heaven left right here on Earth. Can you hear, I hear that fresh, fertile cadence coming out of the forest, ruffed grouse in the forest, blue grouse in the forest, dancing on trees, fallen trees. We too can dance on the floors of decaying wood. Can you hear, I hear, that wide-open joy singing on the sage flats, meadowlark, meadow vole, hidden, it can be hidden, all this is hidden, until the faith of falcons, peregrine falcons appear mid-air, drop and break through a haze of indifference, *the greatest sin is the sin of indifference,* and dive past our sluggish hearts and we are jump-started again by beauty, rising and falling in beauty, our native pulse restored. The falcons restored. I thought they were dead. I thought I was dead. Have you ever felt dead? This world, this mysterious, unknowable world is so lovely, all creation, this fleeting, ephemeral world, where we live and die and decay and evolve into who knows what our next step might be?

> *What it all comes down to is that we are the sum of our efforts to change who we are. Identity is no museum piece sitting stock-still in a display case, but rather the endlessly astonishing synthesis of the contradictions of everyday life. . . . I believe in that fugitive faith. It*

*seems to me the only faith worthy of belief for its great likeness to
the human animal, accursed yet holy, and to the mad adventure
that is living in this world.*

I am the figure walking the tightrope between two volcanoes,
one erupting, the other the haunt of ghouls. The iron rod I
hold on to for balance is beginning to melt. The flag on top of
the outpost, once white, is now charred.

Below me on the River of Sorrows is a boat with a blood-
red sail. What was once fueled by passion is now powered by
regret. There is no way to know the outcome of our lives.

I stand on the tip of my toes to see beyond the flaming horizon of the Millennium looming in the future.

2 0 0 0

1 5 0 0

Fin de siècle.

Hieronymus Bosch must have lived with these prophecies of
doom in the twilight of the Middle Ages, as well. He too must
have performed the tightrope walk stretched across the dualities of Heaven and Hell, right and wrong, Good and Evil, the
sacred and profane. And as the rope became even more taut,
did he feel the pulled loyalties of his art and his religion? Or did
he use the same muscles to paint as he did to pray?

DID HIERONYMUS BOSCH PRAY?

As I stand on a bridge spanning the boiling waters of Hell,
armies of men march past me. They have not awakened from
their embattled nightmares.

Leap

Bosch endured the aftermath of the Plague; the shadow and
flames of the Spanish Inquisition under the reign of King Ferdinand and Queen Isabella in 1479; the Spanish conquering of
Granada and demise of the Moorish kingdom in 1492, consoli-
dating the monarchy of Ferdinand of Aragon and Isabella of
Castile; that same year he would have heard of the excitement
of Christopher Columbus's discovery of America; He would
learn, in 1493, of Pope Alexander VI publishing the papal bull
Inter cetera divina dividing the New World between Spain and
Portugal; in 1503 he would have found the Casa Contratación
(Colonial Office) established in Madrid to deal with American
affairs.

And had he lived a full one hundred years, El Bosco would
have lived through King Ferdinand's death in 1516 and Charles
V's, his grandson's, inauguration as the new king of Spain who
inherited Austria, the Spanish Netherlands, and Burgundy. He
would have seen the Spanish empire expand as Hernán Cortés
conquered the Aztec empire in Mexico and, in 1531, Pizarro
overtook the Inca empire in Peru. In 1556 Charles abdicated in
favor of his son Philip II, who inherited Spain, Sicily, and the
Netherlands, who led the charge of the Counter-Reformation
against the Protestant states in Europe. It was an "empire upon
which the sun never set."

Spain was a blood country and El Bosco, a subject of her
empire, painting in his beloved Netherlands, was one of her ac-
quisitions.

And what have we witnessed in the twentieth century?

We turn our heads. The names of the damned are etched on
the skin of the dead whose bodies raised mountains.

I follow El Bosco's soldiers in Hell over the charred bridge
around the blood-soaked soil surrounding the River of Sor-

rows to the site of the Universal Battlefield, where the bodies of all the war dead through time are stacked. The soldiers keep marching as I become just another traveler staggering and stumbling over bodies, bloated bodies, stinking bodies, collapsing bodies, bodies known and unknown, under the weight of decay. I puke and vomit and cover my eyes and mouth with blistered hands, until I see even in darkness the ghosts of Moors, Jews, Aztecs, and Incas—all those who were not Catholic or Catholic enough during Spain's Golden Age—rise from the furnaces like smoke, curling themselves around the throats of the still marching soldiers until they decide when and where to taunt them.

There are more soldiers than ghosts.

Someone in Hell takes my arm and leads me to another ladder, which I climb. My eyes open to a sea of blood.

From afar I thought this lake was simply the red reflection of flames. There appeared to be no end to the resourcefulness of the damned and their knowledge of how to bleed the pores of sinners, wave after wave after wave.

And the sea gave up the dead which were in it; and death and hell delivered up the dead which were in them.

And in the black caves surrounding the sea, what looked like kelp beds rising and falling with the tide are the tangled arteries and blood vessels stripped from the bodies of the Inquisitors. Who will offer prayers over these ropes used to hang those who hung the heretics, the innocent?

The sound of pounding waves is matched by drums made from the skin of miserly men and women stretched tight. Beaten by ghouls, the heads of these drums register screams, wails of grief rupturing from a place so deep within I shake with a terror that threatens to break bones. My descension and ascension in Hell, climbing down one ladder and up another, has given me an aerial view of power and desire gone mad, the chaos created when the heart is murdered.

Bleeding heart. I knew it as a child in my grandmother's yard. It grew beneath the largest spruce tree, hidden. Bleeding hearts, red and white petals perfectly fused to create secret chambers, chambers left closed, only to dangle from the green leafy stems. Bring the color green into Hell. It is nowhere to be found. Bleeding hearts. Perennial. Pink. They appear each spring, growing best in shade. A bleeding heart creates beauty in darkness, dares to stay and send roots down. They were the only flowers my grandmother refused to cut and bring inside.

I have climbed to the highest point in Hell to distance myself from the heat. I see something I have not noticed before: a bleeding heart torn in half standing upside down on the white brim of the Hollow Man's hat. Some might insist it is a pink bagpipe, a medieval instrument turned into an aberration. But what are our hearts if not both an instrument and an aberration when measured against sharp cruelties? I still hold a memory in my hands of tenderness for all the heart-shaped blossoms I picked up after they had fallen on the black, damp soil. Taking the petals into my hands, I would close my fingers carefully around them like a cradle for all that was vulnerable.

Is Hell nothing more than the tortured chambers of our own hearts?

I enter the body of the woman stretched across the strings of an enormous gold harp. Love is the great crucifixion.

There are forests burning in Hell.

. . .

In Bosch's Hell there are forests burning.

I walk into the forest and encounter tree spirits who cry out in pain. Souls torn from their bodies by suicide are transformed into the knotted trunks of trees where harpies now choose to nest.

> *"If thou lop off*
> *A single twig from one of those ill plants,*
> *The thought thou has conceived shall vanish quite."*
> *There at a little stretching forth my hand,*
> *From a great wilding gather'd I a branch,*
> *And straight the trunk exclaim'd: "Why pluck'st thou me?"*
> *Then, as the dark blood trickled down its side,*
> *These words it added: "Wherefore tear'st me thus?*
> *Is there no touch of mercy in thy breast?*
> *Men once were we, that now are rooted here.*
> *Thy hand might well have spared us, had we been*
> *The souls of serpents." As a brand yet green,*
> *That burning at one end from the other sends*
> *A groaning sound, and hisses with the wind*
> *That forces out its way.*

The report from the pathologist reads "benign." I do not have breast cancer. I am relieved, but a melancholy hangs over me. This story tires me, breaks me down, erodes my spine. Mother had breast cancer, so did my grandmothers. They are dead. I am alive. Why?

Last night, I had a dream that the mountain across from where we live had been clear-cut.

My grandmother is sitting on the chaise in our den. I say to her, "How did this happen and so soon?" She is dressed in white and says nothing.

I run outside to see if it is really true.

I am creating a narrative on the forest floor out of found objects—pine needles, sticks, and branches, pieces of bark, cones, stones, feathers, moss—it is a sentence written in the native voice of the woods. I do not know what it says, only that I am its scribe. What I feel as I place these "letters" on the ground is that it is a way to stay the cutting, long, flowing sentences rising out of the duff that acknowledges the death of trees.

A friend sends me a large wooden ball. It is made out of yew, yew that heals the cancers of women. Taxol. This is a tree I know from the Willamette Valley where she lives. Pacific yew, so elegant below the towering cedars and firs. I remember watching the slash piles burn, the pungent smell that inevitably follows the chain saws and timber sales. I recall all the clearcuts I have stood in, walked through in Utah, Idaho, Montana, Oregon, Washington, and British Columbia.

The silence.

The heat.

The mutilations.

The stumps.

The phantom limbs still waving above my head.

The hillsides from a distance look like a woman's body prepped for surgery, shaved and cleared, ready for the scalpel.

I hold this yew ball in my hands, close my eyes. Heartwood. Wood round like the cyst my body created, now removed by a surgeon, the same surgeon who removed my grandmother's breast, his hands holding the knife—cut and release. What have I released?

Where do the clear-cut breasts of women go? Where has the tissue of my body been thrown? I should have asked for it back so I could have buried it in my garden like a sunflower seed.

I want to be buried on Antelope Island out on Great Salt Lake. It is not legal, but my husband and brothers have promised to sneak my carapace onto the land, dig a good hole, then cover it with rocks, a fine perch for horned larks.

Mormons believe you should be buried with your feet facing east so you can rise in the First Resurrection. I want to face west toward the lake, toward the setting sun, toward the unknown, my body easing back into earth, food for beetles, worms, and microbes. I am satisfied to be soil. The songs of meadowlarks and curlews will be my voice. Stampeding bison over my grave are the only eternal vision I need.

White roses sit on our dining room table like doves, the doves I saw cross over our home in unified flight on the morning of my surgery. Are we ever at peace?

Yesterday, my breast was cut open, a cyst removed. I was unconscious as part of myself was taken. I dream of mountains being clear-cut. My eyes open, the hills outside our home are still wild. It is only when I look in the mirror that my body reveals the trauma.

Bear tracks in the snow coming down from the mountain. They are filled with blood. I see the blood of my mother and grandmothers. I smell the potent sap of yew, slash and burn, cut and release. I cup my two breasts, one tender, one firm in my hands.

My friend from the forest and I are canoeing in a lake. The mountains that surround us are burning, the trees are burning.

I hear W. S. Merwin's voice:

> *but what came out of the forest*
> *was all part of the story*
> *whatever died on the way*
> *or was named but no longer*
> *recognizable even*
> *what vanished out of the story*
> *finally day after day*
> *was becoming the story*
> *so that when there is no more*
> *story that will be our*
> *story when there is no*
> *forest that will be our forest.*

What do I do now with the open space in front of my heart?

The severed hand of Christ falls off the gambling table over-turned by Bosch. Again, bets are wagered in favor of our own disembodiment. We will be lonely. We will be hungry. We will be tricked and fooled. Pan for gold on the river's edge. Step into the river and sink. A hand waves above the surface of the water. We wave back. No one sees it is a drowning man's gesture for help.

The Nightjar Magistrate who sits on his golden throne in Hell, a hell where we are consumed not just by flames but literally by the things we love. Birds. I am being consumed by a bird, a nightjar or goatsucker, who knows what violations I have committed on Earth to warrant this kind of punishment. We are all complicit in the destruction of life.

To destroy: *destruir*. Present tense: *destruyo*. Imperfect: *destruía*. Indefinite: *destruí*. Future imperfect: *destruiré*. Conditional: *destruirá*.

Present.

Tense.

Imperfect.

Indefinite.

Future.

Imperfect.

Conditional.

All these tenses at once. I am a body of verbs standing in El Bosco's Hell. How do I speak to this blue-skinned ogre whose feathers have been plucked? Is there time to learn a new language? Am I too old to learn a new language? The Nightjar Magistrate is not going to wait to hear what I have to say. He does not care what I have to say. He wears a three-legged kettle on his head as a helmet. The animals are taking their revenge: hyenas tearing flesh, a rabbit piercing feet, pigs licking, raccoons beating, a wolf molesting, a squirrel strangling, a monkey ringing, a moth-priest is blinding a man with its beak.

The animals are taking their revenge.

A woman (or is she a coyote disguised?) wears a dress made of what appears to be human skin with a collar of human hair and walks down the streets of Madrid. The skin's irregularity upon closer examination is the pinch and pull of where navels were, nipples, and sphincters. The dress is beautiful, chic, and costly.

People walking by suddenly stop and stare. They say behind her back, "What a perverse idea."

Another woman stands in the middle of the city with the letters of the alphabet pinned to her clothes, her shabby clothes. She walks in circles. Some stand on the sidewalk and mock her, call her mad, want her removed from the street. A monk stops and recognizes her as a Buddhist prayer wheel.

. . .

A letter arrives from home. Six men and women, largely scholars and intellectuals, all living in Utah, have been excommunicated from the Church of Jesus Christ of Latter-day Saints for
exercising beliefs contrary to the doctrine. Apostasy. It is being
called Black September.

There is a history of excommunicating men and women
who believe beyond convention. But an institution can never
excommunicate a spirit from its body. Cut the trees down.
Believe the green stand is gone. Then walk among the stumps
when the wind blows through and feel the phantom limbs
bowing to what remains, what can never be destroyed.

We have forgotten the art of a living theology. Look at Hieronymus Bosch to remember. His language of images, visual
poetry, is a lyrical meditation.

We have forgotten that God's declarations are always heard,
seen, and delivered through our own creative interpretations.
Without language, we could not speak of God. We can never
escape our own formulations, conjectures, translations. Religions begin as a salve to mystery, not a manifesto of truth.
We too can interpret the truth and make it our own. It is
our nature to question. It is our nature to create meaning and
make myths out of our lives. Each religion creates an anthology
of stories, some oral, some written, as an attempt to make
the sacred concrete. The Bible. The Torah. The Koran. The
Hopi Prophecy. The Book of Mormon. Creation cosmologies
around the world deliver us to a place of compassion and reverence. We see the world whole, even holy.

Spiritual beliefs are not something alien from Earth, but rise
out of its very soil. Perhaps our first gestures of humility and
gratitude were extended to Earth through prayer, the recogni-

tion that we exist by the grace of something beyond ourselves. Call it God. Call it Wind. Call it a thousand different names. Corn pollen sprinkled over the nose of deer. Incense sprinkled from swaying balls held by a priest. Arms folded, heads bowed. The fullness we feel after prayer is the acknowledgment that we are not alone in our struggles and sufferings. We can engage in dialogue with the Sacred, with God and each other. A suffering that cannot be shared is a suffering that cannot be endured.

*And some feeble-minded children in the kitchens have
discovered tiny swallows on crutches
that could pronounce the word love.*

I think about love in Hell as I am dying. Yes, in El Bosco's Hell, I am dying. I think about the Mormon concept of Hell: *That part of the spirit world inhabited by wicked spirits who are awaiting the eventual day of their resurrection. . . . There they suffer the torments of the damned; there they welter in the vengeance of eternal fire; there is found weeping and wailing and gnashing of teeth; there the fiery indignation of the wrath of God is poured out upon the wicked.*

We are taught *Spiritual death is hell . . . hell must deliver up its captive spirits. Hell will have an end.*

I am the woman half inside, half outside the blue bubble being expelled from the bowels of the Nightjar Magistrate that feels like being caught between the walls of a narrow room whose door is locked when the earth quakes and the ceiling cracks, the plaster falls, the walls are moving, the floor is moving, and suddenly everything breaks open and you are thrown outside, exposed to chaos, amazed to be alive, eyes safe, still breathing, legs free.

I walk these streets of Madrid anonymous, faceless, attached to no one. I do not cast a shadow. If I were to die, no one would know my identity or whereabouts. The sky is grey. The buildings are grey. The mood is grey. *The color of retreat is grey.* Nothing has meaning. I can find no meaning. I stop and lean against a stone wall. Across the street, there are red fliers stapled to wooden posts. *Release him. Free him. Do not forget him.* It looks like an image of Christ. I cross the cobbled street and see it is an image of Leonard Peltier. How strange to see him here in Spain. I wonder who put up these posters—an American, a Spaniard, an Oglala Sioux?

Boundaries dissolve. Teachings dissolve. Where did we come from? Why are we here? Where are we going? *I honestly don't know.* Say it again. *I honestly don't know.* Nothing makes sense. El Bosco's Hell is seeping into the world.

I am afraid. I am afraid of justice, *poetic justice.* I am afraid of license, *artistic license.* I am afraid because in the context of modernity, a path of amnesia is being created, a state where the art of forgetting is perfected in the name of comfort and denial and distraction. Where is the truth? What is the truth? Sanitize the truth. The perfection of amnesia is the erasure of memory. *Clean, clean, clean.* Without memory there is no emotion. Without emotion there is no experience. Without experience there is only abstraction.

There is no solid footing in Hell.

The ghoul in the pink frock is flashing his barbed tongue. His eyes are glazed. He does not frighten me now because I don't care. I am too tired and fractured to care. I wander through this scorched and tarnished landscape feeling trapped and defeated by all the obstacles and stalemates I encounter. Hell, I am certain, is the place where one is afforded no movement.

Motion. Emotion. To remember what moves us, inside, outside. Perhaps the most profound barometer for misery is when we can no longer perceive beauty. To feel beauty. Hell is the Great Forgetting.

What is the key?

My body is draped over the key, the key that is hanging from a hook on a pole that is lodged in the skull. I am always losing the keys, forgetting where I put them, misplaced them, last saw them. It is the key that always brings me back. *Excuse me, I forgot my keys, have you seen my keys?* Keys to the Gospel. I seem to have temporarily lost them. Closed doors. Locked doors. There are rooms I may never enter again. The Temple is closed. I have lost my key. Where is the key, the skeleton key made to fit many locks? Here is the key. I am caught in the doorway of my religious past.

It grows dark around me as I enter the portal behind the red hills. Five blackbirds fly out of the ass of the man the Nightjar Magistrate is devouring. I follow a naked individual (man or woman, who can be sure?) who wears the carapace of a horseshoe crab as a helmet. How do we arm ourselves against that which we fear? It is becoming darker and darker. My mind is unraveling.

I strike a match and stare into the small flame.

What am I afraid of?

A shattered glass broken in rage.
The dismantling of family.
A loss of hearing.

What am I not hearing?
A loss of sight.
What am I not seeing?
Becoming numb.
The dismantling of the self.

I am detached, displaced, disoriented, disturbed, despondent. I am the bruise no one sees. Congealed blood. Stuck. Stuck in Hell. Who is the architect of this nightmare?

I have tried to turn my back and walk away. The painting has not devoured me. I have devoured the painting. And right now, I am living inside the right panel which is the wrong panel which is Hell.

I blow out the candle, turn my back again, and close my eyes.

The house.
The family house is gone.
The house with the comet overhead is gone.

When my grandfather was dying in the darkness of December, I tried to offer him solace by listening to his visions.

"Can you see the man with the wheelbarrow taking away the dirt?" he would say, his eyes open to the ceiling. "Can you hear what he is saying?"

"No," I said. "I am sorry I cannot hear what he is saying. Tell me what the man is saying."

I tried to ask him some questions regarding the man he was seeing, when suddenly the last of my elders sat up abruptly, crossed his two index fingers, and screamed, "Don't do this to me! Don't do this to me! You are breaking up my signal!"

He used the last of his strength to cross his fingers at me, a witch, he saw a witch.

I find myself walking aimlessly in the rain with no place to go. There is a small cemetery ahead on the outskirts of Madrid. I enter the refuge of graves and stop at a garden of headstones. Sitting down on a black iron bench, I read the Spanish names of other people's elders. Mothers. Fathers. Grandparents. Children. Especially the elders that die as children. In the end, we are children. Husbands. Wives. Brothers. Sisters. Friends. Lovers. Everything is buried beneath our feet. Under our feet. Everything under our feet is decomposing.

I am decomposing.

The Hollow Man in El Bosco's Hell looking over his shoulder is decomposing. He has tree stumps for legs. His body is an eggshell, broken. He wears boats as shoes. This unsteady man in Hell is looking over his shoulder. A white flag has been raised. He is on his way to becoming something else.

"It's the hardest thing I've ever had to do—" my grandfather said. "But everyone goes through it." He shrugs his shoulders and lifts his eyebrows. "If you sit here long enough, eventually you will leave with a philosophy."

Now after months of frailty, he has stopped eating. Call it the hunger strike of the elderly, their last act of control. He waits. The family waits. The days slowly pass in autumn.

"I am a falling leaf on our family tree," he tells my cousin and me, his veined hand swaying back and forth in a downward motion.

I savor his words, desperate to know what he sees through the lens of his ninety-one years. He is not a verbal man. He prefers listening, his blue eyes steady.

In 1923, he received his amateur radio operator's license. W7JOE has been his call name for almost seventy-five years. He was the youngest "ham" in Utah and is now the oldest. He was always in his room sitting in his swayback chair tucked between his radios, listening, dwarfed by the huge black machines. The static, the martian-like voices speaking from the metal boxes day and night, taught us as children that there was a larger world outside, a world we didn't have access to but our grandfather did.

His conversations on air required no eye contact, only a turn of hand, fingers manipulating dials, scanning voices until a tone or an idea stopped him. He would roll the silver dial back and forth, sharpening the frequency until the band was clear. Then, he would listen. He would enter in when he wanted to and leave when he was no longer interested.

"It used to be politics and religion were off-limits," he told us. "But the world changed. The rules of civility are gone. No manners. Now, people talk about anything."

Conversation for my grandfather has always been a matter of tuning in and tuning out. He loved the equipment as much as the talk. And he always prided himself in having the finest, most up-to-date technology. Through the years, the transmitters and receivers became smaller and smaller, until now condensed into one transceiver.

My grandmother always said that the day Jack quits listening to his radio he will be dead.

But he is not dead.

He is still breathing: the rise and fall of his chest beneath the down comforter. His eyes are open staring at the ceiling.

"What are you thinking?" I ask as I rub his arm that is more bone than muscle.

"I'm not thinking, period. I'm a blank."

"So you're just existing?"

"That's right. I don't want to think." He makes a straight line in the air.

He turns to me. "You wouldn't be asking me these questions if you were facing what I am. You'd choose to be a blank too. If you think too much you can make yourself crazy."

"Zen masters spend a lifetime striving for an empty mind," I say, teasing.

He lies in bed like a corpse with its mouth open. I close my eyes and listen to the old man's breaths. They have the steady underground surge of a receding tide.

I sit near, reading Krishnamurti's journal, one of my grandmother's books still on the nightstand.

All this is the way of living which is meditation and that is the beauty of it; beauty, not as in architecture, in the line and curve of a hill, of the setting sun or the moon, not in the word or in the poem, not in a statue or a painting—it is in a way of living, you can look at anything and there is beauty.

On another day, I walk in, take off my coat.

"How are you this afternoon?"

"Here."

He wants to know what the weather is like outside, what day of the week it is, and if my husband is in town.

I tell him it is a glorious blue day, a bit chilly, quintessential October, and that the temperature dropped below freezing the night before.

"It's Thursday, and yes, Brooke is in town."

"Good," he says, as he closes his eyes.

We sit comfortably in silence.

"Did you know the average person blinks eighteen to twenty times a minute?" he suddenly says.

"No, I didn't."

"And that a person who is working at a computer only blinks four to five times a minute?"

"No, I didn't know that either."

"What's that going to do to our eyesight?" he asks. "It seems to me, eventually you're going to strain something."

I look at my grandfather lying on his back in bed staring at the ceiling. He rarely blinks at all in these last days of his life.

"Where did you hear those statistics?" I ask.

"On the air, a while back."

More silence.

"Something's not right."

"What do you mean?"

"I mean all this fuss about information on the Internet. We're doing away with human contact. Everyone is so busy. No more rubbing shoulders. No more shaking hands. We want too much and in the process of getting it we miss so much." He pauses. "It's lonely." He turns his head on the pillow and looks at me. "I just want to hear your voice."

I thought about all the voices on the radio he spent a lifetime listening to and now without his "rig" the silence that must be enveloping him.

"How did you become interested in radio?"

"I don't know," he says. "It was another way to reach people. I was always interested in striving for a better signal, a cleaner, crisper, more powerful signal that could communicate with someone somewhere."

He pauses.

"You could say it started with a cat-whisker radio, a little wire sticking out, you hit a sensitive spot and there it is— contact. Then vacuum tubes were introduced; every year there were improvements to follow and implement until today we've got solid-state transistors. Invention is a remarkable thing, really."

"What has radio taught you?"

"Three things," he says without hesitation. (I am surprised by his definitive response.) "First, radio brings people together through the human voice, the most reassuring of sounds. A manner of goodwill is acknowledged and extended across the air. Second, you talk about the rig itself, how you can improve it. After all, it's the equipment that brings you to this hobby in the first place. And third, you look at the radio and think about it, what it is, how it's made, what it can do. I spend a lot of time wondering."

"Wondering?"

"Wondering about sound waves, how electronic waves keep moving outward until they become fainter and fainter, wearing themselves out until they are overcome by something else. Someday equipment will be able to pick these sound waves up. Nothing is ever lost. The sound is still there. We just can't hear it."

Another silence follows. El Bosco's ears. *To cut the air with a knife.* What do we hear? The image of El Bosco's ears returns to me, the sounds of both joy and terror that will never die.

"And I'll tell you another funny thing, you can electrically eliminate all manner of noise on the air—man-made noise—but you can't get rid of natural static, static or interference caused by thunder and lightning, rainstorms or snowstorms. Ham radio operators always pay attention to the weather, light, too. In the day, radio bands expand way out. At night, they contract, shut down. You see that the sun pulls the signals out, while sunspots can cause blackouts altogether. So you wonder about these things."

He closes his eyes and smiles.

"What?" I ask.

"I was just thinking that in spite of all our technologies, maybe we haven't progressed that far as human beings. We still have the same fundamental needs. Sometimes I wonder if we have evolved at all."

I sit with him for another hour or so, kiss his forehead, and leave.

To wonder. To contemplate that which is never lost but continues to move outward forever, however faint.

To wonder. Throw pebbles in pools and watch the concentric circles that reach the shore in waves. Waves of water. Waves of electricity. Our words are still moving, churning, careening through space and time—this sea of spoken languages oscillates around us.

What do we hear?

Harold Schapero writes in "The Musical Mind": *A great percentage of what is heard becomes submerged in the unconscious and is subject to literal recall . . . a tonal memory.*

What sounds do we hold in our bodies and retrieve when necessary? What sounds disturb and what sounds heal? Where do we store the tension of traffic, honking horns, or the hum of fluorescent lights? How do we receive birdsong, the leg rubbings of crickets, the water music of trout?

I sit before the trio of giant instruments in Hell: a lute, a harp, and a hurdy-gurdy. They are so beautiful, even in Hell they are beautiful, perfectly rendered in their elegant designs, instruments adored and savored in the Middle Ages. None of them are sounding. No music to soothe or join souls here. Herein lies the perversity. Through their silence, these instruments torture, each a grotesque apparatus of pain heightened by the memory

Hell

of pleasure that still reverberates in their strings that strangle and bind the bodies they have attracted. Addiction. Affliction. Torment. In silence, we suffer.

The shawm, a reed instrument akin to an oboe, is leaning cruelly against a man's back (who incidentally has a fife jammed up his ass) and is being played by another man wearing a white cradle cap with a crescent-moon banner attached on top. And a bombardon, a brass horn, is being blown, adding to the chaos of a pounding drum.

El Bosco's residents must endure the discordant, tuneless, repetitive din that leaves them shaking on the ground, knees brought to their chins like babies abandoned as they rock back and forth in agony, impossible to deny or deflect the blare, blast, bang, boom, rumble, crumble, groan, clatter, scratch, brattle, screech, tin, cling, chink, clank, clang, chime, peal, knell, toll, tinkle, drone, creak, grate, grind, until even the ice shatters as a violent plea to stop.

But it doesn't stop.

My body holds the dissonance. The clanging, banging, and blowing threatens to incite some savage response inside.

How to overturn the chaos?

Hold the dissonance and remember the calm, the hiss and hush of summer grasses cured by the sun that become knee-high rattles. Hear the ridge winds shake the tiny seedheads like gourds.

I hear my grandfather's voice and wonder why, here in Hell, it is his voice I yearn for, that it is his presence I look for in this lost landscape of heartbreak. He was always home. On the surface of the overturned table in Hell, there is a white etching that resembles an antenna. I look down at my feet and see two pieces of broken flint and begin striking the edges together.

My grandfather's desire is for voices, to be held as he dies in the comfort of conversation, even if he rarely contributes words; it is his constancy of being that shapes my thoughts. Under the glass that protects his radio table, he keeps a yellowed quotation that reads, *There is no one true church, no one chosen people.* He inspires me now, even as he lies dying. His mind has always found his own calm. To him, sound is eternity, a form of music that allows him to remember he is not alone in the world.

Our evolution is the story of listening.

A bone flutelike object was found in a cave in northwestern Slovenia recently, dated somewhere between 43,000 and 82,000 years old. It is a piece of bear femur with four holes in a straight alignment. Researchers say the bone flute may be the oldest known musical instrument.

I wonder about that cave, the fire that flickered and faded on damp walls as someone in the clan played a flute. Were they a family? What were their dreams and inventions? When did we start imagining a future?

Returning to my grandfather's home, our family home, the home where Heaven and Hell hung above the grandchildren's beds, I notice the fifty-five-foot antenna that towers over their roof. I recall my grandfather telling me as a young girl how important it was for the antenna to be grounded in the earth, that as long as it was securely placed it could radiate signals in the air all around the world. Transmit and receive. I walk into his dim room and place my hand on my grandfather's leg. My fingers wrap around bone and I feel his life blowing through him.

There is a girl kneeling on the edge of the garden in the cemetery. She is kneading bone meal and blood pellets into the soil beds, mulching it with her hands. With the death of our elders, we search for who remains. New elders emerge. We see them in the eyes of our children as they look into ours.

EYE SCANNING TAKES ATMS HIGH-TECH

USA Today reports PIN numbers and bank cards soon could become obsolete for millions of automated teller machine users. Eye-recognition technology straight out of *Mission Impossible* is expected to be installed this year at dozens of automated teller machines in the United States and about 400 ATMs and teller stations worldwide.

Moorestown, N.J.–based Sensar has developed an ID system that takes a photo of the iris and, in about two seconds, digitizes it and compares it with a photo on file. . . .

The iris is the most data-rich part of the body, with more than 250 unique wrinkles, freckles, and ridges that remain constant over the years, Sensar says.

Sitting outside at a table in a neighborhood café, I continue to read how iris identification works. First the customer stands within three feet of the ATM. Using ordinary video cameras, Sensar Iris Identification finds the customer's face and determines the exact position of an eye. Then the camera takes a black-and-white digital picture of the eye. Next, the Sensar system lays a circular grid over the picture of the eye and generates a unique "human bar code" using the light and dark areas of the iris. The bar code is checked and verified against the one on file. If it matches, the money requested is released. The entire process takes about two seconds.

Surveillance. Who is watching us? God? Satan? Our Dead? Or is that simply another piece of our mythology that keeps us in place, the thought that we are being monitored ensuring our good behavior. We are being filmed at the bank, the grocery store, the convenience store, at stop signs, schools, health clubs, libraries, shopping malls, airports, and elevators. Our lives are on tape.

Who is watching?

Can one recognize a heretic? What might their irises reveal? Whoever deviates from the consensus can be called a heretic, whoever holds an opinion contrary to generally accepted beliefs commits heresy.

When did we forget that the root translation of "heresy" is *hairesis,* the Greek word for choice?

Did we ever really know?

I was taught that during the Great War in Heaven, two plans were offered to God from his sons Lucifer and Jesus as to how human beings were to conduct themselves on Earth. Lucifer wanted to ensure obedience; they would be told how to act and what to do. Jesus wanted to ensure choice; let men and women decide for themselves what is right and what is wrong. A debate ensued. A vote was taken. Jesus won and Lucifer was cast out of Heaven. Call him now Satan, the Tempter. Mormons, along with most Christians, believe he is on the loose to this day. Call him the Devil. Call him the Outsider. The one who can find no peace, save the turmoil of others.

In Spain, they call him *Ángel Caído,* the fallen angel, and he resides in the Parque del Retiro in Madrid. I enjoy visiting him, especially on hot summer days. His is a fountain that is rarely crowded. The statue of Satan is dark, a black shadow in the midst of green. Most people walk by never realizing they have passed the Devil. *Madrileños* claim this is the only homage to Satan found anywhere in the world. They say this site is an occult point where traditionally witches met throughout the centuries.

Ángel Caído looks as though he has been impaled by his own wings, his struggle internal. The fountain from which he rises is surrounded by demons, spurting water from their mouths and the mouths of those they are devouring. The Outsider is held captive by the grip of serpents who are strangling his legs and crushing his shoulders. Their mouths are open. The sound of falling water is the sound of serpents hissing, violently, in their fight to bring him down.

Sitting on the pavement beyond the spray of water, I look up at the black statue, almost blue in its casting, and cannot help but feel a certain sympathy. This fallen figure struggling to free himself, this dark angel who once had a voice in Heaven and now moans in exile, this presence pulled between opposing forces, is a force I recognize in myself.

If I believe or don't believe in Satan, he is still the dark stranger inside. We cannot give our darkness away. Satan is alive whenever I cause pain. Satan is alive whenever someone else causes pain. This is what I fear, the shadow cast by our unconscious selves.

If the Devil is present, where is he? I tiptoe around each figure. The pink ghoul sitting on his haunches, the one I dreamed about in Paradise, the one whose barbed tongue is extended, the one whose eyes are permanently glazed, that in a moment of resignation I said I did not fear—this monster in front of the hurdy-gurdy, singing the sins of the damned in a discordant key, is disturbing. Too close to the demon's noxious breath, I step back. Now I see that his tongue is not barbed at all but is, in fact, a long white strand of beads hanging from his mouth. It is knotted, an ingested rosary whose circle was snapped and now remains wrapped and lodged inside the organs of Satan himself. Standing behind the lute, I want to grab the string and run. I have never trusted the outward virtue of pearls. They are most seductive when hidden.

Behind the Pink Singer of Sin, there is the man still trapped inside a drum. A raccoon is beating the drum on both ends. And above him, still there, is the man carrying the giant shawm on his back being played violently by a soldier. Misery. Anguish. Despair. Over and over. What are the words, the notes, the music, we have had drummed into us over and over again, all of our lives? What is the burden we carry when we allow someone else to play on the back of our own creativity?

I try desperately to escape, the repetition of images and figures is making El Bosco's world and my world indivisible. I am, she is, spinning in a circle where time is a lie. I am inside Hell. She is outside Hell. The self is separated from the soul. Look here. Look there. Listen to this. Listen to that. Watch your back. Watch the time. What is time? In Hell, there is no place to stand, only to run.

I turn and look upward at this hierarchy of chaos towering, collapsing, crumbling around me. The world begins to spin faster and faster. I am dizzy. One of the Bird Mentors takes pity on me and extends her hand. We circle the pink heart being played as a bagpipe. Faster and faster. The white hat the Hollow Man is wearing is spinning. A millstone. A grindstone. Faster and faster, the world is spinning, spinning out of control, someone grabs a string on the white cloak of a fellow traveler and we all start unraveling u n r a v e l i n g u n r a v e l i n g beforeourverybloodshotandwearyandweepyeyes. The dismantling of family, the crumbling of community, the careening of our senses, a blade between our ears, a knife stabbed through our hands, a knife stabbed through our hands impaled on the center of a satellite dish, a blue satellite dish. How did El Bosco foresee our future? Sequestered in Hell, we're just doing time, your business, my business: busy, busier, busiest, busy body, busy work, busy signal, just trying to keep ourselves occupied. Please leave a message and we'll call you back when we can. We can call back. I call back to the animal mentor I have lost as I am spinning, spinning, spinning, my hand reaching to hold. A woman holds the forehead of a man vomiting bile. Her hand supports his head. *What are we supposed to do? How do we purge all we have been asked to ingest?*

Pangs of hunger have led us to Hell. We are not being fed by anything real.

I stand up from the whirlwind in Hell, my arms like the hands of a clock having been spun counterclockwise, I cannot feel my fingers. I see a round mirror rimmed in gold stuck to the buttocks of a green body whose head is hidden. His feet have turned to branches, brittle and sharp. I see my reflection, the grey hair, the lines in my face, the looseness of my skin, the darkness of my eyes.

Why look?

Do we dare to look?

If we look, can we change what we see?

Satan is not one figure in El Bosco's Hell, he is a visitor, like the rest of us. His two-legged hoofprints are the tracks we call ruts, the ones walked in with our eyes closed.

Running down the stairs to the *metro,* late for an appointment, having spent too much time at the Prado, I fly down another steep flight of stairs. The train arrives. Doors open. I barely slip in. Doors close. I catch my breath and stand holding on to the bar above my head. The train speeds down the tiled tunnel. The underworld flashes by as we rock back and forth on the tracks.

And then it becomes dark. The train screeches. Everyone on the train is silent. Blackout. The train coasts to a stop. No lights in the tunnel. Breathing. All I can hear is breathing. Someone lights a match and shelters a small flame in the alcove of their hand.

Mi cuerpo entre los equilibrios contrarios.

"My body floats between contrary equilibriums," say it again, say it over and over. What is real and what is imagined. Federico García Lorca, his assassins must surely be here. Over there, those men, young, now old, sitting in the corner. I cannot see them completely in the dark, only their cheekbones reflecting back light. What was their age in 1936 when García Lorca was executed by a military firing squad in Granada? A voice like his must be silenced. Who told them? García Lorca's murderers during Franco's Civil War are the murderers of the Spanish Inquisition, the same technicians who fueled the great autos-da-fé in the fifteenth and sixteenth centuries, the public burnings of Jews, Moors, Protestants, and Lutherans, Gypsies, witches, doctors, scholars, healers, and anyone else who was suspected as *contraire* to the blood-red-black-and-gold truth of the Catholic Church.

They are all present in the upper reaches of Hell, burning on the plazas and pillars and inside the buildings of the red-black-and-gold horizon, these stories of deadly theater sponsored by the Church. Was news of the discovery of the New World preceded by news of people being burned mercilessly at the stake? Did El Bosco paint the paradox of a two-handed Spain, the Great Empire with one hand holding a belief in the New World, a hand open to discovery, while the other hand remained a closed fist holding the reins of terror tight around the neck of every heretic found? Are these the processions Bosch painted in Hell, the bloody, boiling sea of Inquisitors and all those who watched in the plazas and cheered?

I am stuck in a tunnel in Hell on a train that keeps traveling around and around through a landscape of suffering.

The train is stopped.

I keep my eyes open.

Who is the man in the corner being kissed by a pig? A pig in drag. A pig dressed up as a nun. A habit; a kiss, the beginning of betrayal. Bosch directs his brush with his own cynicism. Religious swine, not to be trusted. Where are the stories of ecclesiastical abuse hidden, far beyond the night, the right-hand corner of El Bosco's Hell, lodged in the frozen tissues of bodies that one day remember the heat like a hot poker prodding at their back.

The train jolts forward.

I hit my head on the window as other passengers fall forward and back on top of one another. The lights return. We adjust our eyes. No one speaks. It remains silent except for the whine of the wheels on steel and the swaying cars speeding through the tunnel.

What does it feel like to wear an orange sweater? I pull the sweater over my head, loose and big and nubby. What does it feel like to forgo variations of black and white and beige? It is the sun rising over the Atlantic. It is the sun setting over the Pacific. It is a tangerine poised against blue. It is a leaf swirling downriver. It is a fire lit at night in hope of being found.

Orange should be worn with caution. It is a secret commitment to speaking the language of flames.

Imagination works at the summit of the mind like a flame.

Las Fallas. It is the eve of Saint Joseph's Day when all Valencia will burn at midnight. *Fuego. Falla.* Fire. Fire as torch; fire as illumination; fire as that which initiates change.

Fallas everywhere, hundreds of handmade sculptures created by skilled artisans out of cardboard, wood, and wax, polished to a sheen, some ten stories high, literally planted in the narrow streets and squares of Valencia. They are satirical creations that poke fun at clergy, politicians, celebrities, both local and national, or any idea that finds its way into public discourse. Each neighborhood puts forward its own social commentary. There are no rules. Nothing is sacred. It is a Saturnalian ritual that has been in place for centuries. All this in an allegiance to Joseph, the spouse of Mary, the patron saint of carpenters, kindled during the Spanish Counter-Reformation by Santa Teresa de Ávila's deep affection for the one whom she believed taught her how to pray. This celebration was her idea.

And so, Saint Joseph is honored as fires are lit each year on March 19.

Philip II, king of Spain, entered Valencia through a gauntlet of flames in the early 1500s, communal fires lit to honor his presence in the city. The bonfires of summer solstice burn on the longest day of the year, heralding the coming of winter.

We stand before the flames with our hands open, facing the heat. We say one thing, *warm us,* but our gesture pushes fire away. The fire obliges and we back away. Too much. Yet the flames hold us captive, our eyes fixed on flames. Move in. Move out. Be close. Be distant. Our dance with fire is a two-step with desire. Call her the Devil, the one who ignites our longings. Call him the Devil, the intimate one who betrays our heart.

Strike the match. How long can we hold the small fire burning before we give it to another source or blow it out completely? The persistence of our own annihilations is perhaps the genius of El Bosco's Hell. The flare-ups of thought, the glowing coals of fear, the aftermath.

Staring into fire.

Staring into memory.

Staring into the future.

It is noon. Tens of thousands of Valencians have gathered together to experience the *mascleta,* the mortar explosions that build to a climax.

I sit on the sidewalk with my knees pulled in toward my chest, my head buried. I am being smothered by the masses. The sweet smell of violets that I hold in my hands keeps me from collapsing under the weight of claustrophobia.

1–2–3–4–5–6–7–8 . . . Pop! Pop! Pop! Pop! Pop! Pop! Pop! Pop!

The pounding of gunpowder in my throat through the soles of my feet renders me mute. Cannons, rockets, firecrackers strung together in a row light each other in rapid succession. My ears are ringing.

1–2–3–4–5–6–7–8–9–10–11–12 . . . Pop! Pop! Pop! Pop! Pop! Pop! Pop! Pop! Pop! Pop! Pop! Pop!

The pavement trembles as the force rattles the roots of my teeth. Sparks dance and transpose into an orange, green, then blue haze. The smoke becomes more dense and slowly crawls through the city like a dragon. The breath of the beast overtakes the crowd. I cover my mouth but coughs cannot be suppressed. My eyes burn as everything in view becomes obscured. The crowd inches closer to the center of explosions. I cannot move and bury my head deeper between my legs, bringing the violets in closer as the smell of gunpowder and human beings intensifies. We are all in danger of being crushed.

Too much. Too much. I want less. More, more gunpowder, greater explosions. These tremors are cracking me open. Open. Let me be open to these earthquakes in Hell. I am breaking. My body is breaking. In this City of Fire, everything is breaking.

The thundering continues. It is relentless, relentless, relentless. I feel each flare and rumbling in my cells, the membranes of my cells are rupturing. Gooseflesh. I close my eyes more tightly, hug my knees, and still the sparks enter—I can feel someone else's knees rocking my back.

And then it is over.

Silence.

I raise my head. Open my eyes. The crowd is motionless and then suddenly, spontaneously, everyone bursts into applause.

In El Bosco's Hell, I rise, a solitary figure, a black silhouette in a doorway of light. I am the heretic in Hell who is weeping.

The Virgin of the Forsaken towers over the people in the plaza. She must be twenty feet tall, her robe created out of red and pink carnations, her dress made of white carnations with yellow ones to emphasize the folds in her skirt. She holds the Christ Child in her arms. At her feet are endless bouquets, floral offerings left by the devoted: tulips, lilies, iris, roses, many wild, handpicked from the country nearby. By the end of the *Fallas* Week, a blanket of petals weighing over twenty-five tons will have been laid at the Virgin's feet.

A river of women, all ages, are carrying these bouquets to the Virgin on the Eve of Saint Joseph. They are stoic and erect, each footstep a deliberation in poise and pride. Miles and miles of maidens are walking, a stream of grace and beauty in the midst of chaos and explosions. The women are known as *falleras* and are dressed in the traditional costume of their village. A banner with the name of their district is draped across their breasts. Their hair is parted in the middle, braided over their ears and wrapped into a labyrinth-like bun at the napes of their necks. The braided buns are secured by ornate gold combs and pins. Many of the women wear tiaras, the scaffolding for the lace veils that cascade below their hips. Pearl-drop earrings like clustered grapes dangle above their clavicles as multiple strands of pearls adorn their throats. Their dresses are designed with lace bodices attached to floral skirts with white voile aprons. The women are finished by white or black *mantones de Manila,* the embroidered shawls that create a natural history of flora and fauna draped around their shoulders. Each woman embodies the Garden as they walk to La Plaza de la Virgen. The blur of white lace stockings and satin-petaled slippers is hypnotic.

I stand on the bank of the River of Falleras and watch, watch these women whose only intention is to adorn the façade of the Basílica with flowers. A song rises from the crowd, *"Valencia es la tierra de flores y luz y amor."*

White doves circle the Virgin. Her eyes made of wax that weep in the heat seem to watch each one of the thousands of individuals moving through the narrow streets, moving through the plaza, moving in and out of one another's way trying to find their path to her. All Valencia is in motion. I dissolve into this sea of devotion, the masses breathing, touching, pushing, shoving, sighing, kneeling, crossing, praying, rising, turning, bumping, pardoning one another, they continue on their way.

On the periphery of the Plaza de la Virgen, in the shadow of the cathedral, flamenco music is being played by Gypsies. They pat the side of their beaten guitars, close their eyes and moan, one woman dressed in black with green eyes watches her feet, lifts the corner of her skirt with one hand, exposes her slip and slaps a tambourine on her hip with the other, she throws back her head, turns abruptly to the singer, the *cantador,* stops, stares, then laughs, and resumes dancing again, her feet thundering on the pavement, her feet throbbing on the pavement, her arms, hands, fingers like serpents invading the Garden, seducing the Garden. Her eyes flash fire as she turns and turns and turns. The singers cry her on. Her feet dance her in place, she is going nowhere but here, her feet dance her in place, her head turns, her eyes stare down. Whoever sleeps below is awakened.

Children run in and out of the crowd throwing bangers which explode as they hit the ground, and the steady flow of proper girls and women carrying carnations continues, it all continues, in the chaos, the procession continues, and the Gypsies sing their songs on the edges.

There is no place to sit.

I take up residency inside the Hollow Man. Still looking over his shoulder, I hear him say, "Look at this endless procession. We know what we want. We know what we believe. We don't know what we want. We don't know what we believe. What do you believe?"

WHAT DO I BELIEVE?

. . .

I have taken up residency in an egg broken open. Life is a process of being broken open. A silk moth emerges from her heat-resistant cocoon with gunpowdered wings. Let the fires roar.

I slip on a pair of rowboats for shoes and launch into the blood-red lake. Watch me sail. I sail from the Old World to the New World. Looking back, the millstone is spinning. Looking ahead, the Earth is spinning. I believe I can steady myself by balancing my arms like the extended wings of cranes. What should I look for? Look for the Gypsies even at sea. Clap with the Gypsies. Don't trust the Gypsies. Moan to the strumming of fingers on gut. Leave. Move. Wander. The boats on my feet are wavering. I pick up a dead branch floating in the water, and paddle. Will I ever be found, I am lost in the waves of this endless procession of bodies stating truth. Each of us wears a banner across our chest. I am from here. You are from there. I think this. You think that. Agree. Disagree. Prove me wrong. Prove me right. The boats rock back and forth. El Bosco rolls in the Canon of Ears supporting a knife. Slice the Age of Reason. Slice the Age of Enlightenment. These dueling ideologies are sinking my ship. In the name of rationality, sever the body from the soul. Cut the mind from the body. Leave the heart for wolves. El Bosco's wolves are puncturing the armor of the knight. I cannot watch. I cannot watch one more cruelty.

My boat is drifting away. On the faith of these boat-shoes, I am drifting away. The blood-red waves are splashing my knees. I had no idea the water was so shallow. If only I can keep maneuvering my way out of Hell.

La Albufera de Valencia. One of the largest freshwater lakes in Spain. There are birds everywhere. I look out over these wetlands and whisper the names of the birds I see: mallard, teal, shoveler, godwit, avocet, stilt, egret, night heron. It is a mantra for my soul. Flight. I had to flee the City of Fire.

There is a bird that is new to me hovering over the reeds, swallowlike. With my binoculars, I follow the shorebird and note a black line that originates from the eye and falls like a tear down its cheek and under its throat, creating a mask of melancholy. In truth, these wetlands have been abandoned.

In the fifteenth century, La Albufera would have been over ten times its present size, but gradually, farmers have taken over these marshlands and turned them into rice paddies. It now covers around seven thousand acres, much of it taken up by reed beds and small islands called *matas*. The average depth varies from three to eight feet. The water level is controlled at the southern end of the lagoon where there is a canal that can be opened and closed at will, allowing the water to flow into the Mediterranean so flooding does not occur.

I take out my bird book and flip through the pages. Here it is, yes, exactly. *Pratincole.*

As serene as these waters appear, they are suffering from neglect as sewage and agricultural and industrial waste seep into the ecosystem.

The controversy has escalated in the past few years over conflicting interests between farmers, duck hunters, and conservationists. It was declared a national park and then recently stripped of its protective status because of a legal technicality. Politics. The bottom line: locals wanted the lake back under their domain. The legislated boundaries were too restrictive. Felipe González, prime minister of Spain at the time of the scrimmage, said, "If it is between a farmer and a duck, the duck is going to lose."

.   .   .

The sun is mirrored in the marsh. La Albufera is a critical passageway for migrants that flock to these waters by the tens of thousands. Over 250 birds have been reported at the ornithological station with nesting records documenting around ninety species. Lapwings, red-crested pochards, black-tailed godwits, golden plovers, little ringed plovers, snipes, dunlins, and redshanks have been counted in the thousands. These birds breeding in the reed beds of Albufera include around a hundred pairs of great crested grebes, black-necked grebes, bitterns, avocets, stilts, and various species of plovers. With increasing insecticides, industrial toxins, and urbanization, these marshes become even more critical to the well-being of Europe's avian population. A harrier floats over the pampas grass. Terns, gulls, rafts of mallards, sandpipers piercing the mudflats—the number of species here is remarkable in spite of the polluted waters. A turquoise kingfisher akin to El Bosco's dives into the water head first, splashes, then rises with a minnow in its beak.

Walking around the shoreline, stepping over heaps of garbage braided into the bulrushes, the familiar grief I know at home returns. I came to Spain to get away from my torn heart ripped open every time I see the landscapes I love ravaged, lost, and opened for development.

There are too many of us, six billion and rising, our collective impact on fragile communities is deadly.

No wonder El Bosco's birds torture us in Hell.

Pink light. The marsh is suddenly very still. *Marisma.* That wildness exists in the midst of such abuse is the forgiveness of birds. They ask so little of us. The palest semblance of life flourishes given half a chance.

Bats criss-cross Saint Joseph's sky, which is gradually intensifying to red at sunset thanks to the gunpowdered City of Fire.

Quarter moon. The silhouettes of herons are reflected in the undulating water as they stand on old moorings. Seven wooden boats rest in the canal just in front of the Comunidad de Pescadores El Palmar, the fisherman's church. Each boat has its own net and a long oar with a forked tip that pulls the fishermen forward in the lake.

Stillness.

Albufera is red, blood red. And on the horizon, Valencia is preparing to burn.

Eight herons fly west. A dozen fish float belly-up, silver scales shimmering in moonlight. The sound of firecrackers on the nearby beach shatters the silence.

It is a few hours before *La Crema, La Nit de Foc,* the Night of Fire, when all the *fallas* will be torched at midnight. I wander the streets to witness these grand, macabre, satirical monuments, the proud artistry of each neighborhood, for the last time. Families and neighbors gather beneath white tents to eat *paella valenciana,* huge hot cast-iron skillets simmer and hiss with saffron rice, peas, and sea treasures: mussels, clams, and crayfish. In a "festival of paellas" the elderly are served first as a tribute to the stories they possess.

Further into the heart of the city, the procession of petaled women continues with the marching brass bands following closely behind. With my head turned toward the women, I keep walking and almost bump into a gigantic dragonfly, half a block long with transparent wings that stretch from one side of the street to the other. It is painted metallic blue, hovering over a pond of ice.

Around the corner and a few blocks west, there stands a four-story wedding cake with naked nymphs cavorting above the betrothed couple. An old man offers me a glass of *orgeat,* a traditional fiesta drink. We toast the *falla.*

Protect the flame. Flame to paper. It is only paper.

Brooke and I are sitting on the shore of Great Salt Lake. The morning is ethereal with a faint mist slowly rising from the inland sea. Clouds appear as the pink petals of roses floating across the sky. The sun has not yet peaked over the Wasatch Mountains.

We lay our marriage certificate on the salt flats of the receding lake. He strikes a wooden match on stone and ignites one corner. I light the other. I watch it curl with a single flame, the burning theology of my childhood, a black burn racing, erasing our fathers' names, disappearing simultaneously, their signatures before God. Gone. We have no witnesses before God.

The small fire sweeps across the parchment. . . . *were by me joined together in the holy bonds of matrimony for time and all eternity, according to the ordinance of God and the laws of the state of Utah. Signed, S. Dilworth Young, an Elder of the Church of Jesus Christ of Latter-day Saints.*

The ornate border dissipates, the engraved gothic spires of the Salt Lake Temple with our names, vanish in flames, turn to smoke as black ashes cartwheel across white sand.

Emotion swells inside me. This piece of paper mattered. I look to Brooke for a similar response. He is elated. It frightens me. I turn to the lake. Something steals my attention. Pink on

blue. I squint. I squint again against the glare of water. I stand
to get a better look to be certain of what I see and then slowly,
gently, take my husband's hand. He stands as I point to a flock
of gulls standing twenty yards ahead.

"A flamingo?"

I smile.

"Who could imagine?"

Phoenicopterus ruber. The Latin genus translates to "the
Phoenix," the firebird rising from the ashes.

We walk to the edge of Great Salt Lake. I take off my platinum wedding bands and hurl them as far as I can into the lake.
He has brought an antique dinner plate, a souvenir from our
wedding breakfast, and skips it across the water like a flat stone.
It shatters on the third run.

We turn. We follow the pink flamingo along the shore as it
feeds on brine—a rose petal on the water.

What happens when our institutions no longer serve us, no
longer reflect the truth of our own experience? We sit on pews
and feel a soul-stirring disconnect as we are preached sermons
spoken from the dead. What we know is not what we hear.
We mistake our confusion for guilt. Our hearts close. Our
minds wander and then we walk away. Inspiration returns when
another voice is heard, one that recognizes that the past and the
future are contemporary. How can we learn to speak in a language that is authentic, faithful to our hearts? The ceiling is
raised by our imagination. Authentic acts reform.

It is only an hour away from midnight. I am still walking the
streets of Valencia in a trance, slowly meandering through the
city, shoulder to shoulder with the masses.

A branching tree covered with odd, deformed fruits provides shelter. I failed to see until I stood beneath it the garish serpent with gold fangs wrapped around the trunk. Eve with gilded nipples minus her fig leaf sits comfortably on a cushion and feeds Adam (dressed as a sultan) grapes.

Finally, I see the *falla* I choose to adopt as my own: a five-story pile of hospital beds, each one stacked precariously on top of the other. I think of the hours spent in literal hospitals attending to the sick and dying.

"This is the *falla* I want to see burn," I say to myself.

With the help of the *llibert,* the *falla* verse which accompanies each sculpture to inform the public, I begin to understand the voice of this particular artist, Ortifus, crying out against the ills of society.

Forty-eight beds, *camas,* each bear a label ranging from *"agonía patológica"* (dying ducks) to *"embolias"* (embezzlers) to *"estado crítico"* (with the country of Spain under the covers) to *"cancer de plumón"* (a plumed pen lying in bed); *"sordera"* (deafness); *"polución nocturna"* (night pollution); and many beds of humor and puns such as the *"camasutra"* and the *"camakaze."*

And here, in this City of Fire, the Seven Deadly Sins are also sick in bed, precariously piled on top of each other, teetering. Avarice, sloth, gluttony, lust, anger, envy, and pride, by now feel so familiar I worry they are my only true companions in Spain.

El Bosco nudges me again as fireworks explode at random in the night sky.

Welcome to the Temple of Confessions. We incarnate your desires. We incarnate your fears. We know you are experiencing cultural deprivation, political disenchantment and sexual loneliness. ... At times, this "border zone" between cultures, peoples, and languages

*becomes a dangerous minefield. . . . We respectfully invite you to . . .
share with "the living saints" your most intimate thoughts, memo-
ries, and mythologies.*

Inside one of the rooms there is a body bag wrapped in black
plastic with red roses tossed on top, a white rooster, strangled,
dangles above on a twisted rope.

New World. Old World. A World in Transition.

Living Saints. Latter-day Saints. A Saint does not dwell in
comfort. Teach us how to pray. If we are to repent of our collective sins, to whom do we acknowledge the pain we have
caused?

Welcome to The Temple of Confessions.

One of the Living Saints is dressed in a jaguar skin with
a burlap tie, looking like an Aztec God in bondage. I hang
my head. I hear voices. There are voices speaking all around
me in a language I do not understand. I am unable to speak.
Mute. I kneel in a circle of confusion. Hieronymus Bosch.
He is speaking to me again. "If you continue to follow me, I
will tell you there is no way out." Mad, I am truly mad. Abuse.
Spiritual abuse. Why is that revolver placed on top of the
American flag and the crucifix, too? A voice behind me says,
"It wasn't so long ago when a woman was murdered by a man
who raped her with a crucifix because she refused to bear any
more children." These voices, there are voices, can you hear the
voices?

Another Living Saint is naked wearing a butcher's apron
with a black stocking cap over his head. He is a cook who has
used the kitchen of the Spanish Army to create a corpse made
of gelatin. He has a machete in his hand.

"This is the body of South and North America," he says.

He begins to cut off of the genitals, the heart, the eyes, the hands, the soles of the feet, random cuts and mutilations. People line up behind him. He hands them pieces of the body on a paper plate. "I invite you to eat."

The cutting becomes more systematic as he slices up the legs and arms, the line grows longer for those who come back for seconds.

He looks at me. "I was once a spiritual tourist like you, go home."

I turn. In an empty room, a single candle burns.

It is only a few minutes before midnight. The masses are mingling in the streets, two million or more, they gather around their preferred *falla*. I am still standing before the tower of beds. Last-minute touches are being made as the *tracas* are checked, the lines of explosives that run like mycelium through the interior of the *falla* which will be lit at precisely the right moment.

Firemen surround the *falla* with hoses in hand should the fire suddenly break out of control. There is tension circulating among the crowd like an electrical current. We are tightly sandwiched between strangers on all sides.

The clock strikes twelve.

The City of Fire explodes! The beds burst into flames! Fireworks ignite as the crowd presses in to one another out of fear, out of excitement, awe, terror, as we witness the ills of society burn. The *tracas* are deafening, the fire gains momentum, the heat intensifies, pushing the crowd back slowly.

I cannot take my eyes off the *falla*.

Yo soy la desintegración.

I watch these words go up in flames. I will paint them on the walls of our bedroom where I dream at night and choreograph each day.

Yo soy la desintegración.

I will sing it in the foyer of my church. I will write it on my hands with reversible ink and shake the hands of everyone I meet.

Yo soy la desintegración.

The blaze is now on the verge of being out of control, an inferno raging, reflected in the windows of the apartment buildings that line both sides of the street. The firemen begin to manipulate the fire with their hoses, spraying water on the outer flames, but the beds are blazing, collapsing on top of each other. As each one falls, we applaud and cheer, as if our own illnesses are being exorcised. The crowd moves back quickly now as one giant organism recoiling in the name of its own survival. The fire is roaring. The heat is searing. My eyelashes are singed. The entire structure is threatening to fall. Panic presses against my ribs. I turn around. There is no place to run. The threat of being crushed is controlled only by people's faith in the history of this ritual. Everyone takes rapid steps backward, eyes on the *fallas*. There is no violence, only a disciplined, collective retreat. All around Valencia is burning. An unearthly red glow rims the city just like El Bosco's Hell.

How do you paint your own conversion?

I touch my forehead. It is a self-induced fever, the hallucination that Hieronymus Bosch envisioned five hundred years ago in his upper reaches of Hell.

But Hell is here, now, burning joyously, as millions stand in this City of Fire and bear witness to the transformation of their own communities. They are not voyeurs to change, but participants striking the match. Individual sparks emancipate from the flames in the Old World to the New World. Orange wings flapping in the darkness.

Monarch butterflies are migrating across North America, south to the creases in the mountains of Central Mexico. Michoacán. They fly fifteen thousand feet above the Earth to the Sierra Palone, an active transvolcanic range. Orange. Black. Monarchs wear the topography of flowing lava on their wings. The butterflies' final destination was a secret, not discovered by lepidopterists until 1974. Of course, the locals knew but they never told anyone that forty million monarchs were sitting on the mountaintops above their village opening and closing their wings in private conversations.

I am walking up a mountain along a steep, thin path. The path is dry and dusty. There are burning fields, cleared fields, and farms that appear as quilted squares on the steep hillsides. Gullies cut deep from rains expose red soil. A few monarchs are sipping nectar from roadside flowers, some called seneceo. *I have a guide. We pass men on the trail who remove monarchs from the path; they pick them up, blow the dust off their wings, and place them in sunlight safe from foot traffic. This is their job. This is their work.*

I stop. I think I hear rain. The guide smiles. We continue walking until the forest darkens, cools. Suddenly, we look up through a canopy of wings, wings fanning the air, creating the sound of rain, the sound of wind, the sound of wings, butterfly wings. The fir trees are laying down their arms. Here. Now. Millions of monarchs hang from the trees like frostbitten leaves, the underside of their wings exposed, burnished, and bronzed.

We are dressed in butterflies. The longer we stay inside the winged forest, the more we see and hear, the settling of peace, the rupture of peace. The sun appears from behind a cloud, there is a frenzy of flight.

Another voice speaks, "Here we stand inside the mind of God."

Why must we leave?

We walk back down the mountain. I trip on an exposed root, my foot falls on a butterfly. I have killed a butterfly. My guide bends down, picks up the still life with cradled hands, brings the monarch to his mouth and with one quick pop of his breath, blows it back to life.

In a miracle, it flies.

"Ciclo de vida," *he says.*

I want to believe. This is what I believe. In the middle of the road is a tiny vein of water crowded with monarchs. I continue walking down the mountain until the sound of wings is no longer audible. We stand outside the miraculous. Loneliness creeps down the hillside as I return to the smoke-filled clearing and the sounds of chain saws, the forest freshly felled.

Sparks are ascending and descending in the upper reaches of El Bosco's Hell.

I am in Spain. I am in Mexico. Old World. New World. It is the year 1500. It is the year 2000. Time is alive. Time is a lie. I am present to quivering wings. Monarch butterflies light on my hands and burst into flames.

Bouquets of fireworks are thrown to the sky. Valencia is burning. The masses are dancing arm in arm, in the streets they are dancing and singing. Across the bridge, the people dance, fireworks exploding in the river.

I stop and lean over the railing and make prayers to my gods, male and female, human and animal, recalling privately the vows I once made and burned.

. . .

Strike the match.
Protect the flame.
Ignite the hymns.

The spirit of God like a fire is burning. Start the city burning feel the
stomach turning the ache that keeps returning *count your many
blessings name them one by one* it is never enough give us our bread
our daily bread more more slice the bread slice the wrist that's
threatening to raise the hand against the hand who is destroy-
ing the Earth for the beauty of the Earth see the Earth see the
servant Adam slumped in his damp Eden dead from words
dead from Eve serenely drinking swallowing the sap of the
dragon palm mistaking it for blood blood blood knowledge
choking before she coughs up the seeds plant the seeds *we are
all enlisted till the conflict is o'er: Happy are we! Happy are we!* Her
health all health is as precarious as ladders raised against heaven
up-down fall into hell the rungs of ladders are the frames of
our own experience one step at a time how high do we dare to
go how low do we dare to go these ladders in El Bosco's Hell
stretch heights and depths until we fall free fall our souls travel
without brakes no breaks no time no space or pause to feel or
find or be true to anything but here we go to work and work
and work and work eat work sleep work and work and work *put
your shoulder to the wheel push along do your duty with a heart full of song
we all have work let no one shirk put your shoulder to the wheel.* Clear-
cut. Cutthroat. Cut. Cut the road into the mountain. Cut. Take
one. Take two. Take three. Take out the entire hillside for a
house for a subdivision of the future. We are developing. See
how we are developing. Six billion and rising. The rungs on
the ladder, become the frames of our film. Speed them up.
Run. The place where I was born is now a prison. Cut. Take

four. The place where I was born is now a prison. Cut. Run the film again in El Bosco's Hell. Play my precious images of pain over and over again on the backs of the dead who lead me in Hell, who welcome me in Hell, my eyes watch as each frame rolls down their spines. Stop. A vertebra is exposed. My dying mother. Roll. Stop. My ghostly lover. Roll again. My own rapacious appetites play themselves one after the other for free, this is all free, free fall until images collapse in the boneyard of crimes and cruelties. Lay me down to sleep on fire and millstone. I cannot sleep. *Come, come, ye saints, no toil or labor fear but with joy wend your way.* The stakes are high. High on the ridge. Pull the stakes. One by one by one. *Count your many blessings see what God has done.* Take the wooden stakes out of the Earth into our hands one vertical the other horizontal tie them together with orange plastic tape turn them into crosses plant them in the soil see how rage grows see how rage flies dragonflies be calm they say sit at the table they say come to consensus they say with the power vested in them they say *oh say can you see* my body a clear-cut my voice a serpent wrapped around the tree the power vested in me *like a fire is burning.*

It is never enough.

Whataboutthecovenantswehavemadenottobebrokenweare
brokenwearebrokenthisrecordofoursisbrokenisbrokenis
brokenwearebrokenthisrecordofours

God forbid. God forgive.

III

EARTHLY DELIGHTS

Paradise or not paradise, I have the very definite impression that the people of this vicinity are striving to live up to the grandeur and nobility which is such an integral part of the setting. They behave as if it were a privilege to live here, as if it were by an act of grace they found themselves here. The place itself is so overwhelmingly bigger, greater, than anyone could hope to make it that it engenders a humility and reverence not frequently met with in Americans. There being nothing to improve on in the surroundings, the tendency is to set about improving oneself.

—Henry Miller, *Big Sur and the Oranges of Hieronymus Bosch*

The body of the butterfly is still, the wings are steady. I am lying on the ground in the Garden of Earthly Delights, looking up. Someone is taking my pulse. My neck is being supported on the calf of another man who kneels, arching his back as he waves a blue thistle over my head.

Why why why joy enjoy joy joy
Why why why joy enjoy joy joy
Why why why joy enjoy joy joy
Why why why joy enjoy joy joy
Why why why joy enjoy joy joy
        Why why why joy enjoy joy joy
Why why why joy enjoy joy joy
Why why why joy enjoy joy joy
Why why why joy enjoy joy joy
Why why why joy enjoy joy joy
Why why why joy enjoy joy joy
        Why why why joy enjoy joy joy
Why why why joy enjoy joy joy
Why why why joy enjoy joy joy
Why why why joy enjoy joy joy
Why why why joy enjoy joy joy
Why why why joy enjoy joy joy

El Bosco's men and women are uttering chants, healing chants, offering me the chance to live after I was almost dead, have you ever felt dead to rise again in joy, enjoy this Garden of Delights? There is a desire in my soul to see, a desire in my heart to be, here, finally, in peace.

My left hand reaches to touch, what can I feel but a blue blackberry. Earthly blue. They say my pulse is returning. I am returning to the place I feared was gone. I can touch and taste my own irrepressible hunger. Rise to eat this lip-luscious fruit, the flesh of these berries: blackberries, raspberries, blueberries, and strawberries. *This triptych was once called "The Strawberry" in medieval days.* Ripe on the vine, heavy on the bough, I pick each one, a delicacy in my hand, a redvioletblue weight on my tongue, on this day, I taste the joy, explode with joy, smear the joy all over my face. Feed me cherries and I will feed you grapes, deep red-purple grapes, one grape at a time. Time. The most luxurious gift in this Garden is time. Time to talk, time to eat, time to love, time to drink, discover, uncover, expose, explore, ponder, dream, create, time to do nothing but sit and stare, look and listen and wonder how it is, why it is, that we have strayed so far from this world of *Naked Truth*.

What is Naked Truth?

I am clothed in delight. In naked delight I am clothed. Wearing my own skin of joy and two cherries as a hat, there is no shame in this earthly stance of love. One foot forward, it is easier than I thought. Before my friends and fellow creatures, I say yes, yes to this open, delightful body.

I will take my stand in *El jardín de las delicias* and breathe.

I dreamed this center panel long before I saw it. I was walking through the Hayden Valley of Yellowstone. It was autumn and the grasses along the river had turned to gold. Steam was rising from pink and blue furnaces. The stench of sulphur was strong. Mudpots hidden in the forests were bubbling. There were people everywhere, human beings engaged in Earthplay.

Everyone, everything was in motion.

Yellow Grizzlies. Blue Bison. Red Ravens. Elk wearing bridles of silver led by Coyotes in pink capes at dawn. Flying Trout. Pelicans levitating above the river. Moose trying to hide behind the all-seeing aspen. Something was said to me. I have forgotten the words. What were the words? I awoke in a sweat. That is all I remembered until I stood before the triptych in the Prado and realized El Bosco had painted my dream.

What the heart desires can be dreamed.

I dreamed the panel withheld from me as a child, never knowing this was the landscape between Paradise and Hell, never knowing as children who slept beneath images of Good and Evil, that there was another way of being, another way of seeing in this Garden of Earthly Delights.

There is almost too much to witness in the endless choreography of the curious. I am struck by the androgynous nature of human beings, how I feel myself united, woman-man, man-woman, neither gender taking leadership over the other. Couples are lying on the ground, raised up by elbows in conversation. Others are dancing inside the hollowed bodies of fruit. And still others are gathered around berries, floating in berries, talking, listening, wondering what it might mean to engage in creation. To partake of these fleshy fruits is to swallow the seeds of our own inquiry born of the body, sensed of the body, the body broken open through beauty. They are singing. They are sighing. And still others are simply standing in a state of awe, looking outward at all that moves. Everything moves. Their nakedness allows the body to be in open dialogue with the world, not hidden, so little is hidden in this Garden of Delights.

Why was it hidden from me?

> *I went to the Garden of Love,*
> *And saw what I never had seen:*
> *A Chapel was built in the midst,*
> *Where I used to play on the green.*
>
> *And the gates of this Chapel were shut,*
> *And Thou shalt not writ over the door;*
> *So I turn'd to the Garden of Love,*
> *That so many sweet flowers bore,*
>
> *And I saw it was filled with graves,*
> *And tomb-stones where flowers should be:*
> *And Priests in black gowns, were walking their rounds,*
> *And binding with briars, my joys & desires.*

William Blake. I memorized this poem as a child, had forgotten it until now. Might this be the Garden of Love before the Chapel, before the Priests, before the briars? Did Hieronymus Bosch visit the dreams of Blake?

A magnificent pink tower stands to the west. Is it a fountain or a furnace? Do I dare to enter the organic structure that dwarfs everything below? I touch its flank and quickly withdraw my hand. *Furnace,* I think to myself, stepping back and stretching to feel the radiant heat emanating from the walls.

I walk away from the tower and stand on my hands (I've never stood on my hands), I am walking on my hands through this Garden of Delights. I am upside down, eyes lower, feet higher, head throbbing, rushing, reeling down, head down, my legs are up, wavering like the antennae of a beetle who feels the future.

I've always felt like an insect equipped with antennae. I prowl and, mysteriously, along the way I come upon new discoveries.

Here with my legs waving above the Garden, I suddenly sprout wings, insect wings (what is happening to me?), panes of light in flight, translucent and strong, that will allow me to hold a fish or carry a cherry above my head and soar. I drop to my feet, stand up tall, and spread my arms, yes they are wings. I accept this invitation to fly and ascend or float (I cannot be sure) in this airborne aquarium of hybrid human beings, half-bird, half-horse, half-fish, watching them slide down the curves of crescent moons, blue moons, swifts and swallows circle the acrobats. I glide through the sky, in between clouds, feeling the maneuvers of my own imagination for the very first time, how agile I have become when the fears I have lived with seem to have vanished. For now, I see them as blackberries bobbing downriver.

No one figure stands out. No one voice is raised above another. All are in concert with their own curiosities that contribute to the whole of wonder. El Bosco has created a democracy of discovery in a time when Catholic kings ruled.

. . .

Feed me. Nourish me. Remind me what I have forgotten. Within this red tent we conspire, receive instruction as to how one bows to love. The birds remember Eden without sin, the Earth before greed.

Communion in *El jardín de las delicias* is administered through the birds, one berry at a time.

> *We are many, a whole tribe swarming,*
> *And so like each other that our lovemaking*
> *Is as sweet and immodest as a game of hide-and-seek.*
> *And we lock ourselves inside the crowns of flowers*
> *Or in transparent, iridescent bubbles.*
> *Meanwhile a flock of lunar signs fills the sky*
> *To prepare the alchemical nuptials of the planets.*

Let the mind fall in favor of the heart, I swoop, let the heart sing like the scarlet bird in its ivory cage of bones, I rise. I steer through the upper reaches of the Garden, fearing only the time when I must return to solid ground. Are we ever on solid ground for long?

I am a traveler hovering in place, watching, watching pleasure, pleasure pursued through the body, my body rising and falling, rising and falling, until I am carried away. Let us be carried away. A red bird is carried across the sky, on a branch of a tree, held up by a man who is riding a griffin, who is carrying a creature resembling a frog. In the blue of El Bosco's sky above the Garden, who is afraid of feeling the weight, carrying the weight, lifting the weight of each sovereign species like a barbell pressed up and down, up and down, against our chest, raised above our head and then held steady, so steady, steady for how long, nobody knows, we all take our turn. We can be light even with the weight we carry.

Hieronymus Bosch allows us to play in the Garden. With Paradise on my left and Hell to my right, I can play in the middle of my life, with the middle of my life I will play. Run. Jump. Leap. I will leap with my eyes wide open and land without knowing anything except my feet are on the Earth, this beautiful Earth where we live and breathe and love and work and play and pray that we might never lose sight of how delicious it is to open our mouths *while of these emblems we partake* of all the bounties of the Earth, a jay drops a berry into a mouth that is open. We can remain open.

To open is not a sin.
To play is not a sin.
To imagine is not a sin.

Do you see the couple making love inside a mussel shell?

There is a traveler who walks beyond El Bosco's blue horizon. The town is Ribadesella, a northern port of Spain where deep caves hold the images of horses. She walks along the beach. It is low tide. Among the rocks, she is aware of a strange hissing. She stops, bends down, and locates the sound. It is the musings of barnacles, creatures who stand on their heads with their feathered feet filtering food as the sea overtakes them. Tiny armored shells protect the flesh inside. She looks more closely. A double door whose sides disappear when opened is tightly sealed. Only their voices whisper life. The traveler rises, looks ahead, and finds mussels, saturated blue, also attached to the rocks. A herring gull has pulled one of the bivalves from its base, breaks it open with its beak and tears the orange body into sinewy strands and eats. Long, thick strands of eel grass grow below, green.

The traveler stops at the Gran Hotel, where seventy-eight lanterns round like the moon illuminate the beach. It has begun to rain. She takes a small room with a balcony and sits on a pink plush chair until the sun sets. She enjoys a shower, slips into a chiffon dress, puts on her pearls, and walks down the spiral staircase noting the carved spindles in the shape of sea horses.

Inside the dining room, she asks for the table in the corner. It is still raining. The tide is rising. She orders paella. The waiter informs the traveler that it will take forty-five minutes to pre-pare. She says that is what she would expect from such a lavish dish. She relaxes and watches the waves reach, crest, and break in small elegant intervals. The traveler wonders why such harsh, direct lighting is used inside when everything outside is muted. She wishes for the light of candles to comfort the food.

It rains and rains.

While waiting for the paella, the traveler whispers to the waiter after he has filled her glass with wine that if a gentleman should walk into the dining room looking for a table and would like to join her she would be delighted to share the shellfish. The waiter nods. The traveler takes her first sip of wine. Rioja. Red. Black cherries. Plums. She reaches for the baguette, tears off the heel. There is a wedge of cabrales wrapped in leaves on the table. She spreads the cheese on the bread. As she takes it into her mouth the sound of bells through the high Áliva meadows in the Picos returns to her. Harebell, columbine, iris, lilies, ferns, penstemon, gilia, orchids—the transformed hayfields of Asturias are the florid backgrounds of medieval tapestries.

The waiter pardons himself and introduces a dinner companion to the traveler. She extends her hand to the man, who takes it generously and sits down across from her. The waiter pours him a glass of cabernet and refills hers. They both lift their glasses and then avert their eyes.

It rains and rains.

The paella arrives steaming.

The waiter, with two covered hands, carries the cast-iron pan sizzling and carefully places it on the table between the two eaters. As he moves away the traveler motions him forward one more time and whispers something in his ear. She returns her attention to her guest.

The City of Longing appears.

On her plate: mussels, barnacles, clams, squid, crab legs, and crayfish. Saffron rice: yellow-orange. Green olives stuffed with pimentos. Peas. Sliced hard-boiled eggs. Olive oil, some still simmering at the bottom of the pan.

On his plate: mussels, crab legs, clams, crayfish, barnacles, and squid. Saffron rice: orange. Perfectly sliced hard-boiled eggs. Black olives. Peas. White asparagus.

They lift their forks and begin to explore, to taste, to tease, to touch, to play, to romp, to knead, to court, to want, to do, to dare, to ride, to rock, to swim, to float, to fly, to feed, to toy, to try, to say, to hear, to see, to dare, to do, to break, to burn, to eat and be eaten. With saffron-stained fingers they break open the last mussels, blue-orange, and feed each other what is inside moving to the outside.

Explorar. Probar. Agitar. Palpar. Jugar. Retozar. Amasar. Cortejar. Querer. Hacer. Osar. Montar. Mecer. Nadar. Flotar. Volar. Nutrir. Juguetear. Intentar. Decir. Oír. Ver. Osar. Hacer. Romper. Incendiar. Comer y ser comida.

They drink coffee black with no cream. To be curious. To imagine. To question and be questioned. To desire. *Desear.*

The tide is rising to stand on one's head and feed.

Upside down, I can see the world upside down. Hanging by my knees from a tendril erect from the top of a mushroom that is moving, *everything is moving,* someone inside is crawling toward the pool of bathers.

> *Let it be*
> *like wild flowers,*
> *suddenly, an imperative of the field:*
> *Wild Peace.*

Wild Peace. Naked Truth. Change is possible with a wild heart.

What if the Seven Deadly Sins in the Garden of Love became caterpillars that metamorphosed into Earthly Delights? Leaf by leaf, they devour the color green.

Invidia. Envy, a feeling of discontent becomes a feeling of gratitude, knowing what one has we all can enjoy.

Up and down the branches, they eat, eat, eat, more, more, more.

Gula. Gluttony, an insatiable appetite for more, becomes the gift of needing less.

They do not sleep, they only crave larger leaves for themselves.

Avaritia. Let avarice, greed for gain, become the sustained, slow pleasure of being satisfied.

The caterpillars are full. They stop eating. They stop altogether.

Accidia. Let slothfulness finally hear its own desire to move willingly toward others.

They only want to dream. Each finds its own branch to hang from and sleep.

Luxuria. Will lust, the obsession to possess, find an honest desire to share?

They spin a chrysalis around their tubular, elastic body until destroyed by their own will.

Ira. The heat of anger that burns and destroys becomes the heat that nurtures and warms.

The caterpillars dream for days until their dreams become too small for what their bodies have become. Freedom becomes their beauty. A chrysalis is shed for wings.

Superbia. Let the attachment of pride become humility when given away.

I desire to live differently.

Inside and outside the pink and blue fountains and furnaces, something is happening, something slowly is happening. A man-woman, woman-man tiptoes across a glass tube. *Opus contra naturam.*

In love we learn the pleasure and pain of love inseparable one without the other we come to give and receive the body does not lie in love we surrender to instinct to animal smells to taste to touch to see the map revealed on the body through contours of flesh and flashes of fever the fires turned high by a chemistry registered in the brain in the blood it simmers and boils and bursts the bubble bursts the ruptured hearts a man and woman and woman and man and man together sit inside the hollow shell of convention and point to the pond of passions the parade of men and women beast and fowl circling their desires flirting with their fantasies pleasing their hearts as they laugh and sing and play and indulge all the whims and wonders and topical wisdom that surfaces through motion bodies in motion around and around *motion can be a place too* like the man with his hands over his ears, the woodpecker, the robin, the goldfinch he sits on, cannot tell him whether to do this or not he is thinking he is remembering the guilt that comes in love when you open to sex and when you do not, either way the soul is stretched to imagine what if only if another man opens his mouth to the very red berry about to be dropped on his tongue by a jay the bird that told him so so so what if the world were free to love why would we need to live in the mind of heaven or hell?

A woman in the lower right-hand corner holds an apple in her hand, the only man clothed in the Garden of Earthly Delights points to the apple.

"There has never been any forbidden fruit," writes André Breton, "only temptation is divine."

Tentar. To tempt. What is real and what is imagined is always the question of love. El Bosco tempts me to imagine what is curious and what is desirable on a grand scale, a mythic scale. Love is a visual orgy of abandonment. Breton calls it "lyric behavior."

Lyric behavior. To bite the apple. To peel the peach. To suck the orange. Call it "convulsive beauty," a beauty that "will be veiled-erotic, fixed-explosive, magic-circumstantial."

There are three individuals talking inside a transparent dome just beyond the orchard to the right of the jay who is dropping the berry once again into the mouth that is open. Call it a bubble of conversation, a dome of conversion. I lean closer. Yes, there is an echo, a reverberation of ideas, an amplification of what they are discussing, considering, questioning. Yes, I hear the words alive on their tongues, "Above all, the senses."

From where I stand (you will not find me, for I have learned the art of invisibility) this chamber appears as a jellyfish. The human legs are tentacles, the heads and bodies inside the transparency become one organism capable of simply drifting with the current. To drift in the collective, even the sea, to send out tentacles—

I, you, we—whisper—my, your, our—longings, protect them, protect our longings, find the dark opening in whatever appears bright. *Darkness is just a memory of light.* Our secretly dashed hopes and stellar fears become neurons of bitterness capable of propelling the tentacles to sting anyone, anything who dares to do differently or something other. These tentacles of the collective can bring down the healthiest of creatures in the smallest of ways. What is seemingly invisible rises to the surface and strikes—it has been pulsing with direction all along.

The Reformation was a movement that broke the bubble that held the Middle Ages in place. Martin Luther, Erasmus, Leonardo da Vinci, Michelangelo offered a personal vision of what was to come, the inevitability of a free, sovereign mind. El Bosco painted his Garden on the threshold of this leap.

. . .

Never trust the artist, the writer, the philosopher. They will betray the truth that raised them. Through their curiosity and the fire of their imagination, they will evoke change. They are religion-breakers, myth-makers, and alchemists. Their loyalties are to the lapis stones they carry in their hands at birth.

If I dare to take an even closer look at the three individuals conversing inside the dome, do I see the Holy Trinity disguised in the middle of *El jardín de las delicias*? The Father. The Son. The Holy Ghost. The Trinity is standing just beyond the grove of trees. Which one is speaking? Which one is listening? Which one will lift the canopy to include those not allowed inside?

I turn. There he is again, Joseph, Joseph Smith kneeling inside the Garden. His Sacred Grove. His Canopy of Visions. I recognize him as the original that he was, a charismatic, a geomancer, eyes open focused on the Earth, watching the Earth, eyes closed focused on the Heart, listening to his Heart. Joseph—a mystic. Joseph—a diviner. Joseph—a restorer, a Man of the Signs, a student of the occult, a practitioner of magic. Mormonism is magic. He opens his hand. A stone of lapis rests in his hand.

Close his hand.

As Latter-day Saints, we have closed his hand and let it fall in the name of respectability. We are honest, earnest, hard-working people, not people prone to roaming naked in gardens plucking fruit, eating berries, kneeling under trees, or searching for water with two quivering sticks. No, we can the fruit. Chop the trees. Do something useful, practical. Work. Don't dream. Take the beehive to heart and adopt it as a symbol of industry. As a people, my people, we have dropped the hand of Joseph and grasped the hand of Brigham who led us to the Promised Land, this land of little water, to organize, colonize, proselytize, and grow.

The pragmatism of Brigham Young is our religion now. Communal. Corporate. *Mormon, Inc.* There is little mystical about us. As a people, my people, we have abandoned the vision of Joseph, his vision culled of the Earth, our sacred texts opened and pulled from a hillside, the birth of an alchemical text, gold, translated, sublimated, a solid body turned into Spirit.

Ralph Waldo Emerson and Walt Whitman were great writers, Jonathan Edwards and Horace Bushnell major theologians, William James a superb psychologist, and all these are crucial figures in the spiritual history of our country. Joseph Smith did not excel as a writer or as a theologian. . . . But he was an authentic religious genius, and surpassed all Americans before or since, in the possession and expression of what could be called the religion-making imagination.

In the days after the American Revolution, Joseph fostered another revolution, born out of his own spiritual confrontation with longing. He dared to see the possibility of a Utopia where if men "are not equal in earthly things," they cannot be "equal in obtaining heavenly things."

He believed that the scientific method could be applied to religion, that spiritual knowledge is not something to be acquired simply through books or being told something is true, but rather obtained through actual experience.

Just as Galileo climbed the tower to test Aristotle's theory of falling bodies, Joseph Smith sought the serenity of a grove of trees to test the words of James: "If any of ye lack wisdom, let him ask of God, who giveth liberally." It was here he had a vision of the restoration of a living gospel.

> *Perhaps God having foreseen that Mormon mainstreamers would develop a fetish for self-righteousness, called, as the founding prophet of the church, a prodigal. Perhaps, having foreseen that Mormon independents would develop a fetish for the urbane, God launched the Restoration through a magician. Seen from this perspective, Joseph is not just a problem to both camps, he is an antidote: a corrective to the idea that Christian salvation is the wages of either human righteousness or human intellect, but that it remains always the gift of God to all who will, like Joseph Smith, struggle to repent, struggle to forgive, and struggle to bear the crosses of the world.*

Joseph Smith created both a religion and a people out of the sublime. He recognized the eternal in the temporal.

On a mountain trail in the Adirondacks, not so far from Palmyra, New York, I encountered a golden eye that blinked inside the Earth. It was a salamander, true not counterfeit, God staring from below.

How have we forgotten our origins?

El Bosco has created his own utopia in the Garden of Delights, a perfect world in harmony with discovery, not vulgar, not profane, but a responsible inquiry into the fruits of our own experience, the knowledge transmitted through a blackberry placed on our tongue.

This is the delicacy of a sensual life, not in the service of the Self, but in service of the Sacred within a shared community honoring the dignity of all its members.

In trying to wrap my arms around my own religious beliefs, I am aware I pick and choose what feels right to me, adapting as I go, adopting what I like and discarding what I don't within my own ethical framework, which is a simple one, to help more than harm and contribute to the well-being of my community with love, good works, and compassion. I accept the Organic Trinity of Mineral, Vegetable, and Animal with as much authority as I accept the Holy Trinity. Both are sacred.

How do we remain faithful to our own spiritual imagination and not betray what we know in our bodies? The world is holy. We are holy. All life is holy.

I hear the voices of my Elders: *You can't have it both ways.*

Again, must it really be all or nothing? Right wing or left wing? Paradise or Hell?

Instead, couldn't this religious adaptation be another form of natural selection along the path to a spiritual evolution?

See the mermaid grabbing her tail. She is a waterwheel, turning, turning, a wheel in the water turning, *hen to pan,* her body half-light, her body half-dark, self-sufficient, she chooses to propel herself through waves, her divine nature awakened, a wheel in the water through a phosphorescent tide.

I swim behind her in a gold-emerald wake following the sound of her musical scales, rising and falling, rising and falling, it is never all or nothing.

As Mormons we practice CTR, *Choose the Right,* and place these letters on rings. We remember to purchase our rings in silver or in gold, with diamonds or without, large or small, pick the finger of our choice to wear these letters in code, so we will not forget to *choose the right* with the time we have left—children and adults, let us join hands together and pray that this religion, original at its core, will not become another advertisement for God.

But I am not immune. I have charms and fetishes in every place imaginable, including turquoise stones secretly sewn inside my cowboy boots. I am well protected every day of my life. Joseph Smith could call forth the spirit in humble ways. He carried stones that helped him to see; he was adept with divining rods as they quivered in their search for water. He was a true seer. The danger is in what we codify, commodify, and exploit. The symbol becomes the sign. Praying hands no longer real become a decoration above the bed of the elderly.

The origin of my religion, any religion, is a true impulse, one I want to keep pure in my blood.

Practice CPR. We are lying on our backs in the Garden. El Bosco's Garden. Hands over our hearts, can our institutions be revived?

I shake my head inside the Prado. How strange to think of Joseph Smith inside the Garden of Hieronymus Bosch. How peculiar to place the birth of Mormonism inside a painting of the Late Middle Ages.

How can I attain an original or at least an individual relationship to truth or God?

How can I open the traditions of religion to my own experience?

I need to touch soil.

. . .

On the train to Ávila, tamarisks are in bloom, yellow not pink. Native to Spain. Exotic to Utah. Pines. Junipers. Arid shrub country pocketed with boulders. Magpies. Poppies. The *meseta,* or plateau country, of central Spain looks much like home in the American Southwest. Little excess. Nothing wasted.

The medieval walls surrounding the *ciudad antigua* of Ávila are the threshold to the world of Santa Teresa in the early sixteenth century. Even though the walls were built five hundred years earlier by an estimated nineteen hundred men miraculously in nine years after the town had been reclaimed from the Moors, it is her presence that lingers.

Hundreds of swifts circle her city; pink, white, and yellow roses flourish against the stone wall. Bouquets of wildflowers carefully picked are left in her honor. Overhead three storks fly toward the bell tower of Carmen, where they nest. Did Santa Teresa know these birds, these mediators between Heaven and Earth? These swifts and storks must have swayed her thinking. Surely the Holy Spirit appears in more incarnations than doves.

To whom do I pray?

A Spanish woman sits in the row across from me in the Iglesia de Santa Teresa, reciting her prayers in whispers as she rotates each bead of her rosary through her fingers. Her hands are folded beneath her chin. She alternates her prayers with the reading of scriptures.

To whom do I pray?

I kneel before the statue of Santa Teresa, gilded and animated by the soft light in this small dark alcove. Her right hand is outstretched as though she were about to touch Spirit, her left hand covers her heart.

I close my eyes and listen.

After many minutes of silence, what comes into my mind unannounced is the phrase *"wet not dry."*

I close my eyes tighter and concentrate more deeply, let these words simply pass through as one does with distractions in meditation. Again, I hear the words *"wet not dry."* The woman across the aisle from me is weeping. Her private utterings, *"para ti, para ti,"* for you, for you, are audible. I open my eyes feeling little emotion and look down at the worn tiles beneath my feet. The Spanish woman faces the saint, bows, crosses herself, and leaves.

Wondering if I should be here at all, I try once again to pray. In stillness, the phrase returns to me.

All I can hear in the sanctity of this chapel is what sounds at best like a cheap antiperspirant jingle. I do not feel my heart. Am I numb to these things of the Spirit? Even the white gladiolus arranged as offerings appear as the bleached vertebrae of deer. Filled with shame, I look up at Santa Teresa's face.

Later that afternoon, I steady myself by sitting beneath an old cottonwood tree, similar to the ones I have sat under a hundred times in the desert. I open Santa Teresa's autobiography, *The Life of Saint Teresa of Ávila by Herself: . . . and God converted the dryness of my soul into a great tenderness.*

I turn another page: *Only once in my life do I remember asking Him for consolation and that was when I was very dry. . . .*

And another: *It is my opinion that though a soul may seem to be deriving some immediate benefit when it does anything to further itself in this prayer of union, it will in fact very quickly fall again, like buildings without foundations. . . . Remain calm in times of dryness.*

Santa Teresa's book articulates "the Four Waters of Prayer."

She says simply that wetness brings us "to a recollected state."
A well. A spring. A fountain. To drink deeply from the Spirit
and quench the aridity of the soul is to retrieve, revive, and
renew our relationship with God.

Where are my tears? Where is the rain? I ask myself. *I am now
speaking of that rain that comes down abundantly from heaven to soak
and saturate the whole garden.*

The leaves of the cottonwood tree shield me from the heat
as I read her *Confessions* slowly:

*Who is this whom all my faculties thus obey? Who is it that in a
moment sheds light amidst such great darkness, who softens a heart
that seemed to be of stone and sheds the water of gentle tears where
for so long it had seemed to be dry? Who gives these desires? Who
gives this courage? What have I been thinking of? What am I
afraid of?*

The smells of lavender and rosemary collide in the garden.
Something breaks open in me. My soul is brittle, my body a
desert. I weep. What might it mean to honor thirst before
hunger and joy before obligation?

"Una botella de agua. Necesito una botella de agua." These are the
first words out of my mouth this morning as I awaken from a
dream.

I go to get my hair cut and, without my realizing it, the
woman shaves my head and plucks my eyebrows. When I look
in the mirror, I am stunned. My eyebrows are now in the bold
shapes of swallows.

"How could you have done this?" I ask.

"It is the shearing of a woman's hair before she commits to
the Habit," the woman replies.

. . .

The Monasterio de la Encarnación, a dignified granite fortress north of the Wall, is not far from the *parador* where I am staying. In 1534, Santa Teresa walked through these doors when she was twenty years old. It is closed. I sit on the stone steps outside the corridor. *Hace calor.* I settle in the shade and read more of Santa Teresa's words: *All its joys came in little sips.*

The mystic writes about women and the importance of discretion in speaking of one's spiritual experiences, the need to share with others of like mind for solace and safety, reflection, and inspiration.

Joseph Smith believed so fully in Santa Teresa's visions that he had himself sealed to the Carmelite nun in "the everlasting covenant of marriage," not uncommon to "the spiritual wife doctrine" he initiated through the revelation and practice of polygamy. He recognized her as a spiritual soulmate, trusting that revelations from God have been and will be continuous through time, that the truth is soul-wrenching, having said himself that he shared only a hundredth of what he saw when the heavens opened up to him. Schooled in the hermetic traditions of Santa Teresa's time, he might have felt as though they were contemporaries, sympathetic to her roving states of being.

El corazón que
mucho ama no
admite consuelo sino
del mismo que le
llagó

I am weak, light-headed, perhaps because of the heat, perhaps because of the intensity of Santa Teresa's story: a child who at the age of ten vowed to be a nun, but at fourteen blossomed into a vibrant young woman enraptured by the sensory pleasures of the world, gifted in poetry and literature. She fell tumultuously in love and was so frightened by her own sexuality that she confessed to her father, who immediately sent her to the convent; there, struggling with the disciplined life set by the nuns against her own instinctive nature, she succumbed to violent seizures and bouts of hysteria that eventually left her paralyzed for years, seized by the darkest of visions. Unable to move, her pain at times barely tolerable, she renounced all medical treatments and relied solely on prayer, never giving up hope of being healed. At one point, when she was deep in a coma mistaken for death, the nuns dug a grave for her. And then the miraculous day arrived. In 1540, she awoke to find her arms and legs no longer paralyzed. She had successfully passed through her journey through Hell. Teresa de Ávila stood up and walked. It was proclaimed a miracle, a cure that reached the masses, whereupon people from surrounding villages came to see the nun whom God had healed.

Her life from that point forward was a testament of austere devotion and simplicity, but she never gave up her pen.

Inside the *monasterio,* there are relics: a wooden log which Santa Teresa used as a pillow; a small statue of Christ "covered with wounds," said to have been very important to her spiritual awakening of great compassion and sorrow; a statue of Saint Joseph, who taught her how to pray. The nuns have passed down the story that this statue used to talk to Santa Teresa. Whenever she left on her travels she would leave him on the prioress's chair. Upon her return, he would tell her everything that had gone on in her absence.

The key to her cell where she lived for twenty-seven years begs to be turned. Turn the key. Santa Teresa's hand opens the door.

. . .

Stillness.

Downstairs, there is a tiny revolving door made of oak. It was the only access the nuns had to the outside world, sending messages out with one turn and receiving them with another in silence.

I descend further into the stark parlor where San Juan de la Cruz and Santa Teresa were *suspendidos en éxtasis,* lifted in ecstasy. Once again, I sit quietly. The word *casado* comes into my mind—married, a prayer of union, a state of oneness with God and with whom we confide our bodies. The Divine Lover. Santa Teresa knew these moments of pure union, where body, soul, and spirit fused.

Ecstasy. Elevation. Suspension.

> *Este saber no sabiendo*
> *es de tan alto poder,*
> *que los sabios arguyendo*
> *jamás le pueden vencer;*
> *que no llega su saber*
> *a no entender entendiendo,*
> *toda ciencia trascendiendo.*

> *This knowledge by unknowing*
> *is such a soaring force*
> *that scholars argue long*
> *but never leave the ground.*
> *Their knowledge always fails the source:*
> *to understand unknowing,*
> *rising beyond all science.*

Y si lo queréis oír,
consiste esta suma ciencia
en un subido sentir
de la divinal Escencia:
es obra de su clemencia
hacer quedar no entendiendo,
toda ciencia trascendiendo.

And if you wish to hear:
the highest science leads
to an ecstatic feeling
of the most holy Being;
and from his mercy comes his deed:
to let us stay unknowing,
rising beyond all science.

The bells of the Monasterio de la Encarnación begin ringing. In the courtyard, two young girls are singing, one is playing the guitar, the other is clapping with her eyes closed. I walk down the road to the plaza where there is a fountain bubbling up from a stone basin, and sit down.

Teenagers play in the pool below the fountain. They flirt and splash each other, then the young men and women, soaked, hoist each other up and over the stone wall and disappear. A man interrupts their frolicking to fill two jugs tied together by a rope that he swings over his neck.

The small plaza is quiet. I walk to the fountain and wash my face and hands and arms. The water is cold and invigorating. I wash my face again.

An old man with a black beret, dressed in a white shirt with an olive green cardigan and grey slacks, comes to the fountain carrying a plastic sack with two one-gallon jugs. He is wearing blue canvas slippers.

I learn he is from one of the outlying *pueblos* in the mountains, that he makes this journey once a week to collect water for his wife from this particular fountain. His wife is especially devoted to Santa Teresa de Ávila. She believes this water restores the spirit and all manner of ailments. He invites me to drink the water with him.

I watch him walk carefully over the uneven cobbles and cannot guess his age. He is a small and handsomely weathered man. He lifts his weary legs over the steps of the fountain, stoops down, and then with great deliberation begins to fill each bottle. He fills one with about an inch of water, shakes the bottle, then pours it out, filling it the second time as he sits down on the stone ledge above the spout. The old man enjoys several sips, wipes his mouth with the back of his hand and fills it again.

Joining him from below, I cup my hands below the running water and drink.

The old man gestures to one of the two bottles he has just painstakingly filled. It rests on the ledge like a prism separating light as the sun shines through.

At first, I do not understand. Perhaps he is offering me another drink?

"Gracias pero no."

He persists.

"Para mí?"

He nods. He hands me one of his bottles. I hardly know what to do. The old man has walked so far for this water. What will his wife say when he returns home to the mountains with only one bottle? How to receive this gift? What can I give him in return? I hold the jug of water close and feel its refreshment even against my skin.

"Gracias, señor, por su regalo."

"De nada."

The old man nods and smiles and slowly shifts his weight on his right hand to ease himself up. He bends down and puts the other bottle in his bag.

After he is gone, I look back toward the fountain.

For tears gain everything; and one kind of water attracts another.

"I surrender myself to Bosch," Mariko Umeoka Taki says over tea. "Before El Bosco, I ask, ask, ask for my original vision and nothing comes. Now after my apprenticeship with Bosch, I wait, even no wait, and it comes. I can't stop my paintings—they come like—how you say, water, yes, like water, more and more, my art has become a fountain, if you have a fountain in your house, you can always take the water. . . ."

She stops and leans forward.

"But you must take care because the artist is always working in the desert and in darkness; it is in those two places that the imagination is the most beautiful, so you take care of the water when you find it."

Mariko belongs to a traditional family from Osaka. Her father runs a successful family business manufacturing clothes. She attended a Catholic school for fourteen years from the time she was four years old until she was eighteen. The emphasis was on language, which her mother believed was important, so Mariko learned both English and French.

"The choices an artist makes are the same choices a human being makes each day. Finally, they all become choices of spirituality." She pauses. "I felt this in Bosco."

"How?" I ask.

"He would direct me as I was painting. I would tell him,

'I will be faithful to you but you have to help me paint.' He would tell me, 'I will teach you where Hell is, you know when you feel bad, you know when you feel good, Hell is inside the heart."

"I remember asking you when we first met in the Prado years ago, what you thought Bosch was trying to say. You said you didn't care much about what he was thinking but rather how he made you feel. Looking back from the perspective of this finished copy of the triptych, have you come to any insights as to what his painting might mean?"

"Many people say many things, but I honestly believe El Bosco was addressing humanity more than religion. I came to believe that the center panel was a diary, that he wanted to tell another generation about what he had experienced." She sips her tea. "I know nothing about El Bosco to this day—only what I feel from his work. I have not read any criticism or history or biography of him. It's all just people's opinions, anyway. Nobody really knows. I know what I felt in my daily encounter with him, that is enough."

"Did you ever get tired of what you were doing?" I asked as I poured us both more tea in the café at the Círculo de Belles Artistes.

"No," Mariko says. "As I told you, I surrendered to him. I willingly committed myself to a fast of the heart. I cut out everything, opened the door only to El Bosco. Zero. I have to make myself empty."

"Is this something you learned from your Buddhist tradition?"

"It is true my family are Buddhists, that is our tradition. But what is Buddhism? I mean to say, I had to be an empty vessel open to Bosco's directions. People come in this world alone and die alone. I am alone. I am empty to my art."

The waiter asks us if we would like something to eat.

"*Un bocadillo de jamón y queso, por favor.*"

"*También para mí,*" replies Mariko.

"*¿Dos bocadillos?*" checks the waiter.

"*Sí,*" Mariko and I say at exactly the same time.

"I will tell you the greatest lesson from Bosco—to be myself. He would say, 'This is your life, have confidence in your life.'"

Mariko explains how every day she listened and then she painted. Bosco would tell her, "Today you will paint a thousand flying birds," or "Use this color, not that color."

Our sandwiches arrive. We continue our conversation.

"I grew accustomed to seeing the triptych through the shadow of five centuries; suddenly, almost without my realizing it, a light would appear and I would see the pigment, the color, in its original and Bosco would direct me; if wrong, he would say 'no' and I would change it."

She begins to laugh uncontrollably and covers her mouth with her hand.

"What?"

"I was so lost in the triptych for so many years that nothing else existed outside the Garden. Nothing. One day inside the Prado, I noticed there were many more people in the gallery, I was having a difficult time concentrating. I asked the guard why all these crowds suddenly. He told me the Olympics were in Spain. I had no idea that summer that any of that was happening."

Feeling more comfortable with Mariko, I ask her a personal question. "Do you mind me asking you how you support yourself?"

"My husband."

"You're married?"

"*Sí*. Does that surprise you? We've been married for over twenty years."

A silence sits between us.

"My husband also comes from a traditional family in Osaka who have a family business as well. He is a chemist who shares the same philosophy as me. He knew when he met me I was possessed by something larger. His mentality is different from normal thinking in Japan. He says, 'I want to help someone who is serious in the world, especially my wife.' "

"And he understands why you have to be apart?"

"He understands and he doesn't understand."

We both laugh and toast with our water glasses.

"I understand. And how does your mother feel about your work as an artist? I met her this morning at the gallery."

"That is more complicated," Mariko says, sighing. "My mother had a plan for me. When I was seventeen years old, I was afraid. I wanted to paint but I was afraid to go inside of art, too dark, too deep. My family, very traditional, said no to art, be a traditional woman, be happy. I went to the university. My mother said to my art professor, 'Tell my daughter she has no talent.' "

"You're kidding?"

"No; he was my mentor. I just learned this from him last time I was home. Of course, he did not honor my mother's request, instead he kept encouraging me, saying, 'You can choose your life.' "

The waiter replaces the teapot with another.

"*Gracias,*" Mariko says as he warms our cups.

"Many can master technique," Mariko continues. "But true art is more than technique. I wanted to find my own way. I was tired of realism. It was easy to sell. I was good at it, but it did nothing for my spirit. I kept hearing my mentor. 'You have to be yourself and remember what you want.'"

She sips her tea.

"Too much contamination from too much education, too much family pressure, too much religion, until I forgot what I wanted to do." She pauses. "In Japanese culture, you conform, you go down the same worn path. My mother says to me, *Don't make a problem, drink your juice afterward.* And so I became a lawyer, somewhere believing that law would satisfy my desire to be in the service of humanity. But it didn't, my struggle became darker."

She stops talking, takes a full breath, and excuses herself.

Mariko could be telling my own story, I thought as I sat in the café by myself.

"I have struggled with the same constraints," I say to her as she sits back down. "Perhaps that's why both of us have been drawn to Bosch, to his strange, eccentric vision."

"I think that is true," says Mariko. "I was touched by Bosco because his imagination was free. I decided to reproduce *El jardín de las delicias* because I believed Bosco would teach me how to paint, that he would lift me out of my artistic crisis. I believed he was laying the door key to the exit from my painting problems. I was undertaking this activity for the purpose of overcoming what, perhaps, I most hated—copying. In Japan, we copy everything." She laughs, shaking her head. "I just didn't know how far he would take me, how much he would push me."

"What do you mean?"

"I thought I was finally finished with him after I completed the triptych at the end of 1994. *Finis!* Now I am free. I have been a slave of his—no more! But something in my heart said, no, you are not finished. I went to Holland to the place where he was born. There I heard a voice inside me say, 'You must do another Bosch.' No, please, I thought, no. And then, again, I surrendered. 'All right, I will do.' It was then I had the vision that I must paint another triptych from my own tradition, something akin to Japanese paper, very delicate. It took two months just to create the base; yellow, brown, pink, grey. Preparing the canvas was very much like making paper layer after layer after layer. It took one year. This is where I had my own conversation with El Bosco. He was no longer directing me, I was in dialogue with him. I wrote to him literally on the canvas, using the Japanese characters true to his era."

"How so?"

"The Japanese characters are exact to that epoch of the late fifteenth century. If I could not find them, I turned to the Chinese characters that were. After I completed my homage to Bosco, I say to him, 'The marriage is complete. Now we can separate. Don't come to me no more!' "

We laugh.

"And after that?"

"The fountain . . ." Mariko says. "I cannot stop the flow of my own paintings. I am no longer afraid."

It is a white room with wooden floors on the main floor of the Círculo de Belles Artistes. On one end is Mariko's completed reproduction of El Bosco's *El jardín de las delicias*. On the other end of the gallery is *Homenaje a El Bosco,* Bosch's triptych translated into what appears as a Japanese screen in tones of grey and taupe. Twelve original oils painted by Mariko surround the room and hang between the two large triptychs.

I stand before the triptych of the triptych. The colors are bright and pure, as though Bosch has been brought into focus at the close of the twentieth century. There is no craquelure. No patina earned through time. The surface is smooth. The wildness is gone. The copy feels much more innocuous than the original; El Bosco's wit and wickedness remain in his hand alone.

What are we to make of the act of mirroring a masterpiece? Jorge Luis Borges explores this notion of the copy, the mimic, the reproduction, or more exact, the individual interpretation of art.

In a short essay, "Pierre Menard, Author of the Quixote," Borges reviews Menard's rewriting of Cervantes's classic, *Don Quixote*. The method of Menard was straightforward: "Know Spanish well, recover the Catholic faith, fight against the Moor or the Turk, forget the history of Europe between the years 1602 and 1918, *be* Miguel de Cervantes." Instead of blasting the presumption of a twentieth-century writer's desire (not to mention ability) to recompose a seventeenth-century tome *word for word,* Borges praises Pierre Menard.

"The text of Cervantes and that of Menard," he writes, "are verbally identical but the second is almost infinitely richer." Borges's thesis is this: No author owns her words, just as no painter owns his painting, each reader involuntarily rewrites in his own way the masterpieces of past centuries.

In Menard's own words to Borges, "Thinking, analyzing, inventing are not anomalous acts; they are the normal respiration of the intelligence." To explore a masterpiece thoroughly is to renovate our own understandings through the understandings of another. It can be dangerous work, but as Borges suggests, "This technique fills the most placid works with adventure."

Like Pierre Menard, Mariko Umeoka Taki undertook something which was "excceedingly complex and, from the very beginning, futile." Nevertheless, she maintains her own integrity in her mimicry like the viceroy butterfly who patterns itself after the monarch. In the end, it is a separate species. By copying Bosch with great rigor and devotion, paying attention to ancient techniques, the mixing of paints and pigments, acute attention to detail of color and form, Mariko ultimately breaks out of the disciplined conformity into her own creativity.

Directly across from *Copia de El jardín de las delicias* hangs *Homenaje a El Bosco*. I find this the most beautiful of Mariko's paintings, the canvas where she has both found and left her own signature. She has translated El Bosco's triptych into a Japanese silkscreen. Outlines. Silhouettes. It is a delicate sketch of the original washed with monochromatic tones of grey, taupe, and beige. I recall Mariko's story, the year she was in dialogue with Bosch. And there are the Japanese characters from the fifteenth century overlaying Bosch's figures. A private conversation. Painted poetry. The delicacy of the black characters on the canvas falls as rain.

In Mariko's own words, "The soul is transparent in color and is hidden in water."

This is *El jardín de las delicias* rendered in spirit before the body. My Mormon theology is surfacing, the belief in a preexistence. First in spirit, second in flesh. We were an intelligence before we were a body born on Earth.

I walk backwards to the center of the gallery and turn and face the full color *Copia* and then turn back to the *Homenaje*. I find myself standing between a shocking celebration of dualities: East—West; Internal—External; Stillness—Activity; Silence—Music; Gauze—Glass; Heaven—Earth; Eyes closed—Eyes open.

From this vantage point, Hell is not Hell, Paradise is not Paradise, the Garden unites the two panels. Truth is in the mean. Bosch has created a continuous horizon between the three panels. If we could view our existence from the same distance, would we come to a similar understanding?

The gap between Heaven and Hell is fear.
The dialogue between Heaven and Hell is prayer.
The marriage between Heaven and Hell is Earth.

My attention shifts to one of Mariko's new paintings, *Nacimiento, 1996.* She has painted nerve endings, synapses, bubbles black breaking open to gold, the ripened fruit of alchemy, lapis, the philosopher's stone, blue, turquoise, aqua in the foreground, the bronze forest in the background, the forest floor is burning, the Tree of Life is emerging, floating orbs, ganglia, droplets of gold exploding. How many times must the artist break before giving birth to creation?

I remember asking Mariko when she brought me into the gallery if there was a place inside *El jardín de las delicias* where she felt most at home. Without hesitation, she pointed to the upper corner of Hell.

"Here," she said. "Where this procession of people are walking over the bridge in Hell through a doorway backlit by fire. This is where I found my opening."

She translated that particular section of her dialogue with El Bosco: *Men wander throughout the desert in the night of truth. Only he who finds his castle can escape and become its owner.*

Santa Teresa also used the castle as a metaphor for the self:

Let us now imagine that this castle, as I have said, contains many mansions, some above, others below, others at each side; and in the center and midst of them all is the chiefest mansion where the most secret things pass between God and the soul.

Is this where art and spirituality intersect at the junction of a secret self? Who can ever know what is at the heart of an artist or a human being in prayer? We can only bow to our own moments of reverie.

At the exit of Mariko Umeoka Taki's exhibition, her mother sits with her hands folded neatly on her lap.

There is no one in the Bosch Room; even the guards are absent, the ones who call me *"la mujer que mira a El Bosco,"* the woman who stares at Bosch. I step forward freely and close one eye for a heightened perspective, then bring my two index fingers to the top of the Garden, touch the tips together, then begin drawing an imaginary triangle inside the center panel. I begin at the red spire on top of the blue bulbous fountain known by some as "the Marriage Chamber" and then fan my fingers down to the left- and right-hand corners. On the left side, there is a white woman with her hand around a black woman's waist. She releases a nightingale as the other woman hides a cherry behind her back. There, again, is the man in an animal skin pointing to the woman who rests her head wearily on her hand. She looks very much like Eve in Paradise, only this time she is inside a glass cylinder holding an apple.

With my fingers pointing to both corners. The image where her fingers meet is a hand pressed on Earth. The hand belongs to a figure standing on his head, legs bent, now the perch of a duck, a gadwall feeding a man a berry.

At the heart of the triptych, in the middle of my triangle, is an egg, an egg balanced on the head of a man who is staring directly at me.

Egg. Sperm. *Coniunctio.* The philosophical egg is both the birthplace of and container for the union of opposites, male and female. Held in hand or balanced on our heads, the egg is the sealed alchemical vessel. What takes place inside? It is the alchemist's prayer: *illud magnum fluxum capitis et caudae.* A third thing is born, light conceived in darkness, and then the crack in the shell, new life emerges.

Mary Magdalene stayed with Christ on the Cross when most everyone else fled. It was she who first witnessed His resurrection. After the Ascension, she traveled to Rome and was granted entrance to the court of Tiberius Caesar. At dinner, she told Caesar that Jesus had risen from the dead. He did not understand. To explain, Mary Magdalene picked up an egg from the table. Caesar responded by saying that a human being could no more rise from the dead than the egg in her hand turn red. The egg turned red.

Look for the multitudes in Hieronymus Bosch's Garden of Delights trying to crawl back into the broken egg.

I make another triangle with my fingers, this time smaller and inverted. On the left, the broken egg; on the right, a pelican spearing a cherry (or is it an egg turned red?), the same bird medieval alchemists say can bring its dead young back to life with its blood. The pelican stands on an eggshell. Human beings rise from a blossom like stamens reaching, reaching for the red berry, a drop of blood in their hands.

Bringing my fingers down to a point, I am back to the egg balancing on the man's head.

Can a new alchemy bring into being a union or reunion of opposing elements, a conjunction that may produce a new guiding image?

$1 + 1 = 3$

The union of a spirit of love with a spirit of wisdom lifts the creature into the divine state in which the soul is woman and the body man . . . in which the spirit is supreme over the form.

Inside the Blue Fountain, call it the Blue Moon floating where the Four Rivers of Paradise meet, a couple dwells. *Might they be the Divine Couple locked in an erotic embrace?* A circle is squared in the pursuit of wholeness. The Trinity is transformed. Within these saturated blue walls, painted from the crushed petals of larkspur, *Theologia naturalis* is born.

An eight-inch-tall Indian forest owlet, known as Blewitt's owl, was sighted in a wooded area near Shahada, India, northeast of Bombay. It had been unseen for 113 years and thought to be extinct.

"The last definite report on this bird was when a specimen was collected in 1884," said Pamela C. Rasmussen of the National Museum of Natural History in Washington, D.C.

Who were the ones reciting prayers for the owl's return?

"Teach us how to pray," I ask on bent knees in El Bosco's Garden. I turn to my own small perspective, a perspective that focuses on the place where I live and love, Utah, my home. A harvest moon appears over Adobe Mesa, casting a blue light over the desert where I am camped. Color still registers on the red cliff face. On my back, I watch the moon and contemplate the miraculous, simply this, the daily manifestations of beauty. A mountain lion slips into the layers of sandstone like a passing shadow.

In these moments of revelation, I am flushed with faith.

A man is lying on the grass, face down, arms stretched above his head as a deer licks his neck. This is what I see now as I stand before the center panel of *El jardín de las delicias*. Animals and human beings together. Hieronymus Bosch has created a community, he celebrates a community in discovery. Personal engagement is its own form of prayer.

I can no longer live separately any more. I am Eve. I am Earth. I am the owl who has been hiding and is suddenly found. I am the tortoiseshell in El Bosco's Garden fluttering above the thistle.

Blue Thistle bowing over bodies. A blessing and a burden of all that is introduced to the body, whip my body, whip my body with a thistle, what am I to make of these self-imposed welts?

> *There are two ways of escaping the pain*
> *and despair of life, and of the rarest, most*
> *subtle dangerous and ensnaring gift that life*
> *can bring us, relationship with another*
> *person—love.*
>
> *One way is to kill that love in one's heart.*
> *To kill love—to kill life.*
>
> *The other way is to accept that love, to*
> *accept the snare, to accept the pricks, the thistle.*
>
> *To accept life—but that is dangerous.*
>
> *It is also dangerous not to accept life. . . .*
>
> *Every man and woman is free to accept or*
> *deny life—to accept or reject this questionable*
> *gift—this thistle.*

A thistle is the place where bees rest at night.

Nearby, two together in an apple boat float. A heron watches over their heads. Dare I say there is a "God beyond God"? The Mystery that embraces us may be more than human; every living thing that divides itself cell by miraculous cell is a template of this majesty. Heaven and Hell are not places of residency above and below, rather the pulse and pause within our own veins. Our only judgment lies in how we choose to live.

At the Pool of Desire, three men carry a whale on its back, an orange fish is flailing from its mouth.

I once heard in the halls of Congress that the story of the salmon is a cliché.

Nacer. To be born. *Nadar.* To swim. To swim in the river to the ocean, to dwell in the ocean and then return to the place one is born with courage and devotion to the memory that resides, presides, in the body, to fight and climb and fly up obstacles set in one's path, to bear witness to the loss of one's homeland through greed, through neglect, through ignorance, over the blood of the forest turned muddy in the river, to break one's body in sacrament, just to lay one's body down in cool waters, calm waters, and open oneself to birth, allowing the sweet swirl of sperm to fertilize the future, and to then face the river and surrender to the river, to death, knowing community will be sustained through the intelligence of the body decomposing, dreaming itself to be born again.

If this story is a cliché, then isn't the holy seed of Christ planted by God inside the wise womb of the Virgin, carried with compassion, delivered beneath a star under the watch of shepherds to teach us, his sheep, how to live and how to die and live again with forgiveness, also a cliché?

The sacredness of Creation includes both the courage of a fish and the courage of a human being, struggling to fulfill their destiny, each embodiments of flesh and spirit.

Resurrección es un acto que merece nuestra honra.

When I was young, I fell in love with a fly fisherman. His preference was always toward small streams, tributaries to the Missouri. He dreamed of retiring in Montana.

He would walk the creek's willowed edges, halfway hidden, his fly rod in hand with an eye upstream and down for trout. And when he saw the sweet risings of lips to water, he entered the current.

This fly fisherman would stand thigh-high in the Madison with rod in hand and make the most beautiful undulations, waving with his right arm, pulling line with his left. Back and forth, the bamboo extension of himself would arc above his head seconds before he cast his line of light.

"It is an art that is performed on a four-count rhythm between ten and two o'clock," Norman Maclean writes in *A River Runs Through It*. This I saw on the river and recognized as the hours we secretly inhabited. Ten at night until two o'clock in the morning. We were awake while others slept.

Letting the line gracefully slip through his fingers, he placed the dry fly (I believe it was a Royal Wulf) perfectly inside the eddy where he imagined the cutthroat to linger. The ritual of the cast like a tease was repeated again and again between the man's daydreams. The trout would strike. The man would smile with a quick flick of the wrist to plant the hook and then slowly reel the creature toward him until it was time to land the fish.

Out of the water, the man would kneel on the bank with the rod between his legs, steady the trout (native trout), unhook the fly from its white upper lip (she feels no pain, he assured me), then return the fish cradled in both hands to the river (let her adjust and get her bearings), face the trout downstream, tickle her belly, and let her go.

Cutthroat.

Catch and release.

Our friendship was no different. It wasn't until he slipped with his tongue and said, "I made love to you because it was the only way I knew how to reel you in. I was afraid of losing you."

Catch and release.

To fish is to flirt. To flirt is to fish. Is this the sporting nature of love? Lips to water. We kiss. We bite the hidden barb. We are pulled out of the river and brought to shore barely breathing. Through the lens of a cutthroat's eye, we look up to see who has desired us.

That night, I pulled the hook of the dry fly out of my own lip and swam downriver.

Catch and release.

In El Bosco's Garden, a man's hand is rubbing the side of a fish.

"Forgiveness," says the fish. "Forgiveness is the release."

Do I dare approach the magnificent pink tower behind the cavalcade once more? Do I dare to enter this fortress in *El jardín de las delicias*?

My hands feel the radiant heat emanating from the flesh-colored walls. Heat, heat transformed into warmth. This is not the ravaging heat of Hell, but a nurturing heat, a heat that makes a body glow. I step inside. To my surprise, there is a spiral staircase. One step at a time, around and around, each revolution asks for another step and another. A slow ascension. Everything is beginning to throb like high noon in the desert.

I reach the top of the tower. I leap from one tower to the next (how is this possible?) and slide down a spire, dance around its base, run, twirl, and swing my arms high, singing across the tendrils, they scarcely droop from my weight. Is there no end to this feeling of lightness, my body a feather, my mind a cloud, a slowly shifting shape, a fish opens to a bird that widens to a horse that dissipates into roses, a sky of roses.

On top of another tower, I can see the curvature of Earth. When did Columbus know that Earth was not flat? When did Magellan know that Earth was round?

We are all explorers.

Desire possesses the force of navigation. Its lure is physical. Call it scientific. We have proof. In love, there is proof. The body does not lie. One body registers an attraction to another, through the eyes, through the mind, recorded in the brain. Our limbic system, ancient and trustworthy, sends signals to the hypothalamus, the pituitary, thyroid, and adrenal glands. Adrenaline pulses and throbs through the blood. Raw emotion translates to a heightened sense of being.

The nervous system is engaged. The first flickers of love begin. In the prefrontal cortex of the brain, we can anticipate the joy before love ever finds its way.

To imagine is to prepare for the discovery. What Magellan saw on the curved horizon, land, was what he saw in his mind every night when he closed his eyes. The dreamer draws the map, rolls it inside the bottle, and hands it to the sea. The awakened one standing on shore dares to swim beyond the breaking waves to retrieve the bottle and returns with the plan in hand.

Endorphins fuel the desire and seal the attraction. They dress the risks and sacrifices of love in the red surge of romance. It is a single focus of attention. Nothing matters. We marry our obsessions.

The masts are raised. The wind caught in sail moves. Swirling hormones keep love afloat until the marriage hits flat water, the deadly polite calm. No land behind. No land ahead. Navigation stops when the will and imagination retire. One prays for birds.

The spiritual lure of a new world seen from an old world takes over.

What do we do?

What we do we do.

This is what we do.

Name the world. Paint the world. Adam did. Eve did. El Bosco did. His birds are named and painted perfectly. *Was he a naturalist or a visionary?*

Round, round, round, I go joining the circle of bareback riders, faster and faster I ride the palomino. Putting my arms around his neck, I whisper in his ears, *What do you know? When did you know?* Around and around the Pool of Desire we go. A man arches his back, creating a bow of light. A sliver moon defends the parade. Ahead a porcupine rides high in a bubble. And farther still rides a man standing on one leg, bent over, his head touching his knee, while his other leg is raised like a banner creating a right angle to the circle. Birds perch on human limbs as though they are trees.

I smell rosemary. Rosemary has a past. What is it? It greeted me in Ávila. It welcomes me here. I slide off the horse and walk toward a gathering of pilgrims. The shrub is growing wild.

I bend down and breathe the fragrance into my blood, its green endurance filling me with a confidence I associate with family.

The river of pilgrims swells and I am absorbed into the collective current that is leading us in *El jardín de las delicias* toward what looks like a red hibiscus. As the figures gather inside the cup of the flower, one figure extends his hand to another. Where their hands meet, a white egret stands.

I am watching my own people along the Mormon Trail commemorate the sesquicentennial of the Mormon Exodus when my pioneer ancestors left Missouri for the Great Salt Lake Valley, John Henry Tempest among them, the same name as my father and his father and his father's father.

I will arrive home from Spain just in time to witness eight hundred covered wagons moving through Emigration Canyon where we live, a wagon train of eight hundred and thousands of modern-day pioneers reenacting each step taken toward the Promised Land.

This wide open space is my home . . . we have consecrated this land to the Lord.

Looking over the hill, the canyon road is swollen with people dressed in traditional pioneer clothing. Many are on horses, many more are pulling handcarts behind them, and most are walking. The numbers have expanded greatly as they near Salt Lake City. The original pilgrims have been walking since April, almost three months. I squint my eyes as one hundred fifty years vanish. They are only four miles away from the first view of the Salt Lake Valley where Brigham Young, who had been ill, sat up from the back of his covered wagon on July 24, 1847, and said, "This is the right place."

Peregrinación de deseo.

It is twilight. Brooke and I are standing in the Brigham Young Cougar Stadium with our extended family. We are among the sixty thousand members of the Church of Jesus Christ of Latter-day Saints gathered together in Provo, Utah, to celebrate the Pioneer Pilgrimage.

The singing begins.

> *We thank thee, O God, for a prophet to guide us in these latter days.*
> *We thank thee for sending the Gospel to lighten our minds with*
> *   its rays.*
> *We thank thee for every blessing bestowed by thy bounteous hand.*
> *We feel it a pleasure to serve thee and love to obey thy command.*

The lights of the stadium are dimmed. A spotlight scans the crowd and suddenly stops, broadening its beam on a gauntlet of young people dressed in yellow shirts and white pants and shoes. Everyone rises to their feet as the singing intensifies. The prophet of the Mormon Church, President Gordon B. Hinckley, enters the stadium and walks briskly through the receiving line with the members clapping for their leader. Dressed in white, a vigorous man in his eighties waves to the crowd and finds his honored place on the podium. The faithful know he is ordained by God.

The prophet is followed through the gauntlet by his two counselors, Elder Thomas B. Monson and Elder James E. Faust. Their wives, also dressed in white, are transported onto the field in a golf cart to meet their mates onstage. Again, the followers spontaneously rise to their feet and applaud.

The Mormon Tabernacle Choir, the Youth Chorus and Symphony, the Utah Valley Family Choir, and the Young Ambassadors then perform a medley of songs to celebrate the pioneer's journey into Utah.

The Spirit of God like a fire is burning!
The latter-day glory begins to come forth.
The visions and blessings of old are returning,
And angels are coming to visit the earth.
We'll sing and we'll shout with the armies of heaven,
Hosanna, hosanna to God and the Lamb!
Let glory to them in the highest be given,
Henceforth, and forever, amen and amen!

Inside my veins, I feel the pulse of my people, those dead and those standing beside me, a pulse I will always be driven by, a pulse that registers as a murmur in my heart. I cannot escape my history, nor can I ignore the lineage that is mine. Most importantly, I don't want to.

I know these songs. Brooke and I are singing. We are all singing. I am holding my niece's hand. Together we pay homage to the seedbed of our religious life.

Below on the football field, we witness our religious history as an opera. It is epic theater, beginning in 1820 in western New York with Joseph Smith's first vision to Hill Cumorah where the golden plates were recovered and later translated into the Book of Mormon. From there the play moves to April 6, 1830, when the Church of Jesus Christ of Latter-day Saints is organized in Fayette, New York. In 1830–31, Joseph Smith moves his people to Kirtland, Ohio. The crowd witnesses worship as well as dancing, and the growing commerce of a resourceful community. They see tensions mount within the outside community wondering who these people are. On March 24, 1832, the modern-day prophet Joseph Smith is tarred and feathered by a mob in Hiram, Ohio. Torches are lit, buildings are burned. The heat from the stadium rises as believers' faces are lit. My face is lit. On April 3, 1836, after continued persecution, Joseph moves his disciples to Illinois and founds the city of Nauvoo. From 1839 through 1844, the Mormon Ideal expands, with the Church growing to thirty thousand persons. The football field fills with new members. The music swells and deepens as the crowd witnesses the murder of Joseph Smith and his brother by a militia in the Carthage jail on June 27, 1844. Men riding horses circle the jail and set it on fire. Brigham Young, emerges from the flames. He succeeds Joseph Smith as the new Prophet, Seer, and Revelator. The year 1846 through 1847 marks the Great Exodus of the Mormons from Nauvoo, where "the American Moses" delivers his Saints to the Great Salt Lake Valley.

Enter the covered wagons with their teams of horses driven by twentieth-century pioneers into the arena, dust-covered and worn; having traveled the road of history, their journey is complete.

Materia poetica.

A religion becomes a people.

The Kingdom of God enters the Great Basin.

The voices of the Tabernacle Choir begin to sing the emblematic hymn of the Mormon people:

Come, come, ye Saints, no toil or labor fear;
But with joy wend your way.

Though hard to you this journey may appear,
Grace shall be as your day.
'Tis better far for us to strive
Our useless cares from us to drive;
Do this, and joy your hearts will swell—
All is well! All is well!

Tears stream down my cheeks. I am home. I remember who
I am and where I come from. This is my story, a story of a people in search of God who sought a landscape in the desert
where they could worship freely.

I believe.

Suddenly, the mood shifts. The stadium becomes dark.
The covered wagons drawn by horses appear and disappear as
apparitions.

Two enormous video screens perched above the stadium
flash images of the family, mothers, fathers, children together,
the family grows mythically before our eyes, until hundreds,
maybe thousands of children descend from the aisles carrying
lit candles, singing "I Am a Child of God." It is an endless trail
of lights, children dressed in white, and together we watch the
Church of Jesus Christ of Latter-day Saints slowly transfigure
itself from a family seated around the dinner table into a world
family, a global tribe of Truth.

Spotlights dart maniacally through the crowd, resting finally
on the football field as every country and culture on the planet
appears in the circle of lights: Ute, Paiute, Shoshone, Hopi,
Apache, Sioux, are among the Indian Nations of America to
enter the arena in traditional clothing; Maori people; Samoan
people; all European nations; Asia; Africa; Central and South
American people; the entire world begins to dance in circles on
podiums and pedestals in front of the immense congregation.

And then each distinct culture begins singing at once, "Come, Come, Ye Saints," in their own native tongue.

It is a frenzy of faith and ecclesiastical ecstasy, a spectacle so huge, so perfectly choreographed, on such a massive scale, it renders me dumb.

Attachment. Detachment. I feel myself unhinging from the rest of my clan as they gather closer together. There is a rupture in my heart that nobody sees. My niece is still holding my hand. I can find no place to breathe.

And then through the flashing lights, the rotating stages, the dancing fountains behind the dancing nations, a new song erupts, a song I do not know.

From the loudspeakers sounds the command, "Brothers and Sisters, let us welcome today's Pioneers of the Heart!"

From the wings, where typically the athletes run onto the field, thousands upon thousands of Mormon missionaries file out carrying the banners of each country they have been called to labor in. The stream of missionaries is endless, circling around the stadium like a river. The new song intensifies. The crowd are on their feet delirious, clapping their hands, breaking every now and again to wave to the missionaries below, many of them sons, daughters, mothers and fathers, my husband's father and his wife among them, a man and woman we love and cherish.

What is this song? I do not know this song. Behind me, all around, people are singing. I can feel the surge behind the words "baptize, baptize, baptize."

I weep in the midst of my people. I weep because I recognize I no longer believe as I once did. I weep because I do not believe there is only one true church. I weep because within my own homeland I suddenly feel foreign, so very, very foreign. I weep—my own family cries too, but for different reasons.

I look at Brooke, a descendant of Brigham Young, standing next to his nephew. He is frozen, the only son in his family who chose not to serve a mission. It is something you are never allowed to forget, ever. The missionaries keep circling the stadium, circling him, circling us. The River of Truth flowing strong in the heart of Zion.

The closing words from the Prophet ring throughout the stadium: *We have a divine mandate to carry the gospel to every nation, kindred, tongue, and people. . . . We must grasp the torch and run the race.*

Grasp the torch. Carry the torch. Pass the torch.

The torch I see is not the burning torch of truth, nor the torches lit with the intent of martyring a prophet, but the small handheld torch carried into the cave at Altamira in northern Spain, the torch fueled by animal grease that illuminated the dark so an artist could paint a bison galloping on a ceiling of stone.

The next day, I clean my house in an attempt to organize my thoughts. I find a blue spiral notebook among the piles and open it to find my grandmother's handwriting, one of her journals that I kept after her death.

I sit down cross-legged on the floor and flip through the yellowed pages. In my grandmother's hand, I read:

> *There is more faith in honest doubt than in all the unexamined creeds of past and present. In this sense, each of us must articulate*

their own religion—that is, their own concept of what is of supreme worth in living, their own mode of expressing that concept in their own commitment in daily life to the values he or she believes to be basic.

I know the man sitting on the back of the goldfinch with his head in his hands, his hands cup his ears, the ocean speaks to him, a place he has never seen, *where to doubt and to dream is to open one's heart to a truth unknown.*

I am happy to be home in Spain watching the Garden before me.

All that faith creates or love desires,
Terrible, strange, sublime and beauteous shapes.

A curious egg-shaped object, orange with blue triangles on its skin, shines in the afternoon light. The one holding the bulb is looking at a figure who is wearing a strawberry on his back like a knapsack. What is it we carry that may not be ours to hold?

I walk through a forest of sunflowers, a sea of yellow waves. These flowers, disciples of light, flood the Garden with petaled joy. They will be harvested for their seeds that will later rest in the hands of the patient, *let me be patient, I wish there were answers, not simply questions,* each one like an oracle, a secret to be cracked in the mouth and swallowed.

Two visitors, a man and a woman, are whispering. They point to a particular tableau: a man is bending over on his arms and knees as another man pulls flowers out of his anus and makes a bouquet.

Where do we hide our passions, our positions of truth, when everything around us lifts a finger to our mouth and says, "Hush, do not disturb the peace." *Wild Peace.* What peace is mine to live, to savor, to hold and cherish in this marriage between Heaven and Hell that so fully delivers us from the evils of silence, not the holy silence that is alive and fertile, that stirs our hearts, wakes our hearts, and holds us in a throbbing truth, so that in our ears we *return to here's hear,* but the silence of suffocation, the invisible hand that covers our mouth, covers our ears, our eyes, and keeps us in darkness like the woman in El Bosco's Hell that leans against the gold throne, her eyes closed, a black frog clamped on her heart, the same pale woman with a jackal standing behind her grabbing her left breast, checking her swollen belly for tumors.

I recall how the school board in my community voted to ban all high school clubs in the state of Utah not associated with academics in order to eliminate the organization of one club in Salt Lake City called "the Gay-Straight Alliance."

Kelli Peterson, the teenager who petitioned to organize the Gay-Straight Alliance at her high school, said, "I started this group to end the misery and isolation of being gay in high school. . . . We are not teaching how to have sex. It's not a technique club."

The school board was unmoved.

"It is a divisive issue for the whole society," a Utah state senator said. "It is drawing a line in the sand of what is civil and what is bestial. What is a human being and what is an animal."

What are we afraid of?

. . .

Perhaps what we fear most is nature, even our own.

From the Latin Natura is my birth, my characteristics, my condition. It is my nativity, my astrology, my biology, my physiognomy, my geography, my cartography, my spirituality, my mentality, my corporeal, intellectual, emotional, imaginative self. . . . Natura is the whole that I am.

I see my community's fear of homosexuality, even wilderness, as a failure of love and imagination. Sex is like land. It must be used for something.

In wildness, as in love, we are free, breathing, exploring, discovering creatures. We are simply nature—animal, yes, animal. No separation. If the question of the "Other" is the point of every revolution, even war, is it naive to believe in a place within our own evolving state, even the state of Utah, where we can recognize "Other" as ourselves?

What are we afraid of?

It is the nature of art to offend. It is the nature of art to offer. It is the paradox of the artist to both widen and heal the split within ourselves.

We can reject or accept art. We can criticize or lionize an artist's work. What remains secret is the private intention, the nightmares that accompany the artist, the ecstasy each touches in the dark-bright florid landscapes they travel. And in the end, it doesn't matter. They leave their images behind, their words, their dances, behind. Tracks to follow. But they are not to be found. They are miles away—on to the next scent. Hieronymus Bosch painted what he smelled. Then he moved on. The artist is the traveler.

BYU BANS FOUR RODIN WORKS OVER
DEPICTIONS OF NUDITY

PROVO—Brigham Young University has refused to display four nude works of renowned French artist François-Auguste Rodin over religious and moral concerns.

"We have felt that the nature of those works is such that the viewer will be concentrating on them in a way that is not good for us," said Campbell Gray, director of the BYU Museum of Art.

Gray said the museum and university officials discussed the issue for two months before deciding that the four works—including Rodin's world-famous erotic sculpture, *The Kiss*—would be censored.

The Kiss. The hands that hold the kiss. Tender knowledge translated through the lips. Our first contact with the world is the kiss of our mother's nipple. We find the opening that feeds us. Our attachment to life is through the mouth. It begins with a kiss, the uncensored kiss that turns our body to liquid, a stream of milk and the nourishment of love. And later, in another moment of need, two mouths meet, tongues curl around each other like standing waves, our bodies together, a river.

There is a kiss about to erupt in El Bosco's Garden. A woman draws a man's chin down to her with her index finger and thumb, a gentle gesture to come. Their eyes reflect the other's intention. At what moment do they close? At what moment do they recognize the downward pull of the kiss on their backs, on their bellies, open, they are open, their bodies a river flowing downstream. See love as two leaves twirling in an eddy. The lovers are now tucked inside the bulbous fruit. Fruiting bodies. It all begins with that pause between mouths and the memory of milk.

> *I am woman, I make love, love makes me, a Third Body comes to us. . . . Between our two bodies, our Third Body surges forth and flies up to see the summit of things.*

A fish is flying in El Bosco's sky. Riding the fish is a mermaid holding the tip of her tail over her head. She has a rod in her hand, dangling a cherry. I follow them with my eyes as they circle above. Along the edge of the water, I find a vessel that will carry me out to sea. I am hungry, in need of food. I cast a line. Within minutes, I hook a rockfish. The fish is copper, thrashing with a swollen belly on the surface of the water as I bring her into the boat. I hold her. She is so beautiful. What am I to do? Can a woman's eyes meet the eyes of a fish? I slit her belly open with the tip of my knife. Thousands of live young spill out like clear jelly. Green-blue dots of eyes, iridescent eyes, are staring at me, yellow spines, quivering hearts. These fish are minuscule. Their Motherbody is dead. They are alive. I slip my fingers inside the fish and touch posterity, wriggling, wet, and anxious. Leaning over the bow of the boat, I return the babies to the sea. For a brief moment, the estuary is glittering with turquoise and gold.

I return to El Bosco's banks, build a fire, cook the Mother Rockfish, and eat.

There was a time when we were not separated from the sea, but found a home in salt water. A cell floating in the sea. Many cells navigating through waves of the sea. The Body a vessel. My Body a vessel. Two bodies together become intelligence in flames. Red flames. Coral. We grow. We stretch. We branch out like coral, an aquatic tree touching both Earth and Sky. Water is the medium for growth.

There is a red vessel of coral in El Bosco's Garden. Call it a tent. I see legs inside the tent. Another place to play. Another place to probe. Many legs. Many bodies. Many cures. Did Hieronymus Bosch know in his own laboratory at home that coral crushed cures witchcraft, coral ingested absorbs melancholy, coral filtered through a woman's body is hope against infertility? Could he have kept small branches of coral in his own medicinal pouch to protect him against the plague, to guard him against leprosy, to stop excessive bleeding? Veins of coral, veins of blood, healthy blood, might a semblance of form hold a secret for healing?

Play with combinations. Secret combinations. Observe and experiment. Paracelsus the Great speaks: *The magistery of corals, the virtues whereof I very much and specially wonder at, which God has bestowed on this growing thing, which also do operate powerfully and wonderfully, even as they grow.*

To wonder is to grow, not to know, but consider, consider how the coral reefs are dying, why they are dying, veins of coral, we are coral, veins of blood, our own blood. The health of coral depends on both scientists and seers.

Alchemy is a marriage of opposites, a marriage of science and religion. Their marriage is consummated through wonder. I wonder if alchemy is real. I believe it is real, not a rumor for turning base metals into gold, but for bending our minds. Remember how magic metamorphosed into religion metamorphosed into science became our religion? Do we need a new religion or no religion at all, how great a risk would it be to believe in the alchemical wisdom of coral?

El Bosco's people are giving a coral reading in the Garden.

Man is able, if he wishes, to guide his desire
through a vein of coral or a heavenly naked body.

There are offerings being made to the Alchemical Trinity in the Garden. Everywhere there is engagement and distillation. Alchemy is art. Art is alchemy. Temperance. Once we stop contributing to this Alchemical Trinity—Mercury, Sulphur, and Salt: Spirit, Soul, and Body—creativity turns inward. The ripening process is cut short. Melancholia sets in. The fruit is at risk of becoming bitter. If we want to bring about something abiding, we must make time.

A woman savors a cherry. Delight for the Body.

A man rides a white stag high. Movement for the Mind.

A man listens intently from the headdress of a hoopoe. Inspiration for the Soul.

El Bosco's progeny are giving their time. Time is the supreme offering. Time together. Time alone. Time on Earth wandering, wondering, contemplating. Time to live. Time to reflect on the living. This is the nature of experience. This is the nature of El Bosco's middle way.

The middle path makes me wary. It can be frightening, mistaken for a place of safety and moderation. I am not entirely comfortable here, never having been attracted to moderation of any kind. I have courted an intensity of extremes where I know what I am facing and where I choose to stand. But in the middle of my life, I am coming to see the middle path as a walk with wisdom where conversations of complexity can be found, that the middle path is the path of movement. This interests

me. Life is not so predictable. I am forced to listen more carefully. In the right and left worlds, the stories told are largely set,
there is much to defend at the expense of the other, rhetoric is
charged with certitude; it's safer here, we are sure we are correct. We become missionaries for a position, yes, exactly, no
doubt about it, practitioners of the missionary position. Variety
is lost. Diversity is lost. Creativity is lost in our inability to make
love with the world.

The lovers in the mussel shell are lying side by side giving birth
to pearls. I am gathering blue pearls in the Garden as they fall.
Crushed pearls mixed with red sand. The ocean is joining the
desert in my hand as my palms circle together to create this
potion for our bodies. Add oils of frankincense, amber, and
myrrh, plant oils, to spread over our bodies to strengthen and
rejuvenate. Now, add yucca suds combined with ash. It is
bubbling, cooing. Come closer, lie down, stomach on slick-
rock, warm.

Let me spread this hot pearl-sand potion on your body. My
hand smooths one skin over another. Your body turns red mud
glistens with pearls as it sinks into each pore and penetrates.
Now bake in the sun and dry.

Crack. Cracked skin in the desert, we are broken in the
silence of love, take my hand to the river, ease into the river
that shocks the feet, cold feet, calves, thighs, waist, fall, float
together, rub bodies together, warm the red sand is abrasive,
love can be too as we enter the current. Hands touching hands
touching skin so smooth where does one leg end and another
begin on our backs in the river we move don't move stay.

Indigo. Say it—my breath follows the *o* open—stay open to
indigo blue blue the backside of orange the inside of flames
the kiss against the wall you came from home that is the indigo

I know my head hits church doors as we kiss mouths open to the river indigo don't go when did you come I stay open for another evening until dawn you know that color of indigo— how deep love can carry us when the river is clear.

Pearls and sand, ocean and desert combined wash away, our dead skin washed away in a flash flood of tears, erode and come.

A sensation as pleasurable, tender, horrifying, chilling and pene-trating as love. Could this be the grace you call God?

It is quiet in the Prado.
Hieronymus Bosch is a hallucination.
El jardín de las delicias is a fever.

I cannot take it all in. Hieronymus Bosch is too much for me. Be it a molecule or belief, we can never see it all. To look below the surface is the paradox of painting. It is all surface. But what was he saying? How did he paint the views of orthodoxy in the Middle Ages from his easel in the Low Countries? Not to be understood. *I cannot take it all in, just like God.* An artist uses his intelligence as well as skill. Seeing becomes a process of finding meaning. *Is there meaning?* Call it a devotional imagination. I believe the patron or persons for whom Bosch painted his trip-tych did understand the meaning and it was read episodically, the drama of each movement carefully considered within the triptych worshiped at the altar where it hung.

My eyes focus on the bubble with a man and woman sitting inside the delicate membrane as a strawberry floats. The man has his hand on the belly of the woman. Her hand gently squeezes his thigh.

I cannot penetrate this conjugal cell. It is the one truly private place in the Garden. One can only know what one sees on the surface.

In any relationship, we commit ourselves to the emotional oscillations of a shared life. In the beginning we feel protected. Through time, we do not. The utter bliss of two bodies in love rises and falls through our children. We live together as husband and wife and family. And then, the day comes when what is required is retreat where a sovereignty of soul is reclaimed in solitude. Perhaps it is in these moments of stillness art is created, the artistry of an interior life that allows us to surface in partnership once again.

I am content to be among Bosch's people. If I were sitting under that apple tree and a man approached me holding a giant strawberry, so large, in fact, that it covered his genitals, and this man bowed to me offering his fruit—I would say to him, "The strawberry you hold is my womb, ripe and delicious. Eat it whole, now, swallow the yellow seeds quickly, now, so that when we stand on our heads in love, you can redeposit the seeds inside me, now, like the prophecy of fruit you hold in your hands."

I would tell this contrite man to prepare himself for abandonment, that this is the secret every woman knows and privately carries in her belly. Once impregnated with an idea, a child, a poem, or a painting, she must leave the man in order to give birth.

Winter Solstice. I am leaving the Utah Museum of Natural History because I need more light, more life, than this Palace of Memory can hold. A wild mind cannot be married long to an institutional one. We part as friends with a history.

. . .

I walk toward El Escorial, Philip II's austere palace, a granite fortress that meets the granite of the Sierra de Guadarrama. I cannot help but see my own culture's architecture of belief, the similar granite blocks quarried out of the Wasatch Mountains by my ancestors, used to construct a holy temple in the heart of the American West in Salt Lake City. Gothic spires reach toward Heaven. The impulse is the same: to worship God by extending our vision upward, to create "a dwelling for God on Earth."

> *Philip had begun to live inside his dream. The vast stone pile which he had drawn about himself like a garment spoke of his peculiar self as no other building in Europe had ever echoed the spirit of a single man. . . . The Church of San Lorenzo stands for the embattled defense of orthodoxy by the temporal sword.*

I stand from a distance and try to imagine the magnitude of the Real Monasterio de San Lorenzo de El Escorial begun in 1563 by the great architect Juan Bautista de Toledo and finished remarkably twenty-one years later in 1584 by Juan de Herrera.

Next to me is a heavy-set man with a black beard. He is surrounded by other visitors. We are waiting to cross the street. He begins a historical soliloquy. "You may already know that in 1555, Philip II inherited the Spanish empire from his father, Charles V, who controlled Naples, Milan, Sicily, Sardinia, the Low Countries in the Netherlands, Flanders, and Portugal with overseas claims in America, Africa, and the South Seas. If Philip II's father was irritated by Martin Luther's cry for a freedom of conscience over obedience to royal power, posting his infamous ninety-five theses on a church door signaling the Reformation, Philip II became obsessed with Protestantism in the Low Countries and led the Counter-Reformation, supported by Santa Teresa de Ávila, throughout Europe, revitalizing the second Spanish Inquisition, known as 'the Suprema,' to maintain the purity of Catholic devotion."

A few people are asking him questions. There is so much traffic we are still unable to cross.

"The door to comprehending the complexities of Philip II is opened through the doors of El Escorial."

I am amused at the theatrics of his presentation and turn to him as we finally walk to the other side of the street toward the entrance.

"You seem to know a great deal," I say.

"Thank you. My name is Jennings." He extends his hand. "A pleasure to meet you."

"Are you conducting a tour?"

"No, I'm traveling by myself, but a group of us were all on the same train from Madrid. We started talking, they asked some questions, and well, here we are. I enjoy sharing what I know with people if they are interested. I'm a professor, a medievalist by training. I teach at Saint Francis Xavier University in Canada. I'm in Spain for a month to look at some illuminated manuscripts from the fourteenth century. And you?"

"I'm obsessed with Bosch and want to know why Philip II was as well."

"Did you know he owned over thirty of Bosch's paintings?"

"That many?"

"Indeed. Is there one in particular you are interested in?"

"*El jardín de las delicias.*"

"Of course."

"Philip II was fully nurtured in the miracles of nature and art."

"Excuse me?"

"What I mean is that he possessed an insatiable curiosity about the world around him which was encouraged early on by his tutors."

We enter El Escorial. It is very dark. My eyes try to adjust to the solemn interior. The entrance is flanked by Doric columns and I feel very small.

"It is somewhat ironic that a man who had such a sharp hunger for knowledge chose to cloister himself at home. Did you know Philip II never left Spain after 1559, much less El Escorial, in contrast to his father, who traveled extensively through Europe charming all manner of his subjects?"

He touches my arm. "Do you mind if I accompany you?"

I pause. "Not at all."

"Then let's go straight to the library, if you don't mind. I think it's critical to place Hieronymus Bosch in the context of his own time and not project his painting onto our own era," says Jennings in a hushed authoritative voice. "I would recommend reading Charles de Tolnay's interpretation from the 1940s. I believe he has the most comprehensive view of Bosch and is certainly one of the most credible inside the Academy. There's some real harebrains out there, you know."

"Yes."

"Tolnay believes, and I think it's true of most art historians, that Bosch was depicting the Fall of Man in his triptych. During the Late Middle Ages, the common doctrine was based on the idea that the meaning and purpose of life were to be found only in the contemplation of God, and that all other activities of the senses and mind were snares leading mankind to Hell. All of Bosch can fit inside this formula."

"You really think it's that clear-cut?"

"I do. It can be read through a strict reading of the Bible. Don't forget *El jardín de las delicias* was once an altarpiece created for the purpose of meditation."

"But whose meditation?"

He doesn't answer.

We walk down a long dark hallway. I wish I had brought a heavier sweater.

"And what do you think about Fraenger's theory?" I ask.

"So you do know a little about Bosch."

I can feel his assessment of me shift.

"I think Fraenger was a lunatic. His outlandish theory about Bosch serving two masters, the Catholic Church and the Adamites, a sect, as you know, whose members engaged in strange sexual rituals to become closer to God, goes too far. I find much of what he says absurd." He pauses. "Do you have an opinion?"

We proceed through the Patio of Kings, a large courtyard where the six kings of Judah stand. To the right of the patio is the convent.

"I think it's interesting to imagine Bosch creating a hymn to the sensual pleasures of the Earth. From a naturalist's point of view, he was a very astute observer of natural history. I find his center panel almost encyclopedic in scope in terms of the life around him, both real and imagined. I guess I choose to read the triptych in less orthodox terms. And Fraenger's statement that 'The Millennium,' as he calls it, is 'a historical record of the human soul' rings true to me."

I follow the medievalist to a stone stairway and move through the maze of marbled hallways, which he seems to be navigating with remarkable ease.

"Your notion of Bosch's encyclopedic style is typical of

Flemish painters of that era. Van Eyck, Van der Weyden, Memling. The entire Flemish school is based upon observation and accuracy. All their paintings are drenched in details from the flora and fauna to brocaded wallpapers and tiled floors. In fact, this love affair with their surroundings was perhaps most acutely rendered in the *Kunstkammer,* or art cabinet, where men and women in the Low Countries would assemble exotic arrays of artifacts and natural specimens: shells, bones, feathers, stones, oddities found or brought back from various journeys—like maps, globes, coins, microscopes, magnifying lenses, gemstones, botanical and zoological drawings, even protractors, anything that celebrated the curiosities and wonders of the world. Objects from these *Kunstkammern* were often painted, giving the name *stilleven* to what we now know as 'still lifes.' "

I feel myself softening, realizing my vulnerability to anyone who will talk about the wonder of categorizing and cataloging natural objects, why the museums of natural history have held my imagination for so long.

"But you have to admit there is something utterly unique about the way Hieronymus Bosch imagined the world, his fantastic hybrids that both delight and terrorize us?"

"No question. In that sense, it's true we will never know Bosch's intention because we will never know Bosch's mind."

"So what was it about Hieronymus Bosch that captured Philip's imagination?" I ask.

"It's not so difficult following this line of reasoning why Philip was so fond of Flemish painters, especially El Bosco, religion aside. He was a lover of solitude and held a fervent passion for natural history, finding great pleasures in his gardens and woods. He loved birds and plants. In fact, one of his great pleasures was commissioning the eminent naturalist of his time, Antonio Nardo, to preserve and classify the botanical collections coming out of the New World. Imagine. It was Philip who fostered all the scientific expeditions to the Americas led by Dr. Francisco Hernández and started both the Academy of Sciences and the Academy of Mathematics—"

"That's so interesting," I interrupt. "I've had this strong sense that much of the center panel was Bosch's imagination sparked by the discovery of America, that his enthusiasm and affection toward nature, the gifts of wonder and inquiry that they inspire, were in direct response to the stories coming back from the New World."

"Could be," says Jennings. "Again, we'll never know, but one thing that is certain is that Philip II had a true penchant for geography. He ordered the entire mapping of Spain, every province, and he ordered them to be exact, to note down every river, stream, and mountain regardless of size. Philip is also said to have written a couple of sonnets and a book titled *The Order of Creatures* about the diversity of nature."

"Is that true? Have you ever seen a copy?"

"Yes and no, I've only read about it." He laughs. "If you are obsessed by Bosch, I am obsessed by Philip."

Suddenly, we are standing in the most beautiful room I have ever encountered. I am speechless. Remarkably, so is Jennings. It is a 175-foot-long chamber intricately carved with vaulted ceilings, surmounted by vibrant frescos representing the seven Liberal Arts. The floors are a mosaic of marbled squares: black, white, and pink. The bookcases are made of ebony, cedar, orangewood, and walnut, with the spines of most books facing inward so the gilded edges are exposed in the medieval tradition.

José de Siguenza, Philip II's spiritual advisor and trusted biographer, catalogued and arranged the library. His portrait hangs as a guardian. I am fascinated by the primary divisions, the way the library is organized: *gramática, retórica, dialéctica, aritmética, música, astrología,* and *teología.*

Jennings whispers, "There are more than 14,000 volumes here: 1,150 Greek, 94 Hebrew, and 500 codices among them."

I start to smile.

"I'm sorry, I have a photographic mind, it's not my fault that I remember numbers and various scraps of useless information."

"No, I'm sorry, it's just that I feel like I'm walking with a human reference library."

"But I didn't even bother to tell you that there are 84 miles of corridors, 16 courtyards, 15 cloisters, 86 staircases, 2,000-plus windows, and 1,200 doors, all of which Philip knew intimately." He pauses. "I promise you, I don't know a thing beyond the scope of this period, believe me. Anyway, am I boring you?"

"Hardly."

"Well, what I was going to say is that Philip ordered every book of merit that was published to be sent to him, and it is said that the margins are filled with his careful notations."

Walking slowly along the walls of bookcases, it is easy to enter a trance.

"I'm surprised by the esoteric nature of these books. These must reflect his taste, no?"

"He is reported to have possessed over two hundred books on magic, alchemy, astrology, and other cabbalistic volumes. He had a very open mind about alchemy and gave his approval to transmute base metals into gold. Although he remained a skeptic, he allowed several attempts particularly aligned with medicine. His particular interest in the occult made it necessary for him to appoint a special censor to 'expurgate' the library at

El Escorial in order to keep his own Inquisition from turning on him in 1585, a delicious irony."

"Joseph Smith would have loved this library."

"Who?"

"Nothing, no one, I was just talking to myself." (How could I begin to explain that perhaps the origins of my own religion could be traced to some of these obscure, hermetic traditions that were reviving themselves in post-Revolutionary America.) "Didn't Philip II have a huge collection of animal horns?"

"I don't know about that."

"I read where he supposedly had six 'unicorn' horns, maybe in reality those of narwhals. But where would he have acquired them? Again, who knows? It's all so curious. It's hard to imagine what was being discovered and reported from the New World."

"That's why I have chosen to study and, in many ways, live inside the Late Middle Ages. It was anything but dark. There was this wonderful blend of emerging science, art, and religious traditions all centered around small communities still tied to the pagan rites and festivals associated with the turn of seasons. And then there was this absolute reign of power in Spain in the name of the Catholic Church during the eras of Ferdinand and Isabella, Charles V, and Philip II."

A gold armillary sphere at the end of the chamber is a haunting reminder of the decline of the Spanish empire that occurred under Philip II's rule. Perhaps Philip's highest achievement was the "taming of the Americas." Call it the Spanish Acquisition.

In one of the cases in the middle of the room is a sample of the king's penmanship. His script is dark, heavy, and uneven, and overpowers the consistent script of the friars. Elaborate loops seem to turn back on themselves.

"Philip was known to spend up to eight or nine hours a day writing notes and memos, sometimes signing over four hundred documents a day," says Jennings, studying the handwriting carefully. "He was much more comfortable expressing himself on paper than in person. They say his eyes were red-rimmed more often than not from all his detailed correspondence and exhaustive reading. He was mired in minutiae, choosing activities of the mind over the activities of the body, with the exception of hunting. This was in contrast to his father, Charles, who was decisive, physically active, and conceptual in his approach to governing."

I am distracted by a small handwritten book by Santa Teresa de Ávila opened for display. It is her autobiography, a narrative I have come to cherish. Her script is electric, consistent in its eccentricities, with wild movements expressed in her *f*'s and *t*'s. There is an energetic belief conveyed through her pen, a confidence.

In 1579, it is reported that Teresa de Ávila met the king of Spain, and was taken by Philip II's deep spirituality, his uncanny ability to listen, the silence that he conveyed: *I began to speak to him when his penetrating gaze, of those that penetrate the soul, settled on me, so I lowered my eyes and rapidly stated what I wanted.*

Philip II felt a kinship with Teresa and protected her against all accusations of heresy. After her death in 1582, he had her books brought to his library and chose to keep her works by his bedside. In the last painful months of his life, as he lay dying in his bed unable to be moved or turned, Teresa de Ávila's texts were among those he had read to him.

Another strange paradox to ponder, this tender friendship between a pious king and a revolutionary nun, one devoted to purity, even if it meant the brutal instigations of the "Council of Blood," and the other devoted to peace through prayer. Both feared the infection of Protestantism.

*We must retrace the speaking thread, put back into words that
from which words are withdrawn.*

"I cannot think where this will stop," says Teresa de Ávila. "I
have seen so many changes in my lifetime that I do not know
how to go on. What will it be like for those who are born today
and have long lives before them?"

The king of Spain listens.

"I fear, my king, that if the route of power is pursued at
home we will surely see the defeat of the path of God. I fear
great harm."

He takes the esteemed nun by the arm and gently escorts
her to his study. Before them hangs *El jardín de las delicias*.

"Tell me what you see?"

Teresa de Ávila says nothing for some time.

"The sins of the flesh, Your Majesty. It is a most disturbing
sight. Let me keep my gaze to the left of the Garden of Lust
toward Paradise with our Savior Jesus Christ or be reminded of
Hell where we will surely burn if we cannot retain our compo-
sure in the midst of the great temptations of this world." She
pauses. "I have heard stories of this painting."

"I asked my beloved Siguenza if he understood why this
triptych enraptures me so. He said, 'I see El Bosco's satire in
paint as the sins of men.' That is true, but Bride of our Lord, if
we fail to contemplate the refined intelligence of El Bosco and
see the spirit with which he was creating a moral dilemma for
us, we will see only the surface of this painting."

Philip II seats himself and invites Teresa de Ávila to do
the same.

"We have been embraced by suffering. You, perhaps more
than anyone now or before, have touched the burning coals of

Truth. If we did not understand the beauty of His garden our souls would not survive the depths of our miseries. Each day I gather myself before God. It is here before the aura of 'The Strawberry' that I am able to keep my desires under strictest control."

"Your Majesty, you speak in a manner I am not accustomed to and I am unable to find the appropriate words to respond respectfully. The dreams El Bosco has painted are the nightmares I cannot untie myself from in my solitary cell of the convent. These images of unbridled pleasures and retribution offer me no solace, they only strengthen my resolve to remain pure in the light of our Father. I could not bear the weight of this altarpiece."

"Is it beauty you fear?"

Teresa de Ávila lowers her eyes.

The king stands. "Had there been no Inquisition, no Suprema, there would be many more heretics." He walks her out to one of the gardens and breaks the stem of a red rose and hands it to her. "Remember that and this, most thoughtful sister: I believe you have within your heart the power to make this rose white, though others may fear your unorthodox fervor for reform. Pray for me as I pray for you. Do not fear the ruptures of Spain."

The king of the Spanish empire accompanies a Carmelite nun from Ávila down a long stone pathway. He is dressed in black. She is dressed in brown.

"I will leave you with a question," he says, as he turns to her for the last time. "Is it not possible for violence to become an offering?"

I cannot make myself move from Teresa de Ávila's open pages alongside Philip II's letters.

Morning light begins to stream through the windows of the *biblioteca,* seven face the countryside, five face the *basílica.*

I circle the library one more time, this time noticing the various bestiaries exposed, one etching in particular catching my eye. It is a man riding on the back of a lion, similar to the one galloping in Bosch's cavalcade of riders in the Garden. *Obra anónima de ciencia hermética, especialmente magia de los talismanes y alquimia.* El Bosco must have had access to many of these books during the fifteenth century, finding inspiration from the myriad illuminated manuscripts.

I think back to a small Book of Hours that lives in my own library at home. It is approximately 4½ inches by 3 inches and possibly the most beautiful book I have ever seen. *The Master of Mary of Burgundy* was a gift from my first employer, Sam Weller, a revered bookseller in Utah, who owns Zion's Book Store. I was seventeen years old, mesmerized by the details of the marginalia. Each page is a painting; one in particular is composed of violets scattered on a gold background. There are three butterflies and a large dragonfly also placed within the composition of the border. There is another sprinkled with cockleshells in a pink border, the emblem of all pilgrims paying tribute to Saint James of Compostela, and across from that orange poppies with wood moths scattered on green. The tiny window inside depicts the Descension, Christ being taken off the Cross by Joseph and Nicodemus. The Virgin kneels below with her hands clutching her heart.

But perhaps the most curious images are toward the back, titled "Sequence of a Grotesque Tournament." It begins with the Hours of the Cross and runs into the Hours of the Virgin. A lady waits on a unicorn that she covers in a blue cloak, assisted by a monkey. On the next pages, a bull rides the back of a grey goat, carrying the lion's lance. Opposite the bull and goat is a fox wearing a cape about to set off for the tournament, followed by a monkey riding a stag and a lion riding a unicorn. Then the reader sees a monkey on the back of a boar blowing a trumpet as if to herald the coming duel. The subsequent pages depict the tournament between a lion and a wildman on horseback, both carrying lances. Another wildman is mounted on a griffin, waving a pole above his head. Rooks, rabbits, and monkeys all watch from the margins.

I could not have known then that this tiny illuminated manuscript from the late fifteenth century that contained a calendar of the fixed festivals of the Church, prayers to selected saints, the Hours of the Cross and the Hours of the Virgin, this common prayer book of devotion in the Late Middle Ages painted in miniature, was part of the tradition of the Early Flemish school of painting, and a source of inspiration and influence for Hieronymus Bosch. Here is a seed of my obsession in Spain, this Garden of Earthly Delights.

A border of peacock feathers frames the Annunciation in another Book of Hours in the *biblioteca* of El Escorial. In this depiction, Mary sits on the wooden floor with her hands on her lap, her head turned as the angel whispers the news in her ear.

Possession. Obsession. What is it we carry? What carries us? A rush of wind blows us off course into some other place, unknown, untried, just try and resist, resist and insist on a more logical path, a more sought-after path, all gestures of judgment fail, we walk straight into the storm. I am pushed by the wind, pushed against my will, an invisible force, a fist between my shoulders, a blade against blades, with both arms raised I surrender, without warning a strange calm comes and I follow.

Obsession is what we desire all along.

El Escorial is a fortress of desire. Philip II collected his desires from the New World to the Old World, from art to bones to the relics of saints. Before he died, Philip asked his confessor, Fray Diego de Yepes, and the prior of the Escorial to bring him some of the relics for comfort, his desire for comfort. They returned with an arm of Saint Vincent Ferrer and a knee of Saint Sebastian, touching the king's affected leg with them.

Disembodied desire.

Perhaps we desire things, possess things, in our attempt to touch the ineffable. Or perhaps imagining the Golden Age of Spain, it is just another desire to acquire. Bones, books, land, people, all the same to Philip.

Power.

Are our collections a way of staying death, the relics that we keep around us animated by our own projections? No longer dead, they are alive. They are the physical manifestations of what haunts us, what we want to know, yet can never fully understand. In the name of science, we proclaim and procure our mental and physical catalogs of all that we are certain of. Drawers after drawers of bird skins, animal skins, insects on beds of cotton seen behind glass. Cabinets after cabinets of pots, baskets, sandals, manos and metates, turkey robes, yucca mats and blankets, archaic tools of various kinds, all providing a template of the past. But in the end, these endless drawers of objects, numbered and cared for, are still merely remnants of the real. Without the spirit that moved through them, they are corpses in our hands. And yet, we hold on to them in their dry and brittle beauty. Relics. Bring them to us when we are dying. Our Book of Hours. The beautiful marginalia of our lives arranged perfectly to feign a divine order. Hour by Hour, let us pray that the chaos will subside. Let us believe something of us will remain.

Essence.

We ascend from the crypt to the Hall of Paintings and stand in front of a portrait of the king of Spain, this king who sentenced every man, woman, and child in the Netherlands to death, who created the "Council of Blood" that saw thousands of individuals strangled, drowned, burned, and beheaded for the crime of believing other than Catholicism. His nefarious autos-da-fé in Spain were known throughout the continent, festivals of secular punishments, ceremonies of executions held in large plazas where the public was invited to watch.

Philip II stares with blue eyes. He is wearing a high ruff, stiff and white like an orthopedic neck collar attempting to hold his gaunt face erect. He is fair-skinned and fair-haired, looking more Flemish than Castilian; even so his *hidalgo* reigns, the pride he carries is Spanish and it is cloaked in black, the cape, the hat, the habitual garb and unadorned dress of a dying man. He posed for Pantoja de la Cruz in 1598, shortly before he died in his spartan bedchamber clutching the same crucifix his father had held when he died.

As we continue to walk through the immense picture gallery, I become overwhelmed and exhausted by the magnitude of paintings, hundreds of them, each one a masterpiece, a litany of the Great: Titian, Tintoretto, Velásquez, El Greco, Rubens, Dürer, Van der Wyden. Any one of them would be an event, a vision to be celebrated—together they are too much for one visit, for one man, an artistic hoarding, symbolic of the excesses of the Spanish empire. I tell Jennings I am saturated by the extravagance and exalted taste, too much gold, too much suffering, too many crucifixions.

"How much religion can one hall hold?"

He looks puzzled.

"How many ways can Jesus Christ hang on a cross and bleed?"

Finally, we reach Philip II's bedchamber. It is here I find sympathy with the "Spider King," the recluse who ruled the world from home.

"You know this is where many say *El jardín de las delicias* hung," Jennings says. "Bosch's *Table of Seven Deadly Sins* was also here in Philip's private quarters."

"Do you think it's folklore or truth?"

"After a while, I'm afraid they become the same thing. I don't know the exact documentation. I do know the painting was moved. The painting originally was hung in the Hotel of the House of Nassau in Brussels by 1517, one year after Bosch's death. The triptych was likely commissioned by Hendrik III of Nassau, who built the palace in Brussels. It was still hanging there in 1566 when it was copied for tapestries, one of which is here."

"Then when did it come to El Escorial?"

"Again, if my memory serves me, it was stolen from the collection of William the Silent, heir to Hendrik—"

I start to laugh.

"I know, I know all this is terribly useless . . ."

"No, not at all, go on—"

"I told you I am obsessed with Philip; anyway, it was smuggled into Spain through a series of twists and turns until it finally passed into the collection of Philip II in 1593. His lust for Bosch was well known."

He pauses.

"It is ironic that the artist Philip II most adored came from the Low Countries he most abhorred because of the collective threat and push of Protestantism."

I imagine the triptych hanging as a window across from the king of Spain's bed. "Just think if this was the first image he saw when he awoke each morning and the last image his eyes closed on as he fell asleep."

One can imagine that, as the pious and devout Catholic king, Philip saw in El Bosco his own strict doctrine enacted on wooden panels: Adam and Eve resting in Paradise moments before temptation; their offspring engaged in the sensual sins of lust and slothfulness whose retribution is assured in Hell. End of discussion. Bosch paints Philip's ideological sword.

But Philip II was much more complex than the stereotype that has followed him in death and cast a shadow over Spain. His mind was too hungry and his appetites too varied. I can imagine what Philip loved about El Bosco's Garden was what he cherished in his own: the exuberance and vitality of life, the life he seldom allowed himself to embrace. Could it be that what drew him to the painting was its quality of revelation: the disclosure of a rich and secret inner life? Perhaps El Bosco's wild and daring use of traditional imagery allowed the king to leave the torturous web of his compulsive mind and grief-stricken life and imagine a life of the body where he was free to move and love anonymously in the world and partake of the raw and earthly pleasures he quietly held for himself in his private chambers, even in the private chambers of his own bloody heart.

Did Philip II secretly ride on the back of Bosch's lion, prancing around the Pool of Life free of his Spanish coat of arms? Could he be the blond bareback rider beneath the balanced egg carrying the body of Christ in the form of a fish? He holds the fish like a bayonet ready to lead the Counter-Reformation in the name of Truth. Or is he simply listening to the wisdom of the scales? A wild boar in front of the lion rider turns to take note. Does he recognize Philip as the sovereign who had a man killed for poaching two boars near El Escorial? Above the pink boar stands a small owl on the unicorn's spiral horn. Is this the creature who understands that the windows of the church must be left open?

Through the stained glass
The owl got into
The cathedral.

Saint Christopher
Wanted to chase her away
Because she tried to drink
The oil from the lamp
Of Saint Mary.

But the Virgin said—
"Let her drink,
Saint Christopher . . ."

In the olive
Grove I can see the owl
Flying and flying.

She flies heavily
Carrying a green branch
To Saint Mary.

Philip is lying in his humble bed half-conscious from his stomach ailments and looks up at the Garden. What if, on another day, he saw his own black and white soul bordering the full-bodied explorations of the central panel? In his own hallucinatory state, maybe the king saw the Reformation and the inevitability of the Renaissance circling around him. His belief in an austere life in the midst of gilded privilege and adherence to God couched in his own Catholic pessimism and guilt was indeed counter to the artistic and intellectual joy and spiritual freedom that was emerging.

But Hieronymus Bosch's alchemy as an artist is that he could play Philip's passions both ways as religious zealot and as impassioned lover of nature. Regardless of the king's rigidity, El Bosco enabled Philip to travel through his triptych at whim, which incited and fed his curiosity.

Was *El jardín de las delicias* the private pilgrimage Philip took each day to encounter the exotic, the foreign? And if he ventured too far into frightening terrain, he could always glance more deeply into Hell, where he perhaps felt most comfortable. It would be here in a purgatory of his own making that Philip II could love Hieronymus Bosch most deeply. Only El Bosco's demons were more horrific than his own.

Perhaps *El jardín de las delicias* was Philip II's compensatory dream that even his own Suprema could never decipher.

"El Bosco made me feel less lonely in the world."

I turn but there is no one there.

Outside El Escorial, it is raining. I thank Jennings for the eloquence of his companionship and shake his hand before rushing to the train. Under his black umbrella, he wishes me well.

"Don't spend too much time with Bosch," he says. "He'll

overtake you. You'll never find your way back out. Trust me. He casts a spell difficult to break."

Rain. Rain. Rain. My mouth open. My hands cannot hold all the water that is pouring down. Rain. More rain. I am spinning, spinning, eyes closed, head thrown back. The world is so beautiful, so utterly beautiful. Who else is turning with joy as the Earth is turning? Bosch's androgynes are turning, turning, turning over each leaf, flower, berry, and bird. They are hungry. I am hungry. I want to eat everything that is lip-luscious and succulent. Free me from the shadow of Philip's black cloak. If there is lust in *El jardín de las delicias,* it is the lust for experience. *Luxuria.*

After being inside El Escorial and walking in the landscape of Philip II, I cannot help but look at the triptych differently. What is the difference between a religious life and a spiritual one? Are we the individual with his arms around the owl, this owl whose large black eyes stare straight ahead unmoved by human considerations? What is it we can never hold? Is this the bird that embodies the night, the one that haunts our dreams and causes us to declare our visions? What does an owl do in the day if not stare into the sun, storing light so its eyes will glow after dark?

Owl is the bird of insight. We want to be close to Truth.

Religion brings us into community with a shared set of beliefs, symbols, and songs. We can choose to be internally engaged or not. The religion goes forward whether we are present or not. The rules are written. Those in authority tell us what to do. It is, for the most part, comfortable and supportive. We are known. We belong to a congregation and we are taught to worship a creed "the result and fruit of many minds. . . . Purified from all the oddities, shortcomings, and flaws of individual experience." There are answers to be found. It is a peace we can borrow. We learn compliance, cooperation, and sacrifice. We can bask in the warmth of feeling part of an organism that knows its place in the world.

Spirituality is solitary. Its companion is conflict, a gnawing at the soul that cannot be ignored. We are engaged. There are no rules. There are no maps. We live with the discomfort and ambiguity of our own authority. At times, it is lonely, often informed by pain. On other occasions, it is the body submerged in a phosphorescent tide, every movement sparking a trail of illumination. Afterwards, we sit on the shore in moonlight. No candles are necessary. Spirituality exists when we are present, buoyed up by the waters of attention. We learn the courage of faith. It is a peace that is earned. We can take solace in the heat of doubt knowing this is the pulse of poetry.

Back to the owl and the natural history of predator-prey relations. Religion is a rabbit. Spirituality is an owl. An owl will overtake a rabbit. Find the rabbit in the Garden of Delights. El Bosco has placed a rabbit in Paradise half hidden behind grasses. Another rabbit is in Hell dressed in a friar's frock lancing the feet of a human being, another Tournament of the Grotesque.

I begin to feel my own roots in El Bosco's soil and find my own arms, one, two, transforming into three and four, as many arms as there are in the world branching out, with splayed hands, our own hands the branches of trees reaching out for a living truth that will vivify our blood, blood knowledge. Cell by cell. We can escape our cells. Here I am, a traveler dancing inside the shell of a radish, sprouting arms and legs I did not know I had. I am dancing. I am waving cherries by the strength of their stems, singing, *"Come, come, ye Saints, no toil nor labor fear; But with joy wend your way. . . ."*

In these moments of reverie, I realize how close I have come to death through our petrified inheritance of absolutes, the puritanical instructs of authority threatened by joy and discovery.

Firm on our atoll, desert
Heart of bitter mirage,
Doubting believer, I stand with you
Sipping this brackish communion,
Breaking hard bread of alternatives—
Either a waste ocean
Or an infinite ocean of hope:
Whether these shimmering fronds
Above us, mere palms, are illusion,
Or else or also those petals,
That one Dove hovering descending
Out of the garden of the sun
To brood the hopes of humanity—
Both of such beautiful credentials,
Blazoned on measureless dark.

In terrible splendor of dilemma,
Saints walk into the night
To be washed of fire.
                    They return to us
Saying, "This shade is cool

Under the wings and the boughs.
Let us not forget one another."

I seek the Council of the Kingfisher. He is unmistakably *Alcedo atthis,* recognized by a brilliant, iridescent blue and emerald green plumage, chestnut cheeks and belly, with tiny red feet. I am listening to a language I do not understand. Is this the bird who presides over the Garden, and oversees the pristine discoveries of the heart?

Kingfisher stands on the back of Mallard with his attending birds: female Mallard, Jay, Hoopoe, Green Woodpecker, Robin, and Goldfinch; all are witnessing the exploratory acts of humans.

A white man and a black woman sit on the back of Mallard in close collaboration. Two men, hidden behind Kingfisher, observe the couple. Below them is the man embracing Tawny Owl. Another man listens to Jay as another rides Green Woodpecker like a stallion. Two birds down, directly in front of Robin, there is an individual with his head in his hands who sits on the back of Goldfinch, pondering. Goldfinch holds a blackberry in its beak for three men to eat. They lean back as far as their necks will allow to accommodate the fruit. The man next to Goldfinch is restraining a red-haired woman from reaching, reaching for what? A man who is watching them surrenders inside a blueberry.

Women Surrounded by a Flight of Birds at Night.

The Memory of Birds in Times of Revolution.

Why should we care what birds may want from us?

· · ·

It is most humbling to sit among them. *I will take them as my mentors.* They teach me to be still, to be patient and listen, to observe, to be able to discern when to build nests and of what, when it is time to migrate and when it is time to settle. They show me how to hide and how to be seen. Feather by feather, they instruct through beauty, when to sing and when to forage and what is learned inside the egg. They remind me we too can navigate by stars.

I want to sit with the Council of the Kingfisher where I can consider a reversal of scale and bow at the feet of ducks and finches. The size of Bosch's birds is the size of wild forces within our own lives. I want to forgo my authority as a human being, my self-proclaimed dominance, and be at the mercy of another species' judgment, empathy, and compassion. I want to imagine what the owl hears inside a mouse's heartbeat. I want to understand *halcyon days* as a time when the points of view being considered are the perspective of kingfishers. I want to be teachable.

I stroke the back of Kingfisher and whisper in his ears as he continues to shade the lovers seated on Mallard: "Teach me to put back together what we have dismembered, remind me what we have lost and how it might be reclaimed. No longer numb, let me feel the magnetic pull of my body and the body of another toward something stronger."

I slip behind Tawny Owl.

"Let me see the night through your eyes."

It is no accident women take after birds and thieves just as thieves take after women and birds: they pass through, they fly the coop, they take pleasure in jumbling the order of space, disorienting it, in changing around furniture, things, values, breaking them up, emptying structures, turning the proper upside down.

A woman raises her right hand as a blue bird flutters above. We too can humbly raise our hands in remembrance of what can be reclaimed in wildness.

There she is, my playful self, rocking back and forth like the child she is, holding the cherry high above her head, an offering to the magpie perched on her foot. Her knee is bent, perhaps another game with a bird, up and down, an exercise in trust. How far, how close, will the magpie allow her to take him? Slowly she draws the cherry toward her breast, her knee to her belly. The magpie is still with her. The woman never makes eye contact. Only the magpie watches. What the woman knows she knows through her hands, her feet, her back curved, rocking on the earth.

The bird breaks the skin of the cherry open and drinks the red flowing juice. It spills onto the skin of the woman. Now she holds both the fruit and the bird in her hands. Her eyes still remain closed. She rocks back and forth, in place, a cradle to the world.

Elemental pleasures. Rest in motion. Breathing. *Let me go where I have not yet been.*

There seems to be one orange in the Garden of Delights. It hangs as a weight at the end of a woman's ponytail. Memory, a bird, flies to the place where I was born.

The place where I was born is now a prison.

· · ·

The United States Naval Hospital in Riverside County has been closed, transformed into a correctional facility. My father and I stand before a chain-link fence topped with horizontal coils of barbed wire.

A sign reads "Keep Out."

Guards stand their posts. I look past them and see that the hospital was huge, part of the March Air Force Base in the 1950s, where the wives of the enlisted gave birth. I imagine the windows without bars, the windows my mother must have looked through during labor, the windows I must have looked through that gave me my first worldview.

We are suspect. A security officer approaches us and asks our business. My father says simply, "I wanted to show my daughter where she was born. She turns forty next week. This is the first time we've been back."

I hand the officer my birth certificate.

The guard looks down at the yellowed document and then hands it back to me. "I had another kid your age drop by last week."

He and my father, both men in their sixties, begin to reminisce about the Korean War. For the first time, I actually read the piece of paper I am holding. I am a Utah native but I have never reconciled my birth in California.

It distracts you, history. The more personal,
The more confused. You keep moving as the water moves,
Without a motive, taking every irrespective turn
Against the grain.

The house I was brought home to as a baby is empty, abandoned. 6549 Duke Street, Riverside, California. I look into the windows and see a tiny living room that leads to the kitchen. If

I strain to the right, I can make out a hallway and catch a glimpse of two small bedrooms. The light shifts and suddenly I see a middle-aged woman staring back at me. She is not the child I expected to find.

I turn the round brass door knob. It is locked.

My father is looking across the street. "I didn't realize the train tracks were so close to the house."

We walk around the white-paneled house through a broken gate to the backyard. Orange trees. Six of them. I run my hand down one of the smooth gnarled trunks.

"Your mother used to swing you from the branches of these trees," my father says. "There were orchards of orange trees. Imagine, orchards. This backyard was an orchard. The fragrance of the orange blossoms was what made us rent this house. There were no fences then."

He walks around the backyard with his hands in his pockets.

"Everybody was moving here for the good life." He speaks of his neighbor, Peter Caternicheo. "We watched baseball together. Came from Brooklyn, loved the Dodgers. Peter was a mailman. In 1955, the population of Riverside was around fifty-five thousand. Today, there must be over a million in the San Bernardino Valley."

We walk to the west side of the house. On a concrete slab are the handprints of a family dated 1989: Dad, Mom, Melissa, and Jimmy. Paw prints of Simon are also there. An old broom has been left; the wheels of a bed; nails; and a yellow high-lighter pen. Two hummingbirds buzz the sliding doors and then light on the mimosa tree.

My father tells me he was jealous of the attention Mother gave me as a baby.

"One day, a door-to-door salesman dropped by. He told her that for just three hundred fifty dollars she could purchase a special photography package that would allow you to have your baby picture taken every six months for five years. She agreed to the deal. When she told me what she had done, I was furious. One of the worst fights we ever had.

"Let me take your picture," he says.

Before leaving, I walk back to the fence, find a black-fluted feather and, strangely enough, some bones.

Driving out of Riverside back to Los Angeles, my father talks about Paradise, how after driving through Nevada for hours you would enter Riverside and be struck by its natural beauty, the palm trees, orange trees, and hidden springs tucked in the San Bernardinos like an oasis.

"It held a lot of dreams for your mother and me." He pauses. "I guess you don't remember how your mother used to swing you in the branches of those orange trees."

I wear an orange at the end of my ponytail as a weight.

I am in Los Angeles, 4:19 A.M. Awake in the dark. Earthquake— 5.0 on the Richter scale. A few hours later, I am walking with friends in the Ballona Wetlands, one of the last marshes remaining along the Pacific Flyway. We have our binoculars set on a heron rookery, great blue herons. We watch them flare their wings against midday heat waves. The ocean is just beyond a row of houses. Snowy egrets fly overhead. Angels in this City of Angels.

And there are more. A few miles down the beach is a reserve for the endangered California least terns, a postage-stamp sanctuary for nesting, fenced off, even with barbed wire.

Kenneth Patchen creates a picture poem with a porcupine in a box: "My God the sorrow of it."

A security officer stops us and asks us to leave. We are trespassing.

"This land belongs to those doing the work," he says.

"The work?" I ask.

He hands me a brochure of Playa Vista.

The friends I am with, natives of the Ballona Valley, tell stories of Playa Vista and DreamWorks wanting to create an instantaneous city of fifty thousand residents living in one square mile, which would become the largest density settlement in the United States.

We look over the wetlands, one thousand acres of open space in Los Angeles, where over 589 species of plants and animals thrive, even a chorus of frogs singing in the Centinella Ditch adjacent to Ballona Creek. This is where Steven Spielberg wants to create a sound stage for his production company, DreamWorks.

A few feet away, a movie set has been erected in the ravages of the salt marsh. The city of Shanghai rises in the shadow of Marina del Rey.

We are not giving you the reproduction so that you will want the original, rather we are giving you the reproduction so you will no longer feel any need for the original.

DreamWorks. Steven Spielberg. Virtual Reality in Hollywood spinning celluloid tales of "The Lost World" and exporting them around the world while the Ballona Wetlands are still here—herons, egrets, black-necked stilts dancing the lost world back into existence. Even the least terns.

. . .

Behind the woman with the orange holding down her hair is a man looking directly at whoever is looking at the painting. Could this be Hieronymus Bosch himself, hidden inside his own *Jardín de las delicias?*

I step back from the triptych, turn all the way around, and look at it again. For the first time, I see all the figures below the hedge of trees as mycelium, the white fungal network that holds soil, black with possibilities, together. The mushroom is the mycelium's fruiting body, the delectable and poisonous truth that emerges from the underground.

There it is, this entanglement of white and black bodies. There it is above the man and woman in the bubble. And again above the man with his arms wrapped around the owl. There it is above the man treading water with his head raised upward, no one sees how fast his legs and feet are moving below. There it is a mushroom pushed to the surface above the hedgerow of birds. A woman is hanging by her knees on top of its tendril. Someone, something is crawling inside. Over and over again, I watch each moment, each movement, in *El jardín de las delicias.*

Surfaces. This, that, all of it. Where it is wet, look for mushrooms. Where a fire has roared, look again, more mushrooms. Feel the top of the mushroom with your hand, moist and smooth, note the curvature of its head, soft and fleshy, wet with dew. Feel beneath the hood of the mushroom, touch the gills, separate them with your fingers and imagine the folds of darkness and what may live inside. Now wrap your hand around its stem and decide whether or not this is the one you wish to eat. *Sí, sí, sí, los varios efectos del amor,* courageous, near death, dead, alive.

Morels, chanterelles, puffballs, boletus, *Amanita muscaria,* death angels. One must key out a mushroom in order for proper identification. I kneel in the woods and separate one cap from its stem and place it on the forest floor. Finding another I know to be edible, I partake of its earthy flesh. I fall asleep, dream. I am riding inside a milkweed pod balanced on the hump of a camel. There is no escape. Hieronymus Bosch meets me at every turn, his eyes etched on the trunks of trees, watching, hidden in tall grasses, watching. If I am the woman who stares at Bosch, he is the man who is stalking me, haunting me. When I awaken, I lift the mushroom's cap to find a spore print dropped from its gills.

Inside my apartment in Madrid, I sauté some morels in garlic and olive oil.

No one ever told me olive oil was a blessing on the tongue. It belonged to men in the priesthood and to whom they chose to touch. These men who unscrewed the black lid from the tiny glass bottle had been anointed by other men in positions of power within the Melchizedek Priesthood of the Mormon Church. These men who had access to this consecrated oil looked like any other men. But these men were of God.

Within our household, the sacred oil was a secret inside the refrigerator and used by our father for special occasions, most often in times of sickness when one of us needed to be healed.

The person being anointed would sit on a straight-backed chair with family members gathered round. As we bowed our heads, the one receiving the blessing would look to our father as he drew a small circle on their forehead with the oil. They would close their eyes and he would deliver the blessing by the authority vested in him. After the prayer, they would rise in belief and patiently await the cure. The oil was quietly returned, hidden from eyes of gentiles.

Standing over the stove, my senses are bathed in olive oil. I think of my father's fingers. When I was twelve years old, riding too fast on my bicycle down the steep hill of Commonwealth Avenue, the front wheel of my Sting Ray fell off. I hit head first on the asphalt and flew into a coma. At the hospital, my father gave me a blessing, that I might regain consciousness with all my faculties restored. When I awoke the next day, I smelled olive oil. I knew I had been saved.

I spoon the morels over a bed of pasta and say grace.

WOMEN: OLIVE OIL MAY BE AN
ALLY VS. BREAST CANCER

CHICAGO—A new study adds to growing evidence that eating monounsaturated fats—the kind found in olive oil—may significantly reduce the risk of breast cancer. . . . The findings by researchers who studied more than 60,000 women in Sweden appear in today's issue of *Archives of Internal Medicine,* published by the American Medical Association.

"Our results indicate that various types of fat may have specific opposite effects on the risk of breast cancer," wrote the authors, led by researcher Alicja Wolk at Karolinska Institute in Stockholm. Epidemiologists at Harvard's School of Public Health also participated.

The study involved 61,471 women ages 40 through 76 who were questioned between 1987 and 1990 about their fat intake. During an average follow-up of 4.2 years, 674 cases of invasive breast cancer were diagnosed.

Women who ingested at least 10 grams of monounsaturated fat daily—about three-fourths of a teaspoon—cut their risk of breast cancer in half.

Aceite de oliva. To eat sardines with the fingers and lick them drenched in olive oil. To eat the forest floor in a morel. To sip the arid landscape of Extremadura, a cabernet uncorked beneath the great oaks where Eurasian cranes dance. To finger olives, five on each hand and wave them to the one you love before letting them suck each one off slowly, joyously, into their ecstatic mouth, bless this sweet oil of olives.

In El Bosco's Garden there is a blue cross. I had not noticed it before today. A blue vein runs down the center of the panel: blue spire, blue fountain, blue pool of bathers, blue blossom of thistle, blue blackberry, blue vessel with a man sitting inside being fed by a duck. Cross it with the blue water running east and west joining Paradise and Hell.

The light in the Prado is deepening. I have seen enough for today. Behind me hangs another painting of Hieronymus Bosch, *The Temptations of Saint Anthony*. He is resting on his staff in the wilderness, continuing his solitary vigil.

Tired, I walk up to the Parque del Retiro for some fresh air and sit down among trees. Without thinking, I pick up a stick and draw a cross in the dirt. Crosses are forbidden in my religion. When I asked why as a child, I was told by my teachers that we did not believe in emphasizing the suffering of Christ. *We do not labor on suffering. We seek light over dark. Death is but a twinkling of an eye. It is rebirth we honor. Remember the Resurrection. Roll back the stone, He is risen.*

But I would suffer at night wondering about death, imagining Christ on the cross, his wounds, his blood, the people who watched. And I tried to move my mind away from his suffering.

I couldn't.

I never lost my curiosity about crosses. I became obsessed with dragonflies, winged crosses that skimmed the water. When they would land on shore, I would stare at their enormous bulging eyes that magnified the world. I loved the iridescent colors of their bodies, metallic blue, green, sometimes red, their double reflections over the pond and their translucent wings that created a prism of light.

Everywhere I looked I saw crosses: the divine cross of the dragonfly; the winged cross of swifts; the cross in the night sky of stars in the shape of a swan; a poplar in winter haze with the horizon burning through; Heaven crossed by Earth; the ego canceled through humility; sorrow intersected by joy. This was not a conversion but an ongoing conversation with the natural world that I did not feel separate from.

On my sixteenth birthday, I told a friend I secretly wanted a small gold cross. The gift appeared in a black velvet box. I never dared wear it in public. Instead, I wore the cross to bed when I trembled in the dark. I covered it with my hand and felt a quickening of my heart.

To put one's hand on the cross.

Throughout Spain, there are crosses erected on roadsides, *Tierras Cruzadas,* crossed lands. They are known as *descansos,* markers that locate the place of death, usually of someone who died in a car crash. Elaborate shrines are erected in memory of loved ones, altars are filled and maintained with burning candles, bouquets of flowers, photographs, and all manner of charms.

I see them as the collision points of our dualistic world, a visual remembrance of life and death, body and spirit, good and evil, the split-second change that occurs in moments of transition and transformation.

Descansos. It is the intersection where the vertical and horizontal points meet that interests me, the heart of the cross, the wound, where we feel the world tremble.

We remember the delicacy and strength of our relations.

How do we inhabit this dualistic world that we have inherited without falling prey to either side? Is it possible to maintain a residency within the heart of the cross without denying the paradox of our own souls? Can we embrace both night and day without calling one evil and the other good, but see both as the full range of our vision?

This middle way. What is the way? Hieronymus Bosch paints the way and everyone sees it differently.

I have two eyes and they see the world as one. Could this be the "third thing" Nietzsche is seeking? I am a presence in the physical world and I am a traveler in the world I am creating, inside, outside, a marriage of the imagination to a love that is wild.

We can never be tamed completely.

Moments of spiritual recognition in whatever language we choose to speak, to whatever God we happen to know. These are the seeds of our own renewal, our conversations with a living mystery.

I imagine something like *descansos* planted in the places we wander, perhaps a heart turned upward like a flame, *punta del corazón,* marking not crossed lands but beloved lands, lands where a spirit is located, moments in place where someone felt whole or where a mountain lion was seen. Places of inspiration. Must death be the only thing we honor? There are other forms of passage. That a shrine could be constructed in the name of a salmon's return in fall, or the nesting grounds of curlews, the baptism of a child by wings, an altar could be raised stone by stone to make prayers to Creation, full of fruit, El Bosco's cherries, a piece of turquoise, poems, shells, feathers, the white handkerchief of a mother, in the name of all we surrender when we choose to love, these gestures could be a way to re-vest ourselves in place, a personal honoring of where we live, how we live and whom we live among, our hearts rejoined in wonder.

Standing before Antoni Gaudí's unfinished cathedral in Bar-celona known as El Templo de la Sagrada Familia, I cannot imagine a church more alive to the openness of belief, a church still under construction, a church designed by an earthly genius, an artist, who, far from simply representing his own time, anticipated the following one.

I stand in front of the central façade looking up at the intri-cate detailing of Christ's birth, the Doors of Hope and Faith. The sun is intense and my hand shields my eyes. The weight of the central columns is borne on the backs of turtles, their mouths wide open. The four ominous bell towers rise organi-cally from the façade, reminiscent of wet sand squeezed from the hands of children at the beach. They are whimsical, seem-ingly spontaneous with a sense of humor. Upon closer exami-nation, however, they are the meticulous invention of the thirty-one-year-old Gaudí, a Catalan architect known for his originality, who inherited the project in 1883.

The Expiatory Temple of the Sacred Family became the colossal work in which Gaudí saw his destiny fulfilled as architect, builder, believer, and creator. He never planned on finishing the cathedral but trusted and inspired the hands that would follow his. And so, for over forty-two years, Antoni Gaudí dedicated his life to the construction of this church and no longer concerned himself with anything else. Each day for Gaudí became a spiritual revelation as he perfected the structure and oversaw the construction of the Sagrada Familia.

The Sagrada Familia was conceived as a great mystical poem.

To find one's way inside the Church-in-Progress is to enter the architecture of bones. It is skeletal. Bone by bone, ligament by ligament, an idea, now a collective belief in the name of community, is being erected from the ground up.

Gaudí foresaw and created a structure that has come to be called "equilibrated"—a structure designed to stand on its own without internal bracing or external buttressing ("crutches" he called them). He wanted to create a cathedral that "stands as a tree stands." Observing that there are no straight lines in nature, Gaudí relied on the hyperbolic curve, employing columns that are angled to absorb the necessary loads.

Everywhere there are workers: engineers, contractors, laborers, masons. Cranes are carefully lifting cement forms. Sheets of plastic drape over stone beams like sacred shrouds. The spirit of Gaudí is alive, ongoing, still directing this Earthbound vision.

Some say he was a "revivalist," re-creating through his religious fervor and imaginative genius the same kind of Gothic space possible in the Middle Ages.

Much of Gaudí's distinctive style can be seen as *mudéjar*, Spain's convergence of Muslim and Christian design.

But others say Gaudí's "biological style," with a freedom of form, voluptuous color, texture, and organic unity, has its precedents only in the Earth itself. He bowed to nature. He wanted to create through his architecture a natural object in communion with nature's laws.

My eye is drawn to a shell carved on the wall of one of the bell towers. It is a snail's shell, a moon shell, a shell spiraling slowly around itself. I place my hand on the stone carving and enter the tower.

The chamber is dark and narrow. Up, I look up. One foot on one step, then another. Up. Up. Up. Each stone step curves around the next. My right hand keeps track of the wall. There is no railing, only the smooth, warm wall. Up. Up. Up. It is a spiral staircase so steep, so tight, I feel a shell is curling around me, growing around me, wrapping itself around my soft fleshy body. Up. Up. This organic ascension is tight and dark and secret. My heart is pumping, my head is throbbing, my mind is reeling, steeling against the fear, the claustrophobic fear, mirror of doubt, nothing else to do, one foot in front of the next, around and around, curling, whorling, swirling thoughts, spinning thoughts, this is freedom, freedom of form, freedom from mind, freedom in beauty, man-made on Earth, our daily bread, thread, do not panic, there is an invisible thread, pulling me up, up, do not panic, do not waver, one foot in front of the other, up and up and up and up. Wasn't it a chambered nautilus we had given to our parents when we were married in a chamber, another temple dedicated to God, built block by block of

granite, hand cut out of the mountains, delivered, I am delivered, this invisible strand, deliver me from evil, I am delivered
to a small stone alcove where I stop to look out, out beyond
anything I have ever known before now, now, at this particular
moment, I am in, inside, in turn, in tune with the bell tower,
Gaudí's musical bell tower shuttered for perfect sound, it is
perfectly sound to continue up, up, up, do I dare, up and
around, more steps, how many steps, up, up, up, around, my
feet automatically keep trusting, turning, rising, up, up, around,
rising in this stone shell that is gradually wrapping itself around
me in heat, sweet heat, in silence, it is hot, hot, so very hot, I am
faint, faint, have faith, up, up, around, up, hundreds of steps,
hundreds of feet, above me, below me, circling, rising, ascending, I am in the middle, the middle of my life, the middle of the
tower, hundreds of steps below, hundreds of steps above, circling, rising, ascending, hundreds of breaths freely given, given
freely, I have been given my heart pumping, pulsing, pleading
with my blood, my faith, my belief, right now, I can go no further, you can go further, go still further, up, around, ascend,
look out, look in, hand on the wall, the smooth wall, I am inside
a living organism, I am safe, I am strong, hot, hot, up, up, up, I
wipe my brow, it is wet, wet, dry, the wall is dry, but my hands
are wet, my body is wet, dripping, my hand on the wall, the wall
is turning, burning, learning to trust one step at a time, trusting
one step at a time, dizzy, a bridge arches between two towers, I
leave the spiral for air, beware, the view I see is the perspective I
need to return to whatever is carrying me upward, pulling me
upward, the tree of life is ascending upward, the tree of life that
has been carved in stone, carved leaves, painted leaves, green,
green, the place of green where white alabaster doves are
perched and poised in peace, have I ever known peace, flying,

circling, ascending white doves, white doves, cooing doves, a
feather falls, cradles will rock, what is real, what is imagined, I
return to the spiral staircase, the winding shell that is inspiring
me to go up and up and up and around, slowly I climb, my head
light, my body light, my eyes bright, the light pouring in and out
through the shuttered tower where the bells sing, in and out, up
and around I see the cross, the red cross with the gold letter *X,*
a white dove on top, the Holy Trinity, across there are four
other towers, mosaic-covered pinnacles, that shimmer and
sway, they are adorned with words, "Hosanna," "Excelsis,"
"Hosanna," "Excelsis." These ecstatic words glimmer in Cata-
lonian light.

    I stop.

             up
   Should I go   or
          down?

               I go
          down,
          down,
        down,
          my
            descension
                inside
                    Gaudí's
                    shell
                is
            my
      acknowledgment
        of limits,
          limitations,
          lamentations,

                    joy,
                        my own
                        imagination
                      is full,
                  down,
                  down,
                down,
              down,
              around
              my hand
                guiding
                  each
                    step,
                        a song,
                            a step,
                              another
                              step
                              down
                              around
                            hosanna,
                        excelsis,
                        hosanna,
                I see the white
                carved doves
        circling the tree of
        life carved green,
              each leaf,
              down,
                my feet,
                    going
                        down,

                    my head,
            spiraling
down,
                    around,
        around,
                down,
                    down,
                        down,
                    down,
                down,
        down,
                down,
                    down,
                     down,
                            around,
                            how
                        many
                    more
            steps
        around
    in beauty
    descending
        in a shell
            of my own
                    making by
                        making a shell
                        Gaudí wraps
                            his
                            imagination
                        around
                        every

                                            human being
                                    who dares
                            to descend
                        down,
            down,
                        up,
    down,
                up,
        up,
                I look
                            either
                way,
                    down,
                        down,
                            it is
                    a spiral
                we move
                through,
        aspire to,
            down,
                down,
        feet on the ground.

IV

RESTORATION

And there shall be a new heaven and a new earth; and they shall be like unto the old save the old have passed away, and all things have become new.

—Ether 13:9, *Book of Mormon*

After a long absence, I return to the Prado, this time with my father. He does not truly believe the triptych exists, nor that I would waste my time in such foolish behavior. To leave my home, my husband, and work for a painting with wings over the course of many years defies his pragmatism as a pipeline contractor.

"An excuse," he says wryly, "to leave your life."

Nevertheless, he is determined to see *El jardín de las delicias* for himself.

We enter through the large doors of the Goya entrance. I cannot remember ever having seen my father in an art museum. My feet walk automatically through the maze of galleries past Van der Weyden, Van Eyck, Campion, Bruegel. He follows me. He does not want to stop to see any other paintings.

"Let's get right to it," he says, his cowboy boots creating a distinct cadence on the marble floors of the Prado.

The opening of Gallery LVIII is within sight, a rush of anticipation shoots through my body. I turn the corner with my eyes closed, then open them to greet the painting.

"It's not here." my father says.

I look around the room.

El jardín de las delicias is gone.

. . .

The other paintings are present: *Saint Jerome Dreaming, The Adoration of the Magi, The Haywain, The Table of Seven Deadly Sins.* The marble bust of Philip II is still presiding over the gallery.

"This can't be," I say to my father. "They must have moved it to another gallery, to another wall. I'm sure it's here." He puts his hands in his pockets and rolls his eyes. I ask one of the guards where the triptych has been taken. He shrugs his shoulder and walks into the next room. Another guard simply says, *"No sé, señora."*

No one seems to know.

My father says he will find someone who does.

I sit down in the cradle chair with one hand across my waist. The guard's shadow looms large on the shiny floor. I stare at the bare white wall. My window to the outside world has been closed, bricked up and plastered.

I get up from the chair and walk to the wall where the Garden once was and place my right hand on its surface. It was here, right here. I hadn't even noticed the small plexiglass sign standing to the side where the triptych once hung.

It reads:

P 2823
El Bosco
El jardín de las delicias
Esta obra está siendo restaurada
en el taller del Museo Nacional del Prado.

. . .

I check my pocket dictionary for the precise words: *restaurar*—
to restore—to recover; to bring back to its original state by
repairing or rebuilding; to bring back to good health or vigor;
to put back in its former position; to reinstate or stabilize.

R E S T A U R A C I Ó N

The word that precedes "restoration" in the dictionary is
"restless." I understand the restlessness that precedes restoration. Restoration follows crisis. I have witnessed this movement through the landscape of my own family. Following the
death of my mother and grandmothers, our family had to learn
how to rebuild itself and heal. It is a slow and laborious process
that requires patience.

I stare at the wall, the empty wall.

The word of a Basque sheepherder I met in the Pyrenees for
some reason returns to me. *Aquí.* When I asked him where he
was from, he pointed emphatically to the ground between his
feet. *Aquí.* Here. To begin here. To restore the vision of the
triptych. To reconstruct: *reconstruir.* To reestablish: *reinstaurar.*
To reintegrate: *reintegrar.*
Draw on the landscape of Bosch.
I can restore the painting in this moment, this very moment,
through my mind's eye. One by one, I transfer each tableau,
each face, each gesture, each piece of architecture El Bosco has
created from my memory to the white wall before me.
Without realizing it, I am reconstructing the triptych with
both hands. They appear as a shadow dance on the wall.

I lift my arms. I become a cross. I raise and lower my arms slowly and become a bird.

The empty wall.
Look at the shadow.
Face the shadow.

My shadow, my inseparable attendant, is the dark shape of my body, behind my body, beside my body, everywhere I go, my shadow follows me. Blocking light, it is largely hidden, out of view, yet troublesome because it dwells in the basement of my unconscious mind. I don't want it to come up the stairs. I lock the door. Of course, Hieronymus Bosch lets it out, my shadow here, now, just as I am getting comfortable, projecting my own thoughts on El Bosco. My shadow will stand behind me or in front of me, there you are, here I am inside the Prado, my shadow, my shadow as my friend, my shadow as my father, my shadow as my Church. I will hurl my darkest self on to someone else and compensate for what I choose not to see inside my own heart. We live in the company of projected shadows. We are free to blame, to take no action, to create nothing from our own highest selves.

"What is the principle of the Gospel of Jesus Christ that means the most to you?" Obedience. Free agency.

The painting is gone.
A white wall remains.
What will I create for myself?

I will stay in this room even though the triptych is gone. I will look at my shadow because there is nothing else for me to see.

My shadow is speaking to me. My ear is cocked against the wall. I am listening. I am listening to the moving mouth on the wall.

Obedience.
Obedience as trust.
Trust as obedience.

This is a new pairing of words for me. My shadow is authority, obedience to authority. General authority. I am wary of authority. In ignoring my shadow has my own authority been silenced?

In this dualistic world, I have seen obedience on one hand, free agency on the other. How do I bring these two hands opposed together in a gesture of prayer?

To unite, combine, form an alliance, to make whole: *ligar.*

. . . , the heart of the religious experience, is to bond, repair, draw together, to make whole, to find that which is anterior to the split condition.

My father returns with a guide named Juan Manuel Maquieria Davesa.

"Will you please explain this painting to my daughter and me." He is speaking in a rather loud, slow voice, trying to make certain the guide understands him.

Juan Manuel smiles at me. We have met before. The three of us move up close to see the small postcard in the plexiglass sign. Juan proceeds to give a beautiful description of the triptych, when it was painted, the various theories that surround El Bosco and what he might be trying to convey. He is articulate and engaging. My father leans even closer to the postcard.

"Now, what's all this business going on?" he asks, pointing to the pool of bathers. He makes a wisecrack about the naked figures.

"It has been called the Pool of Adultery," Juan says.

My father is having a difficult time understanding his strong Spanish accent.

"The pool of what?" he asks.

"The Pool of Adultery," Juan replies.

My father looks at me. "What is he saying?"

"The Pool of Adultery," Juan repeats, this time more slowly.

"I'm sorry, Juan, I'm having a difficult time understanding you, could you say it one more time."

In exasperation, the guide says in a very loud voice, "L e w i n s k y !"

"Oh, I get it!" my father says, laughing out loud. "The Pool of Adultery."

Everyone in the Bosch Gallery turns and stares.

It was at this point my father became interested in art. He and Juan Manuel spent the next two hours walking through the Prado focusing on El Greco, Goya, and Velázquez.

As we leave the museum, my father turns to me before we walk outside. "I'm really sorry I couldn't see your painting."

The Age of the Holy Ghost has begun.

That night, I lay in bed thinking about the caves of Altamira.

So this is how we dream the world into existence, a flickering of light, brushstrokes of belief. On our backs with a quivering of lungs, we breathe the great herds into being, we paint the great herds into being, above and below. In the secrecy of caves illumined, we create what we need to survive. An artist's hand on stone. A hunter's heart revealed. The bison's soul restored. The bull's blood runs—the moon pulls its red tide out. And here in Altamira, the paint drips, the blood drips into underground pools of water. Eternal cavernous prayers.

On Monday, my father flies back to Utah. I walk into a small paint store near the Plaza de Santa Ana. I am looking for a sketchbook. My eyes have not yet adjusted to the darkness of the small shop when I accidentally bump into a children's easel with open bottles of paint set up for demonstration. It begins to tip over. I try to catch it, but slip. I am on the floor with the easel on top of me, covered in paint.

The shopkeeper runs over and helps me up as we both lift the easel.

"Lo siento, señor," I say apologetically as I wipe my hands on the back of my pants.

The man begins to laugh. He looks at me and kisses the tips of his fingers.

Tuesday. I knock on two immense carved wooden doors inside the Prado. One opens. A small woman in a white lab coat quickly ushers me inside. We are in the outer sanctum of the museum where conservators are intensely at work. The door is locked behind us.

After hours of telephone calls, faxes, interviews, and form filling, I am finally cleared and taken further into the room of restoration.

Natural light is pouring in through two long windows. *El jardín de las delicias* stands, dismantled and exposed. I am not prepared for its ordinariness.

The middle panel, Earthly Delights, is out of its frame,

unhinged from the wings of Paradise and Hell, which are poised on wooden easels against the wall. The triptych's vulnerability is shocking. For the first time, *El jardín de las delicias* appears as painted wood.

The woman in white invites me to sit on a stool in front of the center panel. The quarters are cramped. I slide sideways between the easels, tables, trays, and carts holding rags, brushes, paints, and bottles of various solutions. I am terrified that I might knock something over. I sit down as I am told and find myself face to face with the surface of El Bosco's Garden of Delights.

Bright lights are shining. The panel appears as an old woman with her makeup removed. Every crack, wrinkle, and age spot is revealed. Stains, discrepancies in paint, ruptures in the wood, chips, and grime are all exposed.

Whole sections from the Council of the Kingfisher have been chipped away, the torso of the bubblehead man who is riding on the back of the Woodpecker—gone; the left arm of the man listening above the Hoopoe—gone.

How had this damage to the Garden escaped me? How had I been so blind to the painting's perilous condition? Had I been so in love that I failed to see its deterioration?

Two women are present, both dressed in lab coats. They are the Dávila sisters, Theresa and Rocío, the primary restorers of fifteenth- and sixteenth-century paintings in the Museo del Prado. As we make our introductions, I hear an echo of names and places: Teresa de Ávila, wet not dry; El Rocío, a place of pilgrimage where candles burn before the Virgin of Dew. "Prayer" and "desire" are the words that enter my mind in this strange Old World setting.

There are no stainless steel tables and counters, no microscopes or protected workspaces for the conservators. It feels more like a medieval workshop that El Bosco might have participated in with some of his students. There is, however, an air of reverence and great seriousness.

The sisters tell their story.

Born in Madrid, Theresa Dávila Álvarez in 1948, Rocío Dávila Álvarez in 1950, they were raised in a family who appreciated the arts.

In the family of their mother there were poets and writers. Their mother was a painter. In the family of their father there were also painters and dancers.

"They educated us in the arts," Theresa says.

"We grew up with art as part of our lives. The feeling of art was all around us," Rocío adds.

They look at each other waiting, prompting each other with their eyes as to who will speak next. I have the feeling they can read one another's minds with very few words necessary.

"I like to paint," Rocío says.

"She won first prize in painting," interrupts Theresa.

"And Theresa won first prize in ballet. She was presented to the British Royal Ballet at age nine from Madrid."

"We went to the British Institute as children," Theresa says. "But our parents would not allow me to travel to London."

"Afraid?" I ask.

"*Exactamente.*"

"After we finished our studies at the British Institute we wondered what to do."

"We had read an article in the newspaper here that mentioned a new career being offered at the School of Restoration," says Rocío.

"What year was this?"

"Let's see—" Rocío looks at Theresa. "Yes, that's right, 1966–67. Anyway, we decided it sounded very exciting and enrolled. We were the beginning class of three."

The sisters look at each other again. Theresa is blond with ice-blue eyes. Rocío has brown hair with the depth of brown eyes.

"We were pioneers. We were lucky," says Theresa.

Rocío interrupts. "We studied with the old people, the old masters, who learned their craft inside their families through the tradition of their grandfathers."

"Restoration was a family tradition," broke in Theresa. "The people we apprenticed with were the old—" She stops and looks at her sister, "*¿Como se dice?*"

"*Artesanos,*" answers Rocío. "It was the same tradition throughout Spain and Italy."

"We studied every day, all day long."

"Every day we studied with the old ones. We practiced with the masters. Pupils and masters worked together like residents and doctors in a hospital. *¿Comprende?*"

"*Sí, sí, sí.*"

"Churches and museums from all over Spain would bring old paintings to the school," says Theresa.

"These old restorers were painters themselves. Many of them had copied some of the great masterpieces in the Prado. They had a different way of looking at things, at restoration," explains Theresa. "We were the first people in Spain to learn restoration as a career. We took courses in chemistry, photography, microscopy, musicology, and art history, as well as rigorous coursework on both contemporary and historical restoration techniques and theories."

"How long was this program, did you say?"

"Three years," says Rocío.

"But then they asked us to complete and pass an examination which took six more months, so it was actually four years total," says Theresa.

In 1974, Rocío Dávila Álvarez became the first woman restorer hired by the Museo del Prado.

"It was strictly a man's profession, very traditional," says Rocío. "The director of the Prado said to me, 'You must be good, very, very good. If not good, we will throw you on the street! You understand?' " She looks at her sister and laughs.

In 1980, Theresa joined her sister at the Prado. They prefer working together.

"We speak in the same language when we are working with a painting," explains Rocío.

"It is very difficult when you are working on a painting, when you are engaged in restoration, you are putting all you have inside, you must give it all your attention—"

"—all your concentration," Theresa finishes. "We can argue and fight, but we understand. Our goal is the same."

"*Sí,* we want the same thing."

"It's a feeling," says Theresa. "You forget the world around you. It is only the painting and you. Not only the hands but the depth of your own sensitivity, *es muy especial,* the hands and head and heart, all together, all work together. *¿Comprende, o es muy complicado?*"

"How do we say—" Rocío pauses. "It's similar to playing music. We are interpreters. We are interpreting music."

Both women suddenly stand. A short man in a black suit rushes in with two gentlemen. I stand with them. He nods to Rocío and Theresa. Rocío leaves El Bosco and follows the men to a large painting hanging in the corridor.

"Rubens," whispers Theresa. "Rocío just finished restoring his *Three Graces*."

"And the men?" I ask.

"The director of the Prado, Fernando Checa, with two men from London who provided the new frame for the upcoming exhibition."

I look at *The Three Graces* closely. The women have their arms around each other, their bodies generous and soft.

"Before Rocío's restoration, the flesh was soiled, now it shines. "*The Three Graces* have been lifted out of the shadows of time," she says.

It is true. The painting has an uncommon sheen, each color seems vibrant and clear. I had seen the painting in the past in my walks through the Prado. I had grown used to the smoky appearance, the deep colors.

Rocío returns with Señor Checa and the gentlemen, who introduce themselves to Theresa. A conversation ensues around the Rubens restoration. I am then introduced as a visiting American. The men leave almost as quickly as they entered.

The Dávila sisters look at each other and raise their eyebrows. Whatever is conveyed between them is lost on me.

"Who made the decision to restore *El jardín de las delicias*?"

"The director with recommendations from the Department of Curators," says Theresa. "I was asked for a report last February in 1997 as to the condition of the triptych and the time of the last restoration."

"Which was?"

"1936."

"During the Civil War?"

"Just before."

"We were asked to work on *El jardín de las delicias* in December," says Rocío.

"And how long do you think it will take to complete the restoration?"

The sisters look at each other.

"There are five panels, counting the doors of the triptych," Rocío answers. "We figure it will take us about two years, *pero porque*—"

Theresa interrupts her sister's Spanish: "We should be finished by 2000."

"El Bosco—" Rocío sighs, then laughs as she extends her hands to the painting. *"Tenemos una imaginación muy grande con que trabajar."*

"Verdad," says her sister. "We have a very big imagination to work with. Both an imagination and a facility."

"Facility?" I ask.

"El Bosco is a very delicate painter. His brush is delicate. The way he uses colors, different colors, one in relationship to the next, affects one emotionally. They are strong, bright, pure colors, yet they are harmonizing. He is a painter—" she pauses. *"Un pintor paradójico, ¿comprende?"*

I nod, watching where her hands are pointing on the panel, the predominant reds, yellows, and blues, how green becomes almost a connective tissue between the primary colors.

"El Bosco's style can be both peaceful and exciting, beautiful and disturbing."

Rocío moves up to the panel and shakes her head as she points to the three individuals under the transparent dome and those sitting beneath the apple grove. "This is in very bad condition, *muy mal, mucho deterioro y daño.*"

Theresa agrees with her sister's assessment. *"Sí,* we know that it came from El Escorial, that it suffered from a lot of humidity there. You can actually see some of the water damage here." She points to an area where the paint has flecked off.

"We have documentation. The first thing we do is look at the documentation that has followed the painting, who owned it, where it has been, what its history is. Then we x-ray the painting to see through infra-red and ultra-violet light what cannot be seen on the surface."

"This is all part of our analysis, the preparation, the pigments, the x-rays, the special photographs, all the material associated with the painting in the Biblioteca del Prado. As Theresa said, we know it hung in El Escorial for many centuries and was most likely moved around a fair amount from Prince Philip's bedroom to the Royal Gallery and elsewhere," says Rocío.

"In truth," Theresa says, "we don't know very much about this painting. But for the most part, we are very fortunate thanks to the good taste of Spanish kings that this triptych was generally well preserved."

"But time delivers a harsh hand."

"And this one came to us in a bad state."

"Who were the first restorers?" I ask.

"A man by the name of Jerónimo Seisdedos. He actually wrote a paper about his work on *El jardín de las delicias* in *Arte Español*," says Theresa.

"Do you know when it was published?"

"I think it was in 1944, but I'm not sure. If I remember correctly, it was published almost ten years after the restoration. He delivered the paper before the Sociedad Española de Amigos del Arte."

Rocío walks to the back of the panel. "*Mira,* you can see here the lattice work that was done in the 1930s to stabilize the wood panel. We now know this is a bad practice, but it would cause greater risk to the painting if we tried to remove it.

So we keep learning as time goes on what works and what doesn't."

"You can see very clearly under these lights the seven original panels that make up this center piece."

"Why didn't I notice these things when it was hanging in the gallery?" I ask.

"We have already begun to clean this panel and removed a lot of the grime. Much of the damage was hidden, especially to an untrained eye. Also, the lights you see here are very cruel to a painting's vanity."

"You see," says Theresa, "El Bosco prepared the wood first; that's what these seven panels are. You couldn't find one large panel of wood then, they had to glue them together for a continuous surface. Then he used the glue and gesso for further preparation so the wood would accept the paint. We know through x-ray technology that he drew the characters first and then painted the panel. We also know he made many changes," she says, delighted at their discoveries.

"This is one of the ways you know it is an original and not a copy," says Rocío. "The artist is making decisions all the time and in the process changing his mind."

They continue to talk about the process of restoration. I am beginning to get lost in the terminology, the techniques and practices, struggling with their Spanish and the rapidity of their speech.

"After our assessment, we begin the actual work of restoration. First we fix the cracks with rabbit glue, which is made from the rabbit's bones and skin. It is the traditional glue of the Spanish masters."

"In Russia, for example, the restorers use fish glue," adds Rocío.

"Whenever we can, we use natural materials, the traditional materials akin to the period of the painting," says Theresa. "Next, we begin the cleaning."

She moves over to her cart and takes out a large bottle of clear fluid, then pulls a long swatch of cotton from a roll and wets it with the solution.

"This is called 'Artist's Spirit,'" she says, turning to me. Theresa then carefully wipes a section of the panel and steps aside.

What was once flat and dull, now shines. There is movement and depth. I feel as though I am watching the process of alchemy before my eyes.

The three figures standing inside the transparent dome, a trinity of their own, are now translucent. White opalescent bodies. I inch forward.

The woman on the right appears to be pregnant, something I never noticed before in the whole of the triptych. She is veiled. The man next to her is holding her arm. One of the other figures has his hand raised to his forehead as if he is wondering what they should do. He is looking through the dome. The line of his vision is now bright and clear through the Artist's Spirit. His gaze seems to be directed toward the pool in the center of the Garden, call it the painting's pupil. There is a woman on the water's edge staring at the man, her chin rests on her hand. Is this the outcome of love?

"Do you see the difference?" Theresa asks for a second time.

"*Sí, sí, sí—claro.*"

A silence follows.

We look at each other.

"It is time for you to go."

.   .   .

Spain's Biblioteca Nacional is a grand building in the heart of Old Madrid near the Plaza de Colón. It was built in 1712 by Philip V to replace the Royal Library and now houses more than five million books. In the basement of the library where the periodicals are stored, I locate the index of *Arte Español* and find the 1944 volume listed with an article titled *"La restauración de cuadros y algunas restauraciones recientes," por Jerónimo Seisdedos, Tomo XV, 1944–1945, p. 100.*

I meticulously write down the citation and hand it to the librarian behind the counter.

She disappears, and in a few minutes returns with a large, dusty volume and directs me to a particular desk.

The spine creaks upon first opening. The smell of old books revives me. I transcribe the article. I pore over the photographs. The four figures beneath the grove of trees are all but obliterated, the arbor of trees, gone, just as Theresa said. This is the section she showed me that had been repainted, the area where they will try and restore the original color.

Another photograph focuses on the sky of the center panel. Much of the paint is chipped off, exposing the wood panel. The flying figure holding the cherry is barely visible.

I continue to study the pictures as long as my mind can concentrate and then close the volume, return it to the desk, and thank the librarian.

Over dinner, a friend helps me translate Jerónimo Seisdedos's words more precisely.

I learn *El jardín de las delicias* was in a terrible state of decay. Señor Seisdedos had to reinforce the triptych with a wooden brace. The paint was crumbling and in some cases completely gone. Seisdedos tried to maintain what color remained and reconstruct what was gone.

Seisdedos removed all of the accumulated grit and grime.

He covered the painting with a thin gesso and gauze. Over that he extended a liquid of rabbit glue, honey, and mule bile. He then covered that with fine paper. When that started to dry and filter onto the painting, he ironed it. Once he completed that stage, he took away the paper and gauze. This was followed by the process of cleaning the painting, the most dangerous part of restoration because you are removing past restorations, smoothing the surface for a base to work on, for watercolors and tempera. It is in this stage that if you are not careful you can disturb the artist's colors and varnishes.

Seisdedos describes working with *estuca,* a white plasterlike substance, what some might call gypsum. He worked with the *estuca* and *yeso.* After that, he relied on watercolors to make the painting "shine."

He provides various recipes, and says these are "the daughters of my experience and practice," that for over thirty years he has been cooking calmly for such a long time, brewing, stewing, perfecting these *"remedios."*

This restorer of *El jardín de las delicias* in 1935 and 1936 worked on this painting like a monk. When the smoke and grime was removed, Paradise was revealed. "Time," he says, "comes right up to its surface, looks at it, brushes over it, but can never change its color."

"Look for the patina," he says. "Look for the silver of each painting."

My friend reads silently for a moment, makes a few notes, then resumes speaking in Seisdedos's words:

"How can we care about pieces of art, especially antiquities, when there is a war raging outside?"

The conservator tells a story about his uncle who was a priest, to whom he owes his love of art. He told him tales of

Spanish wars, of which there were many. One in particular he never forgot. It was during the *Liberales y Carlistas* in the nineteenth century, the civil war before the Civil War. A lieutenant was trying to defend his men, but he would not order combat. There was a standstill. All he had to do to advance his men and lose the enemy was blow up a tower, which he had the artillery power to do. The tower was an astonishing piece of architecture, a rare compilation of both Moorish and Spanish culture. Instead, the officer devised an alternative plan that offered the same results.

Afterwards, in the safety of the bunker, the general asked the officer, "Lieutenant, why did you not blow up the tower?"

"My general," he replied, "it was *mudéjar.*"

Seisdedos tells how he was so filled with despair in the aftermath of the Spanish Civil War and World War II that he was going to quit his work as a restorer, and then he thought of the doctors who worked in the solitude of their laboratories in search of cures to human illness.

"Why shouldn't I continue to work on behalf of the paintings that have helped me so much, these works of art that have healed my wounded soul?"

My friend looks up from the text with tears in her eyes.

Walking home from the Círculo de Belles Artistes, I ponder Seisdedos's words about a love of art and I think about my love of the land back home, about the healing grace of wildness, and how difficult it is to articulate why conservation matters, why wilderness matters to the health of our souls and how a language of the heart becomes suspect. I wonder how it is we have come to this place in our society where art and nature are spoken in terms of what is optional, the pastime and concern of the elite?

. . .

At what point did cynicism replace belief?

Outside the studio, I wait for Theresa and Rocío. I am early.
They arrive after lunch. We enter. The doors close ominously
behind us. There is the same air of secrecy and urgency inside.

They motion me to sit down on the stool by the window
once again, directly in front of the center panel.

I simply watch them work.

"This is a spiritual process," Theresa says. "It demands everything of us. We speak with the painting. The painting speaks to
us. Restoration is a process of respect. We are in the service of
the painting." She pauses and looks at Rocío.

"The painting directs us and instructs us. We have to stand
back and see the painting as a whole. Every day, we have to
introduce ourselves to the painting. You see, for the first hour
you are fighting, fighting with the painting—"

Theresa interrupts Rocío, "You fight because you lose yourself in the midst of a great presence. The artist will eventually
overtake you. Yes, the truth of restoration is that you are working with a singular presence."

". . . and then you finally relax and enter in," says Rocío.

"We feel the intelligence of the painting and the master's
hand," says Theresa.

"How so?"

"With Velázquez, for example, he was very cultured, *muy
inteligente*. My sister and I restored *Las Meninas*. You could feel
his genius as you worked with his painting, the rarity of his perspective." She pauses. "These are uncommon people. With El

Bosco—he is a big artist with a big imagination. And yet, he has a delicate hand. *Mucho misterio.* It stirs our own imaginations. Every day we discover something new. Yes, it will take much longer working with him. The details, there are so many, many details."

A long silence follows.

"El Bosco's technique and taste remind me of Botticelli," Theresa continues. "Others may say, how ironic to find El Bosco delicate and of good taste when his subject matter can be terrifying, but the choice of his colors and the high quality rendered in his panel paintings create jewel-like presentations within his meticulous details. It is very difficult to explain. I don't have the words in English. *¿Muy espirital? ¿Comprende?* El Bosco has tried to tell us about the fight between good and evil and he has tried to tell us through a delicacy of technique with a refined taste and a refined intelligence. *Poner el dedo en la llaga.*"

I smile.

"*Sí, señora,* Hieronymus Bosch put his finger on the wound."

It will be several days before I can visit the painting and the Dávila sisters again. I am sitting on the front lawn of the Prado eating my lunch. Looking up at the classical façade of the museum, I try and figure out where the room of restoration might be, second floor, second bank of windows, and then to my great surprise, I discover I can actually see the center panel through the tall narrow windows, the same windows that Theresa keeps open to allow the natural light to inform the colors.

The Garden of Delights is standing at the window watching Madrid.

. . .

This will be my last meeting with Theresa and Rocío. I greet them with tulips. Rocío takes them and arranges them in a vase with water by the windowsill.

"Come," says Theresa.

At first, I do not understand, then I see Theresa is inviting me up to the painting. She hands me a large cotton swab she has just wet with Artist's Spirit.

I pause.

She nods. "Go ahead."

I hesitate, then slowly wipe the body of the man lying on the grass with a blueberry head in one long delicate stroke. I see silver. He is silver, so beautiful, his skin like the surface of wet pearls, bare back, bare buttocks, his right leg raised in a flirtatious manner.

I am the woman the blueberry man is courting; my eyes, mouth want his lip-luscious face just ripe to place on the center of my tongue. I want, I want to suck every ounce of juice, sweet blueberry juice, from his blueberry head, I rest my head on my hand and listen to what he sees as he sees what I am hearing. His left arm is tender around my neck.

Behind us are the whirling cherry pickers, four legs, four arms, inside the body of a radish, twirling, swirling, waving their cherry rattles, they extend their hands to us, we are dancing, dancing inside El jardín de las delicias, *we are dancing as the yellow-eyed owl perches on top, eyes forward, direct and steady.*

One more look.

My eyes focus on the white skin of the lovers inside the bubble, shining, translucent skin, visceral, like the birth sac that covers us before we are born. Wet, reflective, there is a man who does a headstand under water with his legs spread, a raspberry, so delicate, is balanced between his legs, an ibis dwells inside. And again, the man embraces the owl.

The restoration of nature, even our own, will require a reversal of our senses and sensibilities.

To see with our heart.

To touch with our mind.

To smell with our hands.

To taste with our eyes.

To hear with the soles of our feet.

Brooke and I are standing in a sandstone canyon in the redrock desert of Utah before a panel of pictographs, enormous beings with broad shoulders and tapered bodies, some with birds perched on their shoulders, some red, some white, some black; there are also Winged Ones with eyes so large and open, we wonder what they see and we are missing. This place registers like a portal between worlds, some are leaving, some returning, some staying.

In the presence of the Ancient Ones, we deliver new vows in whispers by the authority of our own remembered hearts. Standing before these Elders of Time, we entrust ourselves to each other. Our vows are simple, spontaneous: *Yes, we are here to love. Yes, we are here to experience the body, in both shadow and light, in forgiveness and joy, we return to each other, rejoined. Together we will love this beautiful, broken world of which we are a part.*

And then we laugh, we laugh over the improbability of how we found our way to each other decades ago, two refugees wandering in the wilderness.

Holding each other, we dance, we dance slowly before this painted panel in the desert.

. . .

On December 12, 1998, Brooke and I move from Salt Lake City to a small village in the red canyons of southern Utah. This is a place where apple orchards were planted by latter-day pioneers.

In the middle of the desert there is a river a red river of sand and silt that has eroded the mountains and mesas where great seas once lapped on their shores in the heat they vanished leaving behind salt immense deposits of salt that were pushed up by a force always a force

deep inside the salt domes a fist pushed upward

the winds blew the rains fell the salt domes collapsed in a paradox of geologic confrontation and controversy there is always a controversy I cannot escape the salt the great salt lake I have moved you see the world does shift its bedrock positions through time and space believe in empty space it is still an ongoing free flowing river that no dam can stop remove the dams forever carrying water to the parched mouths of all those who have refused to drink from the well of enduring change change there is a fire burning help us change and drink from this restored well of artistic collaboration between a body and mind between a body and land and all that is wild this love that is wild wild wild give me one wild word and call it restoration.

R E S T O R A T I O N

Nine months later, I return to Madrid.

The center panel, the panel withheld from me as a child, is returned, restored, completed, hanging breathtakingly alone in the Museo del Prado.

The Garden of Delights hangs suspended in this moment of time, freed from the hinges of a dualistic world, no longer caught between myth and prophesy, it shines as its own sovereign truth.

To discover: *descubrir.* To see: *ver.* To see through the wings of a medieval triptych that move forward and back through history and time, open and close, one can move and still stay in place, open.

With gratitude to El Bosco and the Garden, I leave offerings of turquoise, red sand, and sage.

I step back.

My eyes settle on a figure riding a white boar, head bowed, hands raised high holding the tips of an egret's wings like a sail above the great roundabout of animals.

Another egret stands on top of the blue-pink tower, a white flame; the white egg with a spilled yolk of human beings is breaking the water's surface; a white petal floats a bud of human beings reaching for a cherry speared by a pelican; the balanced egg on top of a man's head is a pearl; a white goat; white herons and spoonbills and storks with their mouths wide open; a white horse; a white stag; the white belly of the goldfinch; all the white bodies of humans more spirit than flesh engaging with the world, this beautiful, thriving, eroding world.

El Bosco has just set down his wet white brush tipped in silver.

Before the restoration, it was the colors I watched, blue, red, yellow, green, pink; the architecture, the meadow, the hedges, the water. Now, what I see is light. White light. Color has been absorbed into form. Form is in the service of surprise. It is the light, the throbbing illumination, glowing on the horizon, rippling in the waters, blowing through the grasses, that touches my lips.

Something has been set in motion.

A figure is swimming, head back, mouth open, drinking from the fountain, the blue fountain floating in the center where the four rivers meet.

This is my living faith, an active faith, a faith of verbs: to question, explore, experiment, experience, walk, run, dance, play, eat, love, learn, dare, taste, touch, smell, listen, argue, speak, write, read, draw, provoke, emote, scream, sin, repent, cry, kneel, pray, bow, rise, stand, look, laugh, cajole, create, confront, confound, walk back, walk forward, circle, hide, and seek.

To seek: to embrace the questions, be wary of answers.

Hieronymus Bosch invited me to seek. Joseph Smith taught me to seek truth in a grove of trees. We can have visions. We can have our own personal relationship with God. We can participate in our own healing. *We believe all things, we hope all things, we have endured many things, and hope to be able to endure all things. If there is anything virtuous, lovely, or of good report or praiseworthy, we seek after these things.* We can obey our own authority through our free agency to choose. I choose to believe in the power of restoration, the restoration of our faith, even within my own Church of Jesus Christ of Latter-day Saints. Faith is not about finding meaning in the world, there may be no such thing—Faith is the belief in our capacity to create meaningful lives.

Hieronymus Bosch put his finger on the wound.

. . .

What is the wound?

Our wound, separation from the Sacred, the pain of our isolation, may this be the open door that leads us to the table of restoration, may we sit around the table, may we break bread around the table, may we stand on top of the table, may we turn the table over and dance, leap, leap for joy, all this in the gesture of conserving a painting, conserving a landscape, conserving a spirit, our own restored spirits once lost, now found, Paradise found, right here on this beautiful blue planet called Earth.

The panel shimmers. The bodies shine. I circle the pool in the pink skin of my body, my body joining the bodies of the black and white women bathing in the water, the black and white women who are balancing birds on top of their heads. Cherries, too. Faster and faster the bareback riders gallop their horses and goats and griffins; bareback riders, bareback on animals, circling, circling, circling my body no longer resisting the galloping of my own blood.

Sunday afternoon in Madrid. It is spring. I sit on a bench near the lake and watch the *paseo*. The *paseo* is in motion, slow motion, a parade of people are strolling through the Parque del Retiro. It is a pageantry of surfaces black, white, red, yellow, green, blue, brown, pink, orange, dogs, cats, boas, iguanas, parrots, ferrets, hedgehogs, horses—human beings and animals are circling the lake. Even a bowl of goldfish is discreetly poured into the pool at the base of the fountain. Catch and release.

Couples are walking hand in hand, the old and the young arm in arm, new mothers are slowly pushing their perambulators, their infants are sound asleep beneath elaborate beddings of pink or blue.

They walk by looking at me as I am looking at them, they walk by the palm readers and puppeteers. They pass by the magicians and dancers and painters, all scenery in motion.

The *paseo* continues to circle the lake slowly, so slowly, everyone is walking, music is playing, there is no need to hurry, there is nothing to rush, only to saunter and savor and see the children hiding behind trees watching the lovers lying on the grass feeding each other cherries, red and black cherries, one by one, sweet on the tongue, to taste on the tongue, this Garden of Delights—I enter the *paseo*.

I now live in a landscape called Paradox Basin where salt domes have collapsed under the weight of time. Our house is small. The view is large. I still believe we are the creators of our own worlds.

I now live in a landscape near the shifting banks of a blood-red river where I can dip my hands in its currents and catch sand. Sand through my fingers, I now have time.

I now live in a landscape where there is enough ground-water in the desert to plant a garden that will feed us, a garden we can share.

I now live in a landscape where more is exposed than hidden, and flash floods are common in the fall.

I now live in a landscape where the wind creates windows, windows that become larger and larger through time until they turn into arches one can walk through.

I am the traveler returning home after having wandered through a painting.

p. vii (dedication)   **"Otro día veremos la resurrección de las mariposas disecadas":** *"*Another day we'll witness the resurrection of dried butterflies." Federico García Lorca, *Poet in New York,* p. 69.

PARADISE

p. 5   **These mountains in time were hollowed:** The Church of Jesus Christ of Latter-day Saints keeps its genealogical records inside the Granite Mountain Record Vault, located at the bottom of Little Cottonwood Canyon approximately twenty miles outside Salt Lake City. It is reported to contain over 2 billion names of the dead. This is also near the granite quarry from which the Salt Lake Temple was built.

p. 5   **my people, Mormons:** On February 25, 2001, it was reported by *The New York Times,* "Same Faith, Fewer M's," that the word "Mormon" will no longer be used to identify the Church of Jesus Christ of Latter-day Saints. Instead, Elder Dallin H. Oaks, a member of the Council of 12 Apostles, said members will now refer to themselves as belonging to the Church of Jesus Christ. This is an effort to quell critics who claim its theology is not really Christian.

p. 5   **the landscape of Hieronymus Bosch:** Jeroen van Aken, who took the name Hieronymus Bosch, is believed to have been born in 1453 (the date, however, is uncertain) in the Netherlands village of Hertogenbosch. He is first mentioned as a painter in 1480–81. In June 1481, he appears to have married Aleyt Goyarts van den Meervenne, the daughter of a wealthy townsman, who was twelve years his senior. The marriage was childless.

Important to Bosch's social position was his membership in the Brotherhood of Our Lady, from whom he received his first commissions. This order (which listed Erasmus as a member for three years) preached the spirit of renewal of religious life, an important step along the path of the Reformation. Bosch is known to have died on August 9, 1516. From Jane Turner, ed., *The Dictionary of Art* (New York: Grove's Dictionaries, 1996), vol. 4, p. 445.

p. 5   **Now it opens like a great medieval butterfly:** The dimensions of *El jardín de las delicias* are as follows: center panel: 220 × 195 cm; side wings: 220 × 97 cm. The medium is oil on panel wood.

p. 6   **the wings of Paradise and Hell:** John Canaday, *Metropolitan Seminars in Art* portfolio 12, "The Artist As a Visionary"; plate 135, "The Garden of Eden and Hell." The twelve portfolios—beginning with "What Is a Painting?"—each focused on a particular course of study, from medieval painting to modernism, from realism to impressionism. What we loved most about these large grey books in our grandmother Mimi's study were the inside pockets that held the color plates. My brother and I would sit next to Mimi as she explained each painting, the feelings evoked by Van Gogh's sunflowers, Monet's waterlilies, Velázquez's crucifixion of Christ.

p. 7   **bareback riders gallop their horses and goats and griffins:** The Dutch word for zodiac is *dierenriem,* which means cycle of animals, the continuous repetition of nature, and the revolving drive of our passions, the procreative forces. Many Bosch scholars believe this circular image represents the zodiac.

p. 8   **In Utah . . . cherries are a love crop:** It is curious to note that the Bosch scholar Dirk Bax has written: "The cherry must be understood as a symbol of the female genital organ, which throughout Europe is often given the name of a fruit." He goes on to say that "eating cherries" means to make love. Bax, *Hieronymus Bosch: His Picture-writing Deciphered,* p. 251.

p. 11   **"It is rumored Hieronymus Bosch belonged to a religious sect":** The British matron of arts was referring to the Bosch scholar Wilhelm Fraenger's theory that Hieronymus Bosch belonged to the movement of the Brothers and Sisters of the Free Spirit, known as "Adamites," who believed in the divinity of the body and that the natural sex act was "a prayer to God."

Laurinda S. Dixon, another Bosch scholar, writes: "the state of scholarship concerning Bosch is as confusing as the paintings themselves." (Dixon, "Bosch's Garden of Delights Triptych: Remnants of a 'Fossil' Science," *Art Bulletin,* March 1981). And Erwin Panofsky states in his review of Early Netherlandish paintings: "We have bored a few holes in the door of the locked room; but somehow we do not seem to have discovered the key." (In James Snyder, ed., *Bosch in Perspective*, p. 1).

p. 11 **"A likerous mouth"**: *Chaucer's Major Poetry*, ed. Albert C. Baugh (Englewood Cliffs, N.J.: Prentice-Hall, 1963). The Wife of Bath's Tale can be enjoyed in its fullness in Geoffrey Chaucer's *Canterbury Tales*. The lines quoted by the British guide are found in "The Prologe of the Wyves Tale of Bathe," lines 466–68.

p. 12 **"I hold a stalk in my hand"**: Virginia Woolf, *The Waves*, p. 182. The two quotations that follow are from pp. 189 and 190.

Virginia Woolf wrote a vibrant essay on Madrid titled "To Spain" for *The Nation*, May 5, 1923.

p. 14 **"While of these emblems we partake"**: This Mormon hymn by John Nicholson, with music composed by Alexander Schreiner, is usually sung by the congregation prior to taking the sacrament, the blessing of the bread and water symbolic of the body and blood of Jesus Christ. *Hymns: The Church of Jesus Christ of Latter-day Saints*, p. 173.

p. 14 **"Oh God, the Eternal Father"**: This is the formal prayer given over the sacrament by ordained priesthood holders of the Mormon Church. It is found in the *Doctrine & Covenants*, 20: 77, 79.

p. 16 **When I would bear my testimony:** Fast and Testimony Meetings within the Church of Jesus Christ of Latter-day Saints are held usually the first Sunday of each month, when members fast from meals in the name of humility, an opportunity to be mindful of all the blessings they receive. The fast is broken with the sacrament, followed by communal time shared in silence, much like a Quaker meeting. As people are moved by the Spirit, they are invited to speak and share their thoughts and testimonies of the divinity of Jesus Christ. This is also a time for members to make fast offerings, usually the amount they would have spent on meals for their families. This offering is absorbed into the overall treasury of the Church, some to be used in the Church welfare program to benefit those in need.

p. 16 **two toes forward, two toes back, syndactyl:** Most birds have four toes: three toes forward and one back, known as the hallux. *Syndactyl* is an ornithological term that refers to a toe arrangement characteristic of kingfishers, where two toes are fused together, usually toes 2 and 3.

p. 17 **Bosch's acute skills as a naturalist:** Bosch was an extraordinary observer and student of nature. When Otto Benesch, a Bosch scholar from Vienna, asked the question "Was Bosch a naturalist or a visionary?" he went on to say: "It is not right to pose the question in this alternative form, for he was both. It was certainly his constant practice to supply reality with mysterious backgrounds. But so well did he understand to give naturalness and verisimilitude to what appears to us as unreal and the offspring of fantasy that his creations have a corporeal and convincing effect." Benesch, *Hieronymus Bosch and the Thinking of the Late Middle Ages,* pp. 106–8.

The birds I identified in *El jardín de las delicias* while sitting in the Prado were confirmed in Jim Flegg's *Field Guide to the Birds of Britain and Europe.* Other less defined silhouettes in the triptych were identified by family characteristics.

p. 21 **"While I was thus in the act of calling upon God":** The Joseph Smith story is recounted in the "Origin of the Book of Mormon," located in the opening pages of *The Book of Mormon.*

p. 23 **"When ye shall receive these things":** Moroni 10: 4, *The Book of Mormon.*

p. 23 **"Yea and are ye willing":** Mosiah 18: 4, *The Book of Mormon.*

p. 24 **within the language of my own sacred texts:** For an intriguing look at ancient Hebrew literary forms and patterns within the text of *The Book of Mormon,* see Hugh W. Pinnock, *Finding Biblical Hebrew and Other Literary Forms in the Book of Mormon.*

p. 25 **"Let the mountains shout for joy":** *Doctrine & Covenants* 128: 23.

p. 26 **"In horror of my darkness":** David Rosenberg, *A Poet's Bible,* Isaiah, chap. 6, pp. 249, 250.

p. 28 **the patriarchal blessing:** The First Presidency of the Mormon Church (David O. McKay, Stephen L. Richards, J. Reuben Clark, Jr.), in a letter to all stake presidents dated June 28, 1957, gave the following definition and explanation: "Patriarchal blessings contemplate an inspired declaration of the lineage of the recipient, and also where so moved upon by the Spirit, an inspired and prophetic statement of the life mission of the recipient, together with such blessings, cautions, and admonitions as the patriarch may be prompted to give for the accomplishment of such life's mission; it is always made clear that the realization of all promised blessings is conditioned upon faithfulness to the gospel of our Lord, whose servant the patriarch is."

I received my patriarchal blessing on May 16, 1973. It was given to me by the Stake Patriarch George L. Nelson in the Monument Park Stake of Salt Lake City, Utah. I have always cherished its words and regarded it as a form of personal scripture.

p. 33 **a world of hybrids and hypotheticals:** Bosch must have been very familiar with the bestiaries of his day, among them the *Physiologus,* an animal compendium of Christian symbols. Otto Benesch writes, "Albertus Magnus, Vincent of Beauvais, Philippe de Thaun were among those who composed such bestiaries, in which every animal, real or fabulous, received a distinct moral and ethical significance." *Hieronymus Bosch and the Thinking of the Late Middle Ages,* pp. 106–8.

Alchemical texts such as *Hortus sanitatis* must also have been a reference for Bosch. "The *Hortus* was a combination of bestiary/pharmaceutical manual containing recipes for the distillation of fruit, vegetables, and animals into medicines. . . . It was first printed in 1485." Laurinda S. Dixon, *Alchemical Imagery in Bosch's Garden of Delights,* p. 100. With his wife reported to belong to a family with an apothecary business, Bosch would have been familiar with herbal and alchemical practices and paraphernalia within the medieval healing tradition.

p. 34   **one rib:**

And the Lord God formed man of the dust of the ground, and breathed into his nostrils the breath of life: and man became a living soul.

And the Lord God planted a garden eastward in Eden; and there he put the man whom he had formed. . . .

And the Lord God caused a deep sleep to fall upon Adam, and he slept: and he took one of his ribs, and closed up the flesh instead thereof;

And the rib, which the Lord God had taken from man, made he a woman, and brought her unto the man.

And Adam said, This is now bone of my bones, and flesh of my flesh: she shall be called Woman, because she was taken out of Man.

Genesis 2: 7, 8; 21–23.

p. 35   **The study of evolution:** "In August 1998 conservative John W. Bacon beat moderate Dan Neuenswander by a mere 15 votes in the Kansas 3rd District Republican primary election for the state board of education, tipping the scales to the religious conservatives. In a 6–4 vote, that extra weight succeeded in removing evolution and other basic scientific principles from the state's high school standards." "Science and the Citizen: Creationism," *Scientific American,* November 1999, p. 22

p. 35   **"A grand and almost untrodden field of inquiry":** Charles Darwin, *On the Origin of Species by Means of Natural Selection, or the Preservation of Favoured Races in the Struggle for Life.* (London: John Murray, 1859; reprint ed.: New York: W. W. Norton & Co., 1975), pp. 120, 121.

p. 37   **"As God now is":** The belief of the Mormon Church regarding the personality of God and our relationship to him has been crystallized by President Lorenzo Snow in the aphorism "As man is, God once was; as God is, man may be" (*Manual,* 1901–2, pt. 1, p. 17). Also see *Millennial Star* 54: 404. To understand the Mormon theological foundations regarding the nature of God, "the plurality of gods," and the potential for man to become a god, read the King Follet discourse, perhaps Joseph Smith's greatest sermon, delivered at the funeral of Elder King Follet before 20,000 saints in April 1844. *Teachings of the Prophet Joseph Smith,* pp. 342–62.

p. 37 **marriage in the Salt Lake Temple:** To describe the Mormon view of a "Temple Marriage," let me quote from Bruce R. McConkie, *Mormon Doctrine,* p. 118:

> Celestial marriage is a holy and an eternal ordinance; as an order of the priesthood, it has the name the *new and everlasting covenant of marriage.* Adam was the first one on this earth to enter into this type of union, and it has been the Lord's order in all ages when the fullness of the gospel has been on earth. Its importance in the plan of salvation and exaltation cannot be overestimated. *The most important things that any member of The Church of Jesus Christ of Latter-day Saints ever does in this world are: 1. To marry the right person, in the right place, by the right authority; and 2. To keep the covenant made in connection with this holy and perfect order of matrimony—thus assuring the obedient persons of an inheritance of exaltation in the celestial kingdom.*

And from the current Prophet of The Church of Jesus Christ of Latter-day Saints, President Gordon B. Hinckley:

> One of the distinguishing features of The Church of Jesus Christ of Latter-day Saints is a belief in the divine nature of the family as an institution ordained of God. Here center the most sacred of all human relationships. Life is eternal. Love is eternal. And God our Eternal Father designed and has made it possible that our families shall be eternal.

To be married in the temple is the beginning of this solemnization of the eternal family, a critical step toward the plan of salvation, which is the cornerstone of The Church of Jesus Christ of Latter-day Saints. Its foundation rests on the Atonement of Christ, that we too can experience eternal life if we live by His commandments. Again, from *Mormon Doctrine,* p. 576:

> The plan of salvation . . . is the gospel of Jesus Christ. It comprises all of the laws, ordinances, and performance by conformity to which mortal

man is empowered to gain eternal life in the kingdom of God. Since the fall of Adam, man has been carnal, sensual, and devilish by nature. By conforming to the plan of salvation, man has power to put off the natural man, to be born again as a new creature of the Holy Ghost, and to become "a saint through the atonement of Christ the Lord."

The steps in this plan are: 1. Faith in the Lord Jesus Christ; 2. Repentance; 3. Baptism by immersion under the hands of a legal administrator; 4. The laying on of hands for the gift of the Holy Ghost, also under the hands of a legal administrator; and 5. Enduring in righteousness to the end of the mortal probation.

Covenants are made inside the temple ceremony between a husband and wife and God which are to remain sacred and private.

There is a fascinating parallel to the Mormon concept of marriage in the Bosch scholar Wilhelm Fraenger's interpretation of Christ's gesture toward Eve: "This cardinal giving in marriage is the guiding idea of the Creation panel and also the basic formula for the whole altarpiece. Not only does it represent the divine command to propagate the human race; it is also to be taken as a mystic *religio*, which strives to rejoin in their original wholeness beings that are separated in earthly temporality and to 'bind them back' into eternity." Fraenger, *Hieronymus Bosch,* p. 32.

p. 38   **"Everything in the world is broken":** Graffiti on the tiled wall of the Banco de España *metro.* The initials FGG were written in red marker.

p. 39   **"Out of the river rides a naked girl":** Kenneth Patchen, "In Such Harness," *Doubleheader,* p. 35.

p. 39   **Hieronymus Bosch has painted the Earth round:** "Bosch sees the universe as a transparent ball of glass in which reflections create the impression of roundness; within its womb rests the primeval landscape of the earth with its fantastic flora, surrounded, according to medieval conception, by a belt of water; a pallid gleam as of moonlight illumines this mysterious vision of a world in which man has not yet found his place." Charles de Tolnay, "Hieronymus Bosch," in *Bosch in Perspective,* ed. James Snyder (Englewood Cliffs, N.J.: Prentice-Hall, 1973), p. 61.

p. 39   **"The angels do not reside on a planet":** *Doctrine & Covenants* 130: 7,9

p. 40   **"Ipse dixit et facta sunt":** This phrase is found in Psalms 33: 9, and referenced once again in Psalm 148: 5,6. Fraenger, *Hieronymus Bosch,* pp. 15, 29.

p. 40 **A stream of light cascades from boiling clouds:** Most Bosch scholars attribute this image to the third day of Creation, "the fruitful moment" when the rains first fell. Another reference can be found in Genesis 2: 4–6: "But there went up a mist from the Earth, and wetted down the whole land."

p. 41 **"Let the waters under the heaven be gathered":** Genesis 1: 9–13.

p. 41 **Earth, an eye, a butterfly:** "Every ending a beginning, every beginning an ending—Open and close the triptych—The rhythms of nature are the rhythms of alchemy. . . . In Bosch's triptych, the alchemical cycle unfolds in the opening and closing of the panels." Dixon, "Bosch's Garden of Earthly Delights Triptych."

p. 41 **Blood drips from its bark when scratched:** This is a reference to the dragon palm found in Tenerife, one of the Canary Islands. Laurinda S. Dixon writes: "The curious tree to Adam's left has been identified . . . as the dragon tree *(Dracaena draco),* an observation enlarged upon by Van Lennep and Koch. Koch labeled it the Tree of Life because of the curative powers of its red sap called 'dragon's blood.' . . . The healing power of the blood of the tree associates it with the power of Christ's blood to heal the soul of Man." Dixon, *Alchemical Imagery in Bosch's Garden of Delights,* p. 70.

p. 41 **my forehead touches stars:** "The woman tastes the fruit of each tree, asking Orpheus the snake how to recognize that which is good. The answer given is that it sparkles, that merely to look at it rejoices the heart. Or else the answer given is that, as soon as she has eaten the fruit, she will become taller, she will grow, her feet will not leave the ground though her forehead will touch the stars." Monique Wittig, *Les Guerillères,* p. 52.

p. 42 **I fear his pink robes might suddenly ignite:** Christ's pink robes in this panel have been described by the Bosch scholar Anna Spychalska-Boczkowska as emblematic of the fullness of his divinity: "Christ's garment, 'luminously red,' constitutes a colouristic parallel to the Cancer-fountain (the pink fountain in the center of the panel). A suggestive explanation of this can be found in a poem by Conrad of Wurzburg, who compares Christ to a lobster. A lobster turns red after death and is more beautiful than when alive."

From an astrological point of view, Spychalska-Boczkowska sees the left panel as Cancer, the middle panel as Venus, and the right panel as Saturn. She goes on to speculate: "It is most probable that the Golden Conjunc-

tion of 1504 is the basis of the ideological concept of Bosch's triptych."
Spychalska-Boczkowska, "Material for the Iconography of Hieronymus
Bosch's Triptych, 'The Garden of Earthly Delights,'" *Studia Muzealne* 5
(1966): 49–95.

HELL

p. 47   **El Bosco's mind:** Dirk Bax writes: "Already at an early stage it
became evident that a reasonable explanation can be reached only by taking
pains to orient oneself in the whole field of the language, literature, folklore
and cultural history of the Low Countries, as well as in the extensive area of
Western European fine art, and all this over the period of approximately
1300–1600. . . . If the scholar limits himself to a one-sided approach, as
some have done, the influence of German engraving, the symbolism of
alchemists, or demon literature, the grossest errors will result." Bax, *Hieronymus Bosch: His Picture-writing Deciphered,* p. xv.

Bax felt that the Tree Man was a depiction of merrymakers eating inside
the goose cavern during Carnival. "A cruel sport in Bosch's day was 'pulling the goose.' It was a practice by goose-riders, members of a goose-riders'
guild, which was a company of rude merrymakers. Their goose-pulling was
a feature especially of Carnival (the entire week before the commencement
of Lent in Flanders was referred to as 'the Devil's week'). . . . A live goose
was strung up by its legs on a rope stretched between two trees or poles, the
dangling neck of the bird was greased with oil or soap, and the riders,
mounted on horses, had to try and pull the bird's neck from its body while
passing under full gallop" (p. 237).

In contrast, Laurinda S. Dixon calls the Tree Man the "Alchemical Egg
Man." She notes: "art historians have declared the image to be a giant goose
whose body houses a tavern, and a combined symbol of the male and
female sexual organs. However, if we believe our eyes, the body of the creature cannot be anything but an egg, the ubiquitous alchemical symbol that
appears in all four panels of the Garden of Delights." She associates him
with a "Saturnine melancholia." "Bosch's egg man is indeed immovably
trapped in the mire of the alchemists' hell, and his face seems to beg the
viewer to intercede for him in his awful predicament." Dixon, *Alchemical
Imagery in Bosch's Garden of Delights,* pp. 49, 53.

And Wilhelm Fraenger believes the Tree Man is "the goose who
brooded the fateful world egg." Quoting him further: "The cosmic tree has

mouldered; the world-egg has putrefied and its shell has burst open; the world sea has frozen up. . . . The demon with limbs formed by these decayed elements stands in the darkness of Hell, embodying spiritual death." Fraenger, *Hieronymus Bosch,* p. 47.

Carl Linfert observes: "Considering how much the painting of Bosch has been probed and pried into, and from every conceivable angle, the sum total learned is not very much. The picture as a whole in consequence remains even more a tissue of riddles." Linfert, *Hieronymus Bosch,* pp. 7, 6.

p. 48 **"Cones and rods—there's nothing mystical about it":** Linda Asher, July 1996.

p. 49 **"Father forgive them":** Luke 23: 34.

p. 50 **the Devil is the intimate near faraway stranger:** The idea of Satan as "the intimate stranger" comes from Elaine Pagels's notion of "the enemy within." Dr. Pagels delivered the Tanner Lecture at Kingsbury Hall on May 14, 1997, at the University of Utah, entitled "The Origin of Satan in Christian Traditions," which I attended with my father. The lecture inspired a lively discussion between us about the nature of evil and how so often the most heart-wrenching and violent situations arise within our own families.

Dr. Pagels invites us to "consider Satan as a reflection of how we perceive ourselves and those we call 'others' . . . and so Satan defines negatively what we think of as human. The social and cultural practice of defining certain people as 'others' in relation to one's own group may be, of course, as old as humanity itself. The anthropologist Robert Redfield has argued that the worldview of many peoples consists essentially of two pairs of binary oppositions: human/nonhuman and we/they." Pagels, *The Origin of Satan,* p. xviii.

p. 51 **a knife that slices my reality in two:** In thinking about *El jardín de las delicias* as a map of the mind, Kay Redfield Jamison was very helpful in defining mental dualities, specifically manic-depression, as "the paradoxical core of this quicksilver illness that can both kill and create." She writes: "The Chinese believe that before you can conquer a beast you first must make it beautiful. . . . I have tried to do that with manic-depressive illness. . . . It has been a fascinating, albeit deadly, enemy and companion; I have found it to be seductively complicated, a distillation both of what is finest in our natures, and of what is most dangerous." Jamison, *An Unquiet Mind* (New York: Vintage Books, 1996), p. 5.

p. 51 **"Flectere si nequeo Superos":** "The revolution is from below, the lower classes, the underworld, the damned, the disreputable, the despised and rejected. Freud's revolutionary motto in *The Interpretation of Dreams:* Flectere si nequeo Superos, Acherunta movebo. If I cannot bend the higher powers, I will stir up the lower depths. Freud's discovery: the universal underworld." Norman O. Brown, *Love's Body,* p. 241.

p. 53 **Must we witness and watch and do nothing:** Lester Brown, president of Worldwatch Institute, gave their forecast of ecological health at the beginning of the new millennium. As reported from *Boston Globe,* Sunday, January 16, 2000:

> From eroding soil in Kazakhstan to melting glaciers in the Peruvian Andes to depleted fisheries off New England and elsewhere, the world's ecological health at the dawn of the millennium is deteriorating, the Worldwatch Institute concluded in its annual State of the World report . . .
>
> Species are disappearing, temperatures are rising, reefs are dying, forests are shrinking, storms are raging, water tables are falling: Almost every ecological indicator shows a world on the decline. And with the global population expected to hit 9 billion in the next 50 years, these indicators are likely to worsen, the report said.
>
> "The scale and urgency of the challenges . . . are unprecedented," said Worldwatch President Lester Brown. . . .
>
> If the population and climate are not stabilized, "there is not an ecosystem on earth that we can save," Brown said. He urged a limit of two children per family and a faster transition to solar and wind power.

p. 54 **they are disappearing before our eyes:** "The very last living Spanish ibex was found dead under a fallen tree in Ordesa National Park, Spain, on January 6, 2000. Forest rangers near the French border found the 13-year-old female with her skull crushed. The animal was one of a subspecies of Pyrenees mountain goats, *Capra pyrenaica,* known in Spain as 'bucardo.' Its population once spanned across the Sierra de los Nieves to the French Pyrenees. . . . Although the bucardo became a protected species in 1973, shrinking habitat and poachers eroded its numbers until only the lone surviving female remained." "Earthweek: A Diary of the Planet," *The News & Observer,* January 17, 2000.

p. 54 **The Natural History of the Dead:** In a short story with this title, Ernest Hemingway writes: "It has always seemed to me that the war has been omitted as a field for the observations of a naturalist . . . can any branch of Natural History be studied without increasing that faith, love, and hope, which we also, every one of us, need in our own journey through the wilderness of life?" Hemingway, "The Natural History of the Dead," *The Short Stories,* pp. 440, 441.

Originally this story appeared as nonfiction in the last chapter of *Death in the Afternoon,* Hemingway's treatise on bullfighting in Spain. It was the recommendation of his editor, Maxwell Perkins, and his friend John Dos Passos that he delete this chapter from the book because it was perceived to be tangential to the main text. It is here that Hemingway recounts the story of the sergeant in World War I who pried out the filled teeth of the dead with a trench knife, or knocked them out with a pipe, and put them inside a German gas-mask can. Those interested in the original story can read it in its fullness in the Hemingway Collection, located inside the John F. Kennedy Library in Boston, Massachusetts.

Within this deleted chapter, there is a powerful lament by Hemingway over the loss of wildness in upper Michigan. He says, essentially, that if you care for new country, your heart will be broken over and over again because of the changes, that you will keep trying to find "other new country and other new country" and that the same thing will occur even in old country. Hemingway turns philosophical, realizing one can only adopt a conscious "acceptance or refusal" of change. *Death in the Afternoon,* 24, insert between pages 5, 6, Manuscript of "New Chapter," Hemingway Collection, JFK Library.

It is interesting to note that between 1992 and 1997 nearly 16 million acres of farmlands, forests, and other open spaces were lost to development, a rate of 3.2 million acres a year. *USA Today,* December 8, 1999.

p. 54 **"the twenty-first century will be the century of Noahs":** Homero Aridjis, "Notes on the Millennium," Morelia Conference, Grupo de Cien, Morelia, Mexico, January 14, 1994.

p. 55 **"These wretches, who ne'er lived":** Dante Alighieri, *The Divine Comedy.*

p. 56 **Kids' Fits Cancel Cartoons:** *Time,* November 22, 1999.

p. 57 **Monkeys Put to Work in Coconut Groves:** *The Economist,* December 1997.

p. 57 **Headless Frogs Reignite Row over Genetics:** *Sunday Telegram* (London), October 19, 1997.

p. 58 **Humans Volunteer to Ingest Pesticides:** "Environmental Working Group Blasts Ethics, Questions Merits of Human Pesticide Tests," *Pesticide & Toxic Chemical News,* July 30, 1998.

p. 58 **Frankenstein Foods:** *Newsweek,* September 20, 1999. "Consumer, Environmental Groups Call on Clinton Administration to Halt Rapid Spread of Bt Corn," *Pesticide & Toxic Chemical News,* August 26, 1999.

For an ecological response to the relationship between transgenic corn and monarchs, see Gary Paul Nabhan, "The Killing Fields," *Wild Earth* 9, no. 4 (Winter 1999/2000): 49–52. Nabhan, an ethnobotanist, offers ten myths about Bt corn and butterflies, pointing out the illogical responses given in defense of biotechnology and what we as consumers can do about it.

p. 59 **Radioactive Mill Tailings Need to be Moved:** *The Daily Sentinel* (Grand Junction, Colorado), July 28, 1999.

p. 59 **Mice Injected with DNA from Fireflies:** National Public Radio, 1996.

p. 59 **War Leaves Poison Legacy:** *USA TODAY,* July 20, 1999.

p. 63 **"I like the idea of a thing to describe a feeling":** Damien Hirst, *I Want to Spend the Rest of My Life Everywhere, with Everyone, One to One, Always, Forever, Now,* p. 285.

p. 64 **"The fact that we designate something as art":** Thomas McEvilley, *Art and Otherness* (New York: Documentext, 1992), p. 164.

p. 65 **"Art's about life":** Hirst, *I Want to Spend the Rest of My Life Everywhere,* pp. 20, 21.

p. 66 **"I always believe in contradiction":** Ibid., p. 49.

p. 66 **Call it *Brilliant Love, 1994–95*:** *Brilliant Love, 1994* is one of Damien Hirst's butterfly canvases, vibrant canvases with real butterflies stuck on the paint, at once disturbing and beautiful. One may question his ethics in choosing to use them as art, but here are his own words: "I wanted these paintings to be more than a painting, where the colour leaps off the canvas and flies around the room. . . . You have to find universal triggers, everyone's frightened of glass, everyone's frightened of sharks, everyone loves butterflies" (ibid., pp. 118–34).

p. 66 **"Art is dangerous":** Ibid., p. 49.

p. 67 **Damien Hirst brought together a community:** "Where the Art Brouhaha Was Born," *New York Times,* October 14, 1999, pp. 1, E3.

p. 68 **"What is in the boxes?":** Damien Hirst interviewed by Liam Gillick, *Modern Medicine,* 1990.

p. 68 **let him bring along his chain saw:** *Cutting Ahead, 1994* is an installation that involves a chain saw. Hirst cut a pig's head down the center and exposed the symmetry of both sides.

p. 69 **the shock of what has always been here:** Hirst's installation *Away from the Flock, 1994* features one white sheep floating in turquoise formaldahyde, again framed in white steel.

p. 72   **Procter & Gamble:** "Procter & Gamble is a uniquely diversified consumer products company with a strong global presence. Established in 1837, P & G today markets more than 300 brands to nearly five billion consumers in over 140 countries. They include Tide, Always, Downy, Folgers, Head & Shoulders, Ivory, Cascade, Comet, Pepto-Bismol, Nyquil, Scope, Cover Girl, Secret, Jif, and Zest. On-the-ground operations exist in more than 70 countries. In the fiscal year ending June 30, 1998, P & G had worldwide sales of $37.2 billion." *Procter & Gamble Investor Fact Sheet.*

The *New York Times* reported on July 29, 1997 that Procter & Gambel had filed suit against the Amway Corporation and 11 distributors for allegedly "making disparaging remarks about Procter products and spreading [accusations of] Satanism in an effort to lure customers to Amway."

In his book *The Choking Doberman and Other "New" Urban Legends* (New York: W. W. Norton & Co., 1984), Jan Harold Brunvand traces the origin of the Satanic rumors back to 1980, when queries first began trickling into the company's public relations department concerning "its ubiquitous trademark depicting the man in the moon and thirteen stars." Evidently those who believe P & G is tied to Satanism find the hundred-year-old trademark logo to be a covert representation of the number 666, the "Mark of the Beast" in the book of Revelation.

p. 75   **"The siesta was over":** This idea of changing culture through corporate controls is further elucidated in an article published in the *New York Times,* "Spain Rudely Awakened to Workaday World," December 26, 1999, two and half years after my conversation with the executive from Procter & Gamble.

p. 78   **one life at a time, please:** This is the title of Edward Abbey's collection of essays published in 1978 by Henry Holt. I wanted to evoke Abbey's name as one of my own "prophets in poetry." He was fearless in his questions regarding a culture's relationship to landscape. "If there's anyone still present whom I've failed to insult, I apologise." Typical words from a true patriot of the American West.

Abbey believed the artist had a social responsibility to provoke the status quo. "I write to oppose injustice, to defy power, and to speak for the voiceless. I write to make a difference . . . I write to give pleasure and promote aesthetic bliss. To honor life and to praise the divine beauty of the natural world. I write for the joy and exultation of writing itself." Abbey, *One Life at a Time, Please,* p. 178.

p. 78   **"What it all comes down to":** Eduardo Galeano, *The Book of Embraces,* p. 125.

p. 79   **The iron rod I hold on to:** The "iron rod" refers to a dream the Prophet Lehi had in the wilderness as described in *The Book of Mormon:* "And I beheld a rod of iron, and it extended along the bank of the river, and led to the tree by which I stood. And I also beheld a straight and narrow path, which came along by the rod of iron, even to the tree by which I stood; and it also led by the head of the fountain, unto a large and spacious field, as if it had been a world." 1 Nephi, 8:19, 20.

The idea of the iron rod is further interpreted by the prophet Nephi, son of Lehi: "And they said unto me: What meaneth the rod of iron which our father saw, that led to the tree? And I said unto them that it was the word of God; and whoso would hearken unto the word of God, and would hold fast unto it, they would never perish; neither could the temptations and the fiery darts of the adversary overpower them unto blindness, to lead them away to destruction." 1 Nephi, 15: 23–24.

p. 79   **the flaming horizon of the Millennium:** The Millennium holds special significance for members of the Church of Jesus Christ of Latter-day Saints. As a child, I was always told to prepare for the Millennium. It was common wisdom when I was growing up that the year 2000 would be an auspicious one, possibly the Second Coming of Christ.

According to Mormon theology: "This earth is passing through a mortal or temporal existence of seven millenniums or 7000 years" (*Doctrine & Covenants* 77: 6–7).

And from McConkie, *Mormon Doctrine* (p. 492):

> During the first six of these (covering a total period of 6,000 years from the time of the fall of Adam) conditions of carnality, corruption, evil, and wickedness of every sort have prevailed upon the earth. Wars, death, destruction and everything incident to the present telestial state of existence have held sway over the earth and all life on its face.
>
> When the 7th thousand years commence, however, radical changes will take place both in the earth itself and in the nature and type of existence enjoyed by all forms of life on its face. This will be the long hoped for age of peace when Christ will reign personally upon the earth; when the earth will be renewed and receive its paradisiacal glory; when corruption, death, and disease will cease; and when the kingdom of God on earth will be fully established in all its glory, beauty, and perfection. This is the period known to the saints of all ages as the millennium.

No one knows when the millennium will occur, but there are signs and important events and conditions that will herald this new era. Eduardo

Galeano writes, "the new millennium is already upon us," and states: "If we can't guess what's coming, at least we have the right to imagine the future we want. . . . Let's set our sights beyond the abominations of today, to divine another possible world."

His list includes:

economists shall not measure "living standards" by consumption levels, nor the "quality of life" by the quantity of things;

earnestness shall no longer be a virtue, and no one shall be taken seriously if he can't make fun of himself;

no one shall be considered a hero or a fool, for doing what he believes is right instead of what will serve him best;

the world shall not wage war on the poor, rather on poverty, and the arms industry shall have no alternative but to declare bankruptcy;

street children shall not be treated like garbage because there shall be no street children;

justice and liberty, siamese twins condemned to live apart, shall meet again and be reunited back to back;

the Church, holy mother, shall correct the typos on the tablets of Moses and the sixth commandment shall dictate the celebration of the body;

the Church shall also proclaim another commandment, the one God forgot: "You shall love nature, to which you belong";

we shall be compatriots and contemporaries of all who have a yearning for justice and beauty, no matter where they were born or when they lived, because the borders of geography and time shall cease to exist;

perfection shall remain the boring privilege of the gods; while in our bungling messy world every night shall be lived as if it were the last, and every day as if it were the first.

> Eduardo Galeano, "The Right to Rave," *Bomb*, no. 69 (Fall 1999).

p. 79 **Fin de siècle:** This phrase was first used to describe the end of the last century and to designate the art of the time. In the years 1000 and 1500 many individuals believed the world might come to an end. There is a sense that something important is ending, and that what is beginning is unclear.

p. 80 **It was an "empire upon which the sun never set"**: For a brilliant overview of the Spanish empire, see *The Grand Strategy of Philip II* by Geoffrey Parker: "The annexation of Portugal and her overseas empire in 1580 made Philip II the ruler of the first empire in history on which the sun never set. Although its core—and its king—remained in Europe, issues concerning Africa, Asia, and America regularly flowed across Philip's desk and required countless decisions" (p. 3).

p. 81 **"And the sea gave up the dead"**: Revelation 20:13. Many art historians believe that *El jardín de las delicias* is a reinterpretation of Revelation. In Bosch's panel of Hell, it is easy to see the parallels: "The fearful, and unbelieving, and the abominable, and murders, and whoremongers, and sorcerers, and idolaters, and all liars, shall have their part in the lake which burneth with fire and brimstone" (Revelation 21:8).

p. 83 **"If thou lop off a single twig"**: Dante Alighieri, *The Divine Comedy*.

p. 83 **The report from the pathologist reads "benign"**: This essay appeared as "Clearcut" in the *Western Humanities Review* 50, no. 4/51, no. 1 (Winter 1997/Spring 1997): 292–93.

p. 85 **Where has the tissue of my body been thrown?**: Date of biopsy: August 6, 1996, my grandmother Mimi's birthday. She would have been ninety years old.

p. 86 **"but what came out of the forest"**: W. S. Merwin, "One Story," *Travels* (New York: Alfred A. Knopf, 1992), p. 126.

p. 86 **The Nightjar Magistrate**: The name of the nightjar family, Caprimulgidae, comes from the Latin *caper,* goat, and *mulgeo,* to milk or suck. Legend has it that members of this family, also called goatsuckers, sucked milk from goats at night. *Nightjar* comes from the loud, distinctive cries these birds make, particularly at dusk. This family also includes nighthawks and whip-poor-wills. Their small bills but large, gaping mouths are perfectly adapted to catch insects in flight. They have very large dark eyes. Most are cryptically colored, with mottled brown and black plumage.

Again, art historians disagree as to what this creature in Bosch's Hell represents. Laurinda Dixon calls it "Saturn-Thoth," recalling the legend of Saturn eating his children whereby the Philosopher's Stone is born from the earth and the putrification process (*Alchemical Imagery in Bosch's Garden of Delights,* p. 61). Wilhelm Fraenger calls this "corpse-eating hawk" a symbol "of useless consumption" (*The Millennium of Hieronymus Bosch*, pp. 58–60). And the art historian Carl Linfert writes: "Bosch's realism led him to invent a whole new world of meaningful signs so much the more effective because of their inherent tendency to deform reality. He no longer spoke the fixed and static language of symbols on which the Middle Ages had relied. Indeed, wherein he actually invented something, it was always as unlike as possible what the eye is used to seeing" (*Hieronymus Bosch*, p. 8).

p. 87   **a moth-priest:** In a letter to *Life* magazine, November 12, 1949, Vladimir Nabokov writes,

Sirs,

It may interest a few of your readers to learn that the butterfly wings in the third panel of the Bosch tryptich, so beautifully reproduced in your issue of November 14, can be at once determined as belonging to a female specimen of the common European species now known as *Maniola jurtina,* which Linnaeus described some 250 years after good Bosch knocked it down with his cap in a Flemish meadow to place it in his Hell." *Nabokov's Butterflies,* edited by Brian Boyd and Robert Michael Pyle, Beacon Press, Boston, 2000, p. 449.

p. 87   **A woman (or is she a coyote disguised?) wears a dress:** Nicola Costantino, an artist from Argentina, had an exhibit of her clothing, "Peleteria con piel humana," at the show "A vueltas con los sentidos" at Casa de América in Madrid, January 29, 1999.

p. 88   **Six men and women:** The names of "the September Six" excommunicated from the Mormon Church during the month of September 1993 for apostasy are: Lynne Kanavel Whitesides, Mormon Women's Forum president; Avrahem Gileadi, an Isaiah scholar; Paul James Toscano, Mormon Alliance president; Maxine Hanks, editor of *Mormon Women and Authority;* Lavina Fielding Anderson, editor of the *Journal of Mormon History;* and Michael Quinn, a historian and author of *The Mormon Hierarchy: Origins of Power.*

Michael Quinn, who received his Ph.D from Yale University and was a professor of American social history at Brigham Young University for twelve years, said, "I'm a DNA Mormon. It's in me, whether they accept or remove me."

Maxine Hanks wrote, "According to the dictionary, apostasy means to abandon one's faith. . . . I have abandoned church policy and false authority, but I am in harmony with my faith in God."

Apostle Dallin Oaks, when interviewed on National Public Radio, explained that what was happening was simple discipline of wayward members who contradict Church leaders and doctrine. "There is no purge of feminists. There is no purge of scholars. There is no purge. A church of about eight million has church discipline of a handful, and people begin to call it a purge. That is an exaggeration and perhaps self-serving characterization."

At 12:30 on Saturday, October 2, 1993, a thousand white roses were delivered to the General Authorities of the Church with the following letter:

> In the spirit of peace, we Latter-day Saints from around the world send these thousand white roses to the General Authorities who have been called to serve Jesus Christ and the members of his devotion to Christ's Gospel of love, mercy, faith and hope. The roses symbolize our support both of the church and of the members who have recently had disciplinary action taken against them. Therefore, in the spirit of peace, we make this appeal: let the fear and reprisals end. Though the times are challenging and difficult, we find hope in the belief that we can face such challenges with dignity and grace and with the belief that God cherishes diversity, that He loves all his children, and that He does not seek to exclude any who love him from membership in his Church.
>
> Paid for by the White Rose Campaign.

For a review of the disciplinary action taken on "the September Six," see "Six Intellectuals Disciplined for Apostasy," *Sunstone*, November 1993, pp. 65–73.

Michael Barrett, a CIA lawyer, was excommunicated in April 1994 for refusing to stop writing letters publicly denouncing Church doctrines in papers such as the *Chicago Tribune,* the *Washington Post,* the *New York Times,* the *Salt Lake Tribune,* and *USA Today.*

On May 10, 1995, Janice Allred, a Mormon feminist, was excommunicated after publishing a speculative essay on the Mother in Heaven and after publicly speaking against the popular LDS belief that God will never allow the Church hierarchy to lead the membership astray. She was the eighth high-profile Mormon to be disciplined for her writings. See "Mormon Feminist Disciplined," *Sunstone,* April 1995.

p. 89 **"And some feeble-minded children"**: García Lorca, *Poet in New York,* p. 73.

p. 89 **I think about love in Hell:** Pertinent to the Mormon concept of Hell is the belief that there are three kingdoms of glory to which members of the Church of Jesus Christ of Latter-day Saints may gain an inheritance inside the kingdom of God, dependent upon their good works in life here on Earth. These are the celestial kingdom, the terrestrial kingdom, and the telestial kingdom.

That law by obedience to which men gain an inheritance in the kingdom of God in eternity is called celestial law. It is the law of the gospel, the law of Christ, and it qualifies men for admission to the celestial kingdom because in and through it men are "sanctified by the reception of the Holy Ghost," thus becoming clean, pure, and spotless.

McConkie, *Mormon Doctrine,* p. 117; 3 Nephi 27: 19–21, *The Book of Mormon.*

"And they who are not sanctified through the law which I have given unto you, even the law of Christ," the Lord says, "must inherit an other kingdom, even that of a terrestrial kingdom, or that of a telestial kingdom. For he who is not able to abide the law of a celestial kingdom cannot abide a celestial glory."

Doctrine & Covenants 88: 21–22.

The celestial kingdom is likened to the sun, the terrestrial kingdom to the moon, and the telestial kingdom to the stars.

To the celestial kingdom go those who have received the word of God and the spirit of the Holy Ghost and have lived in accordance with the principles of the gospel.

To the terrestrial kingdom go: (1) Accountable individuals who die without the gospel; (2) Those who reject the gospel in this life and who reverse their course and accept it in the spirit world; (3) Honorable men of the earth who are blinded by the craftiness of men and who therefore do not accept and live the gospel law; and (4) Members of the Church of Jesus Christ of Latter-day Saints who have testimonies of Christ and the divinity of the great latter-day work and who are not valiant, but who are instead lukewarm in their devotion to the Church and to righteousness.

McConkie, *Mormon Doctrine,* p. 784; *Doctrine & Covenants* 76: 71–80.

According to Mormon theology, most inhabitants on this earth will go to the telestial kingdom. "The inhabitants of this lowest kingdom of glory will be 'as innumerable as the stars in the firmament of heaven, or as the sand upon the seashore.' " This is a result of conforming their lives to this world, a world of their own desires, not the world of God. Hell, for Mormons, becomes the place for the "sons of perdition in eternity" who have been in open rebellion with the truth, aside from choosing to abide in sin, they have chosen "a kingdom which is not a kingdom of glory." *Doctrine & Covenants* 88: 24.

p. 90 **"The color of retreat is grey":** Ernest Hemingway, speaking about the Spanish Civil War. Hemingway Collection #716, JFK Library.

p. 90 **"Release him. Free him":** Leonard Peltier is serving two consecutive life sentences in Leavenworth Penitentiary in Kansas for the alleged murders of Joe Stuntz and two FBI agents, Jack Coler and Ron Williams, on June 26, 1975, at the Jumping Bull Ranch on the Pine Ridge Reservation near Wounded Knee. A large number of AIM supporters with their families were camping on the property at the time. Over 150 FBI agents, BIA police, U.S. marshals, and local police descended on the scene, which quickly became a shootout. This highly contested case is fraught with racism and circumstantial evidence. Amnesty International considers Leonard Peltier a political prisoner and is calling for his release. For a thorough rendering of the incident at Pine Ridge and the case of Leonard Peltier, see Peter Matthiessen's book *In the Spirit of Crazy Horse.*

p. 91 **Keys to the Gospel:** Traditionally, the "keys to the kingdom" in Mormon theology belong to those who hold the priesthood and who have the authority to preside over the kingdom of God on earth. "And the Lord confirmed a priesthood also upon Aaron and his seed, throughout all their generations, which priesthood also continueth and abideth forever with the priesthood which is after the holiest order of God. And this greater priesthood administereth the gospel and holdeth the key of the mysteries of the kingdom, even the key of the knowledge of God." *Doctrine & Covenants* 84: 18–19.

Mormon boys are given the Aaronic Priesthood (known as the lesser priesthood) at the age of twelve and may receive the Melchizedek Priesthood (known as the higher priesthood) when they turn eighteen. They are then worthy of the title "Elders." Mormon women cannot hold the priesthood, but can "enter the gospel in partnership with their husbands through celestial marriage."

p. 91 **It is becoming darker and darker:** President George W. Bush in the first one hundred days of his new administration shows his eagerness to please the oil, gas, and mining industries: withdraws a Clinton rule that reduced by 80 percent the permissible standard for arsenic in drinking water; reverses a campaign pledge to impose mandatory limits on carbon dioxide; withdraws from the Kyoto Protocol on climate change; and Interior Secretary Gale Norton suspends new regulations that would require mining companies to pay for cleanups and has targeted some 17 million acres of public lands, in 11 Western states, now designated as wilderness study areas, for the possibility of oil and gas exploration. The Bush administration has also signaled a retreat on Mr. Clinton's most ambitious conservation measure—a Forest Service rule protecting nearly 60 million acres of forest lands.

p. 92 **The house with the comet overhead is gone:** The residence of Kathryn and Jack Tempest in Salt Lake City, Utah, was the home and meeting place of our extended Tempest family. The comet Hale-Bopp was visible in the Western Hemisphere during the spring of 1997.

p. 95 **"All this is the way of living":** J. Krishnamurti, *You Are the World,* p. 33.

> Discontent is painful only when it is resisted. A man who is merely satisfied, without understanding the full significance of discontent, is asleep; he is not sensitive to the whole movement of life. Satisfaction is a drug, and it is comparatively easy to find. But to understand the full significance of discontent, the search for certainty must cease.
>
> J. Krishnamurti, *Commentaries on Living,* p. 75.

My grandmother was a serious student of Krishnamurti. Both she and my grandfather went to Ojai, California, throughout the 1960s and listened to this Indian teacher speak beneath the oak trees. Tucked inside the pages of the *Commentaries,* I found an oak leaf. I remember many times being in the Uintah Mountains with Mimi, or in the Tetons, or at the beach, and she would stop and say, "Remember this—choiceless awareness of the moment."

p. 98 **"A great percentage of what is heard":** Harold Schapero, "The Musical Mind," in Brewster Ghiselin, ed., *The Creative Process,* p. 50.

p. 98 **the trio of giant instruments in Hell:** Hans H. Lenneberg, "Bosch's *Garden of Earthly Delights:* Some Musicological Considerations and Criticisms," *Gazette des Beaux-Arts* 53 (1961): 135–44. This is a fascinating article on a musicologist's perspective regarding the realism of the musical instruments in Bosch's Hell and the accuracy of the codex beneath the lute. Lenneberg raises the question whether Bosch intended to represent actual music at all or whether he painted "mock-music."

I want to express my gratitude to Leo Treitler, a musicologist specializing in medieval music, who spent a great amount of time explaining the subtleties of Gregorian chant and the lexicon of musical notation. His article "Reading and Singing: On the Genesis of Occidental Music-Writing," published in *Early Music History: Studies in Medieval and Early Modern Music,* edited by Iain Fenlon (New York: Cambridge University Press, 1984), is a brilliant discussion of image and language through musical punctuation.

p. 100   **I feel his life blowing through him:** John Henry Tempest, Jr., died on Sunday, December 15, 1996.

p. 101   **Eye Scanning Takes ATMs High Tech:** *Salt Lake Tribune,* March 19, 1998, p. B 4.

p. 102   **the root translation of "heresy":** Pagels, *The Origin of Satan,* p. 163.

p. 106   **"Mi cuerpo entre los equilibrios contrarios":** The great Gypsy poet, Federico García Lorca, was murdered in his hometown of Granada on August 18, 1936. David Johnston writes: "For whatever reasons—anti-intellectualism, envy, hatred for his homosexuality, resentment, the willingness to believe that his writings were a political campaign against Spain rather than a moral one against ingrained inhumanity . . . he was taken from his refuge on August 16, rapidly processed through a kangaroo court, and in the early hours of 18 August 1936, he was shot by a military firing squad. . . . A few bucketfuls of lime were scattered on top as though to conceal the crime." Johnston, *Federico García Lorca* (New York: Stewart, Tabori & Chang, 1998), p. 126.

García Lorca's essay "Play and Theory of the Duende" (a lecture he gave in 1933 in Buenos Aires) is one of the most riveting discussions on poetics I have ever read. He defines *duende* as this "mysterious power that all may feel and no philosophy can explain . . . in sum, the spirit of the earth." "Whatever has black sounds has *duende*," said Manuel Torres, one of the great *cantadores* of flamenco. "Behind those black sounds," writes García Lorca, "tenderly and intimately, live zephyrs, ants, volcanoes, and the huge night, straining its waist against the Milky Way." Where *duende* dwells, passion ignites and forms change.

Duende is the struggle inside that threatens to make art.

p. 108   **"Imagination works at the summit":** Gaston Bachelard, *The Psychoanalysis of Fire,* p. 110.

p. 114   **"If it is between a farmer and a duck":** Similar sentiments reside in rural Utah regarding wilderness. Ranchers and politicians are still up in arms over the designation of the Grand Staircase–Escalante National Monument on September 18, 1996, which protected almost 2 million acres through the 1906 Antiquities Act and the stroke of President William Jefferson Clinton's pen. They felt they had no say. Those of us within the conservation community felt grateful for being heard after a very contentious debate in Congress over the Utah Public Lands Management Act of 1995, which proposed only 1.7 million acres out of 22 million acres of Bureau of Land Management lands. The bill was defeated in the Senate in the spring of 1996. To this date no BLM wilderness has been designated in the state of Utah, but hope remains in support of America's Redrock Wilderness. See Terry Tempest Williams, "Open for Business?," op-ed piece, *New York Times,* June 20, 1995.

A group known as People for the USA sees any movement toward the preservation of wildlands as part of a United Nations conspiracy orchestrated through "the International Union for the Conservation of Nature," an organization they say promotes "science-based ecospiritual theories of pantheism expressed in the biocentric philosophy that all species have equal intrinsic value—humans are merely one strand in nature's fragile web."

p. 119 **"Welcome to the Temple of Confessions":** This text is from an exhibit called "Temple of Confessions" at the Corcoran Gallery of Art, Washington, D.C., October 12, 1996–January 6, 1997.

p. 120 **One of the Living Saints is dressed in a jaguar skin:** The artists responsible for "Temple of Confessions," who also acted as "The Living Saints" in these "living dioramas," are Guillermo Gómez-Pena and Roberto Sifuentes. They are "continuing their research on 'reversed anthropology,' intercultural relations, hybrid identities, fear of immigration, and the exoticization of the 'other.'" A radio version of "Temple of Confessions" aired on National Public Radio in August 1996.

p. 120 **Aztec god in bondage:** For a "gentile's" perspective on Mormon archaeology in Central and South America, see article "This Is Not the Place," by Hampton Sides, *DoubleTake,* Spring 1999.

p. 120 **"This is the body of South and North America":** *"Enguillir lo semejante es siempre una experiencia enriquecedora"*—"To gobble up one's kind is always an enriching experience." This artist would only be identified as Silva from Chiapas, Mexico, one of the performance artists at the exhibit "A vueltas con los sentidos," at Casa de América, Madrid, January 29, 1999. I later learned his name is César Martínez; the piece was titled "PerforMANcena."

p. 124 **"Here we stand inside the mind of God":** Bill McKibben,

January 8, 1994. The hillside where we walked is Cerro Altamirano in Michoacán, Mexico, once site of 40 million migrating monarch butterflies, now threatened by logging practices, pesticides, and development. This field trip was part of El Grupo de Cien, an international gathering of writers, philosophers, and scientists organized by Betty and Homero Aridjis, January 1994. For more information on monarchs, see the following references:

Lincoln P., Brower, "Monarch Migration," *Natural History* 86 (1977): 40–53.

W. H. Calvert and L. P. Brower, "The Importance of Forest Cover for the Survival of Overwintering Monarch Butterflies *(Danaus plexippus, Danaidae),*" *Journal of the Lepidopterists' Society* 35 (1981): 216–25.

Alison Hawthorne Deming, *The Monarchs: A Poem Sequence* (Baton Rouge: Louisiana State University Press, 1998).

Sue Halpern, "A Fragile Kingdom," *Audubon* 100, no. 2 (1998): 36–44, 99–101.

W. S. Merwin, "The Winter Palace," *Orion* 15, no. 1 (1996): 44–53.

Robert Michael Pyle, *Chasing Monarchs—Migrating the Butterflies of Passage* (Boston: Houghton Mifflin, 1999).

p. 124   **blows it back to life:** My guide was Elías Riveria Gonzales.

p. 125   **Ignite the hymns:**

"The Spirit of God Like a Fire Is Burning"
"We Are All Enlisted"
"Put Your Shoulder to the Wheel"
"Come, Come, Ye Saints"
"Count Your Many Blessings"

These are traditional, beloved Mormon hymns. Whenever I find myself in danger, physically or psychologically, I am in the habit of singing these songs for comfort and gravity of soul.

EARTHLY DELIGHTS

p. 131   **"Why why why joy enjoy joy   joy":** From December 11 to 19, 1994, I attended the *Kalachakra por la Paz del Mundo* in Barcelona, on

Montjuic. The preliminary teachings of the Kalachakra Initiation for World Peace were given by His Holiness the 14th Dalai Lama. It was a deeply humbling experience attended by thousands of individuals, many of whom were Tibetan refugees. Throughout the teachings, monks were creating a large sand mandala known as "The Wheel of Time," that we were able to witness at the end of the ritual, after which the sand was swept up and given as an offering to the Mediterranean Sea. It rained.

The Dalai Lama said, "We can bring about reversal through desire and a quieting of the mind."

To learn more about the Kalachakra see Barry Bryant, *The Wheel of Time,* with a foreword by the 14th Dalai Lama.

p. 132 **This triptych was once called "The Strawberry":** In his essay "History of the Order of Saint Jerome" (1605), Fray José de Siguenza refers to the triptych as "The Strawberry Plant." Snyder, ed., *Bosch in Perspective,* p. 38.

With all the abundance of fruit in the center panel of *El jardín de las delicias* I hear Neruda's voice: "And what did the rubies say standing before the juice of pomegranates?" Pablo Neruda, *The Book of Questions,* trans. William O' Daly (Port Townsend, Wash.: Copper Canyon Press, 1974), p. 14.

p. 133 **I am struck by the androgynous nature of human beings:** I would wager a bet that Hemingway and Bosch would have been friends, that Ernesto en España would have been intrigued by *El jardín de las delicias,* especially the middle panel. I have often thought that bleed-throughs can occur where one artist speaks to another through the thin veil of time.

Hemingway told George Plimpton in an interview for the *Paris Review* (Spring 1958) that Hieronymous Bosch was indeed one of his artistic mentors. This bit of information sent me on a search for more clues, evidence in Hemingway's work that the two had been "in correspondence," that it is in the nature of Bosch's genius to possess people as well as ideas.

I turned to the obvious, *The Garden of Eden,* Hemingway's unfinished novel that he worked on for decades, published posthumously in 1986 by Charles Scribner's Sons. Could the title have been inspired by Bosch's triptych? Certainly the novel is filled with androgynous themes, for example, the sexual games played between David and Catherine. There are countless references to Bosch and his imagery throughout the original manuscript that were edited out in the Scribner edition, I believe to the detriment of Hemingway's story. Perhaps most riveting was Catherine's apology in a letter to David after she had burned his manuscripts. In her impassioned lament, she spoke of her mad love for him, akin only to her love for the Bosch room in the Prado. She felt as if she had "blown up" the two things that mattered most to her, the two things that had ever opened her heart.

Who knows, maybe Hemingway secretly recognized himself as one of Bosch's androgynes cavorting and exploring the natural pleasures of the world in the name of love. Perhaps Hemingway was the man being fed grapes by the birds. One can never know another's evolution.

p. 134   **"I went to the Garden of Love":** William Blake, *Songs of Innocence and of Experience,* p. 44.

p. 135   **"I've always felt like an insect":** Joan Miró, talking about a pencil drawing *Dialogue of Insects, 1924–1925.* Claire-Hélène Blanquet, *Miró—Earth and Sky* (New York: Chelsea House, 1993), p. 28.

p. 136   **"We are many, a whole tribe swarming":** Czeslaw Milosz, "The Garden of Earthly Delights," *Collected Poems, 1931–1987* (New York: HarperCollins, 1990), p. 393.

p. 136   **Let us be carried away:** For a visual delight, see Martha Clarke's production *The Garden of Earthly Delights,* performed at Lincoln Center in 1984, with music by Richard Peaslee. It is available on videocassette and can be viewed at the Lincoln Center Library for the Performing Arts in New York.

p. 140   **"Let it be like wild flowers":** Yehuda Amichai, "Wild Peace," *The Selected Poetry of Yehuda Amichai* (Berkeley: University of California Press, 1996), p. 88.

p. 140   **What if the Seven Deadly Sins:** One of the dominant images in the Bosch Gallery inside the Museo del Prado is El Bosco's *Table of the Seven Deadly Sins.* Tableaus of each of the sins circle around the eye of Christ. This, like *El jardín de las delicias,* belonged to Philip II. He placed the Table inside El Escorial for his own private contemplation, and there the king sat in the eye of the Spanish Inquisition. *Beware, Beware, God Sees* are the words inscribed around the pupil of the eye.

p. 141   **Opus contra naturam:** The *opus contra naturam* is the alchemical work; "a way not of small but rather supreme resistance, the work of the alchemical rockbreakers emerges as a powerful symbol for the *removal of repression* by an ego working its way back into the depths of the unconscious. The chaos of the prima materia testifies the dangers of this procedure." Johannes Fabricius, *Alchemy: The Medieval Alchemists and Their Royal Art,* p. 22.

p. 142   **"motion can be a place too":** Robert Pinsky, *An Explanation of America,* p. 18.

p. 142   **"There has never been any forbidden fruit":** André Breton,

Mad Love, trans. Mary Ann Caws (Lincoln: University of Nebraska Press, 1988), p. 93.

p. 142 **"lyric behavior . . . convulsive beauty . . . magic-circumstantial":** Ibid., p. 19.

p. 143 **To peel the peach:** I hear the echo of T. S. Eliot's voice in "The Love Song of J. Alfred Prufrock": "Do I dare? . . . Do I dare?/ Disturb the Universe . . . Do I dare to eat a peach?" I heard this poem spontaneously recited at the Algonquin Hotel in New York City by a man who called himself "a witch-poet."

p. 143 **"Darkness is just a memory of light":** Breyten Breytenbach, *The Memory of Birds in Times of Revolution* (New York: Harcourt, Brace & Co., 1996), p. 54.

p. 143 **El Bosco painted his Garden on the threshold of this leap:** Might we be on the threshold of an ecological reformation?

p. 144 **Their loyalties are to the lapis stones they carry in their hands:** Lapis lazuli is "the secret stone," the philosopher's stone, indigo blue, associated with water. "There could be no alchemy without this stone. It is the heart and tincture of the gold, regarding which Hermes says: 'It is needful that at the end of the world heaven and earth be united: which is the philosophic word' " (Fabricius, *Alchemy,* p. 186). Carl Jung defines it symbolically as "body, mind and spirit" (Jung, *Alchemical Studies,* p. 102). "We know that the lapis is not just "a stone" since it is expressly stated to be composed *"de re animali, vegetabili et minerali,"* and to consist of body, soul, and spirit (*Rosarium philosophorum* [1550], 2, xii, p. 237). In my grandmother's notations of Jung's *Psychology and Alchemy,* I found a page from her journal with 103 references to lapis.

Laurinda S. Dixon finds Bosch's red cherries or red balls emblematic of lapis: "The most important among these playthings are the round red spheres which float in the water like giant beach balls and are balanced and eaten by the population of Bosch's Garden of Eden. According to medieval medical theory, the 'Elixir of Life,' the alchemical Lapis, was round and red." She goes on to say how the winged beings carrying the red balls upward are indicative of an ancient definition of Lapis as that which is "raised aloft to clouds, dwells in the air, is nourished in the river, and sleeps on the summits of mountains" Dixon, *Alchemical Imagery in Bosch's Garden of Delights,* p. 31.

p. 144 **There he is again, Joseph:** To learn more about Joseph Smith and the origins of Mormon thought in relationship to folklore in post-

Revolutionary America, even alchemy and astrology, I recommend D. Michael Quinn's fascinating book *Early Mormonism and the Magic World View*. Also, John L. Brooke, *The Refiner's Fire: The Making of Mormon Cosmology*, a brilliant account of the roots of Mormon theology and its ties to hermetic philosophy.

p. 145 **Mormon, Inc.**: This is a reference to the *Time* cover story "Mormons, Inc." on August 4, 1997, reported by S. C. Gwynne and Richard N. Ostling. Quoting a membership of 10 million and a $30 billion Church empire, the article reads, "given the scale of the current religious revival combined with the formidable organizational resources of the church, the Mormons could well emerge as the next great global tribe, fulfilling, as they believe, the prophecies of ancient and modern prophets" (*Time*, p. 57).

p. 145 **"Ralph Waldo Emerson . . . the religion-making imagination"**: Harold Bloom, *The American Religion*, pp. 96–97.

p. 145 **"are not equal in earthly things"**: To read more about Joseph Smith's notion of Utopia, see John Henry Evans, *Joseph Smith: An American Prophet*, pp. 234–247. "When the Mormon prophet, in his 'Views of the Policy and Government' of the nation, invited Texas, Mexico, Canada, and all the world to 'come, let us be brethren, one great family,' he meant exactly what he said. Not only was he, in that phrase, re-asserting an age-old longing for a world-union, where swords would be beaten to plowshares and spears to pruning-hooks, but he was expressing his own dream of the future, when 'Christ will reign personally on the earth.' Before he died he would give his people the bracing stimulus of a Golden Age to come, an Era of peace to which they might look forward, and for which they might work in hopeful anticipation" (p. 247).

Joseph Smith's Theory of Religious Knowledge can also be read in full in Evans's book (pp. 341–48).

p. 146 **"If any of ye lack wisdom"**: James 1: 5.

p. 146 **"Perhaps God having foreseen"**: Paul James Toscano, *The Sanctity of Dissent*, p. 34. This is a brave, forthright account of Toscano's views on the holy nature of dissent. He was one of the "September Six" excommunicated in 1993.

p. 146 **It was a salamander, true not counterfeit**: "Mark Hofmann's infamous 'White Salamander Letter,' purporting to be written by Martin Harris to William W. Phelps, introduced a powerful alchemical symbol as the bait in a fraud worthy of any of the great eighteenth-century conning men. In the forged letter, Hofmann changed a 'toad' Smith was reported to have found in the stone-lined pit on the Hill Cumorah to a salamander that 'transfigured' into a spirit that struck Smith and denied him the Golden Plates" (Brooke, *The Refiner's Fire*, p. 300). Hofmann is now in the Utah State Prison, serving a life sentence for murder. For more about the Hofmann counterfeiting saga and murders, see *Salamander: The Story of the Mormon Forgery Murders* by Linda Sillitoe and Allen Roberts (Salt Lake City: Signature Books, 1990).

"The salamander, in the high hermetic tradition, was an emblem of the philosopher's stone, the quintessence of perfection. In the words of Michael Maier, a seventeenth-century hermetic philosopher, 'As the Salamander lives by fire, so does the Stone.' " Brooke, *The Refiner's Fire*, pp. 300–301.

Let the eye of the Mormon Church dilate—open—widen—deepen. My faith resides in this strange, magical, divine, borrowed, creative, evolving religion, even as I encountered this salamander on a mountain lake trail in the Adirondacks.

The salamander appears throughout *El jardín de las delicias,* especially in Paradise and Hell.

p. 147   **I accept the Organic Trinity:** Early notations of natural history classified the world into these three divisions. T. A. Strand writes in her book *Tri-ism: The Theory of the Trinity in Nature, Man, and His Works:* "The earth produces mineral, vegetable and animal forms and these are all a part of each other. Minerals are compressed animal and vegetable matter. Vegetation requires minerals and animal wastes for proper growth. Man and other animal forms require mineral and vegetable substances to survive" (p. 14).

Is there a trinity of design at work in the universe? There is a trinity of color: red, yellow, blue; water as an essential requirement for life consists of two parts hydrogen and one part oxygen, a trinity of mineral composition; the atmosphere is made up of three gases: nitrogen, oxygen, and hydrogen; the earth is the third nearest planet to the sun, contributing from our vantage point to a celestial trinity: sun, moon, and stars; geologic time is defined through the Paleozoic, Mesozoic, and Cenozoic Eras; rocks are created through three processes: sedimentary, igneous, and metamorphic; and there are three stages to a butterfly's life: larva, pupa, and imago. "The theory of tri-ism," Strand notes, "is not a political and revolutionary doctrine. It is an attempt to define Democracy in natural terms" (p. 131).

p. 147   **hen to pan:** "The One, the All," as in the *Codex Marcianus* of the second century A.D. This is associated with the ouroboros, the serpent biting its own tail, a symbol of self-sufficiency.

p. 148 **"How can I attain an original . . . relationship to truth or God?"**: Bloom, *The American Religion,* p. 257. I have benefited greatly from Dr. Bloom's scholarship and thinking regarding Joseph Smith, and Mormonism in general. His definition of hermeticism as "the spirit of fusion between different esoteric traditions" helped me to see Smith's spiritual imagination more fully and to understand my own theology of experience. Bloom delivered a lecture at the University of Utah in the early 1990s where his ideas were met enthusiastically by a largely Mormon audience.

This most American of religions lives on a threshold between this world and Millennium (an undesignated one) and holds on hard both to this world and the next. Their premillenarianism breaks down the discursive dichotomy between man and God, and so helps inaugurate a new sense, at least in America, of fusion between our cosmos and the world to come.

Harold Bloom, Omens of Millennium, pp. 224–25.

p. 148 **"How can I open the traditions of religion to my own experience?"**: Ibid.

p. 150 **"and God converted the dryness of my soul"**: *The Life of Saint Teresa of Ávila by Herself,* pp. 33, 70, 158.

p. 151 **"I am now speaking of that rain"**: Ibid., p. 125.

p. 151 **"Who is this whom all my faculties thus obey?"**: Ibid., p. 81.

p. 152 **"All its joys came in little sips"**: Ibid., p. 155.

pp. 152 **Joseph Smith sealed to Santa Teresa**: Toscano, *The Sanctity of Dissent,* p. 88.

p. 152 **"the spiritual wife doctrine"**: "We are further told that there is an institution of 'Cloistered Saints,' which forms the highest order of the Mormon harem, and is composed of women, whether married or unmarried, as secret spiritual wives." Samuel M. Smucker, *The Religious, Social and Political History of the Mormons or Latter-day Saints,* p. 380.

In the early days of this dispensation, as part of the promised restitution of all things, the Lord revealed the principle of *plural marriage* to the Prophet (Joseph Smith). Later the Prophet and leading brethren were commanded to enter into the practice, which they did in all virtue and purity of heart despite the consequent animosity and prejudices of worldly people. After Brigham Young led the saints to the Salt Lake Valley, plural marriage was openly taught and practiced until the year 1890. At that time conditions were such that the Lord by revelation withdrew the command to continue the practice, and President Wilford Woodruff issued the Manifesto directing it cease. Obviously the holy practice will commence again after the Second Coming of the Son of Man and the ushering in of the Millennium.

McConkie, *Mormon Doctrine,* p. 578.

Polygamy is not recognized today by the Church of Jesus Christ of Latter-day Saints. Gordon B. Hinckley, *Teachings of Gordon B. Hinckley,* pp. 456–57.

p. 152 **"El corazón que mucho ama":** "The heart that loves greatly finds solace only from the one that opened it." I found this quotation written on an old bookmark in the town of Ávila.

p. 154 **"Este saber no sabiendo":** "I Came into the Unknown," *The Poems of Saint John of the Cross,* p. 61.

p. 157 **"For tears gain everything":** *The Life of Saint Teresa of Ávila by Herself,* p. 129.

p. 162 **Twelve original oils:** Mariko Umeoka Taki's show, titled *Encuentro con El Bosco,* was exhibited at the Círculo de Belles Artistes in Madrid, June 1997. The show was in collaboration with the Japanese Embassy in Spain.

p. 163 **In a short essay:** Jorge Luis Borges, "Pierre Menard, Author of the Quixote," *Ficciones,* pp. 45–55. Borges also writes, in "Parable of Cervantes and the Quixote," "For in the beginning of literature is the myth, and in the end as well." Borges, *Labyrinths,* p. 242.

p. 165 **"Men wander throughout the desert":** Mariko Umeoka Taki, *Encuentro con El Bosco,* p. 104.

p. 165 **"Let us now imagine":** Santa Teresa de Ávila, *The Interior Castle,* trans. E. Allison Peers, p. 29.

p. 166 **The Marriage Chamber:** Laurinda S. Dixon defines "the blue-black fountain of life in the upper part of the panel" as "The Marriage Chamber." She writes: "A commonly recurring alchemical image derived from the *Rosarium* is the scene of sexual conjunction, or 'coitus,' taking place in flower-topped flasks surrounded by a flowery marshy landscape. As if to emphasize the similarity of his image to the ones in the *Rosarium,* Bosch places a man and a woman engaged in erotic activity inside his flask, in imitation of the alchemical couple inside their cozy 'bridal chamber.'" Dixon, *Alchemical Imagery in Bosch's Garden of Delights,* pp. 28–29.

Wilhelm Fraenger writes: "In the secret language of alchemy the vessels used for distillation and sublimation are known as 'wedding chambers.'" Fraenger, *The Millennium of Hieronymus Bosch,* p. 118.

p. 166 **Coniunctio:** *Coniunctio* is the act of uniting opposites in alchemy. It can be interpreted psychologically as the end of the separation between body and spirit.

p. 167 **"illud magnum fluxum capitis et caudae":** Marie-Louise von Franz refers to this as "the generation of new light, a third thing born or generated in the *coniunctio.* It is a new light born in the darkness, and then all the neurotic symptoms and illness and weakness go; the new thing appears." Von Franz, *Alchemy: An Introduction to the Symbolism and the Psychology,* p. 174.

p. 167 $1 + 1 = 3$: This is the formula my grandmother Mimi, Kathryn Blackett Tempest, would always refer to whenever she was talking about personal transformation, be it in our waking lives or our dreams.

p. 167 **"The union of a spirit of love":** Honoré de Balzac

p. 168 **"Might they be the Divine Couple locked in an erotic embrace?":** Brooke, *The Refiner's Fire,* p. 302.

p. 168 **A circle is squared:** "The wholeness of the celestial circle and the squareness of the earth, uniting the four principles or elements or psychical qualities, express completeness and union. Thus the mandala has the dignity of a 'reconciling symbol.'" Carl G. Jung, *Psychology and Religion,* p. 96. Squaring the circle is symbolic of making the two sexes whole.

p. 168 **The Trinity is transformed:** Jung talks about the Trinity as being "an exclusively masculine character." He goes on to say: "The old philosophers of nature represented the Trinity, in as much as it was *'imaginata in natura,'* as the three *'spiritus'* . . . water, air, and fire. The fourth constituent . . . was the earth or the body. . . . In this way they added the feminine element to their physical Trinity, producing thereby the quaternity or the circulus quadratus. . . ." Ibid., p. 76.

p. 169 **tortoiseshell:** Vladimir Nabokov, the distinguished Russian writer and lepidopterist, was very interested in butterflies depicted in art. From his novel *Ada,* published in 1969, he writes, "Ada is marrying an outdoor man, but her mind is a closed museum, and she, and dear Lucette, once drew my attention, by a creepy coincidence, to certain details of that other triptych, that tremendous garden of tongue-in-cheek delights, circa 1500, and namely, to the butterflies in it—a Meadow Brown, female, in the center of the right panel, and a Tortoiseshell in the middle panel, placed there as if settled on a flower . . . actually the wrong side of the bug is shown, it should have been the underside, if seen, as it is, in profile, but Bosch evidently found a wing or two in the corner cobweb of his casement and showed the prettier upper surface in depicting his incorrectly folded insect. I mean I don't give a hoot for the esoteric meaning, for the myth behind the moth, for the masterpiece-baiter who makes Bosch express some bosh of his time, I'm allergic to allegory and am quite sure he was just enjoying himself by crossbreeding casual fancies just for the fun of the contour and color, and what we have to study, as I was telling your cousins, is the joy of the eye . . ." *Nabokov's Butterflies,* edited by Brian Boyd and Robert Michael Pyle, Beacon Press, Boston, 2000, p. 665.

p. 169 **"There are two ways of escaping":** H.D., *Notes on Thoughts and Vision,* p. 39.

p. 170 **"a God beyond God"?:** I remember attending a lecture by Joseph Campbell at Brigham Young University with my grandmother Mimi—it must have been in the early 1980s. He had said to the effect: "All of our old gods are dead, and the new have not yet been born." (Joseph Campbell, *The Inner Reaches of Outer Space,* p. 45. After the talk, I asked Dr. Campbell what he meant by that. He said simply, "I am talking about a God beyond God." It was a startling thought to a young Mormon woman.

p. 171 **"Resurrección es un acto que merece nuestra honra":** "Resurrection is an act worthy of our honor."

"Religious leaders in the Pacific Northwest are calling on their congregations to view the Columbia River watershed as 'sacramental commons.' They are asking the communities within the region to work together to restore these living waters." *Beyond the Impasse,* a documentary on the Columbia River salmon produced by the Umatilla Tribe, November 1999.

On March 8, 1999, a Salmon Vigil was held at St. Mark's Episcopal Cathedral in Seattle, Washington, an interfaith service of prayer and reflection for the preservation and well-being of the salmon, sponsored by the Partnership for Religion and the Environment. This prayer was recited together:

We have forgotten who we are.

We have forgotten who we are

We have alienated ourselves from the unfolding
of the cosmos
We have become estranged from the movements
of the earth
We have turned our backs on the cycles of life.

We have forgotten who we are.

We have sought only our own security
We have exploited simply for our own ends
We have distorted our knowledge
We have abused our power.

We have forgotten who we are.

Now the forests are dying
And the creatures are disappearing
And humans are despairing.

We have forgotten who we are.

We ask forgiveness
We ask for the gift of remembering
We ask for the strength to change.

We have forgotten who we are.

U.N. Environmental Sabbath Program.

And here is a letter written by an Oregon resident to the *New York Times* and printed on March 22, 1999:

To the Editor:

In the wake of the Government's decision to list nine types of salmon under the Endangered Species Act (new article, March 17), it should not be so difficult to realize that salmon are a valuable and irreplaceable part of our world.

Those of us who have lived near the home waters to which salmon return to spawn, eagerly await their arrival each year. By the time the salmon return home, they are battered and near death. Still, they are capable of bringing a certain grace to the waters where they have come to lay their eggs.

As someone who has watched the degradation of the landscape that is the salmon's and my habitat, I can say that salmon also bring hope, as survivors of a nearly impossible journey completed through strength, and persistence.

Sandra Lopez

p. 175 **"This wide open space is my home":** "Faith in Every Footstep," Pioneer Sesquicentennial Spectacular and Pioneer Rendezvous, Brigham Young University Cougar Stadium, Provo, Utah, 8:30 P.M., July 24, 1997.

p. 176 **"We thank thee, O God, for a prophet":** This Mormon hymn, with lyrics by William Fowler and music composed by Mrs. Norton, is sung brightly, with gratitude toward the Prophet of the Church of Jesus Christ of Latter-day Saints. *Hymns: The Church of Jesus Christ of Latter-day Saints,* p. 196.

p. 177 **"The Spirit of God like a fire is burning":** Both lyrics and music of this Mormon hymn were composed by William W. Phelps. Ibid., p. 213.

p. 178 **"Come, come, ye saints, no toil or labor fear":** The lyrics of this Mormon hymn are by William Clayton. The music is an Old English tune. Ibid., p. 13.

p. 179 **This is my story:** One of my oldest and dearest friends from childhood, Martha Young Moench, a descendant of Brigham Young, sent me the following poem by Vilate Raile, quoted in T. Edgar Lyon's article "Some Uncommon Aspects of the Mormon Migration," *Improvement Era,* September 1969, p. 33. It is an exquisite example of the history we share.

> *They cut desire into short lengths*
> *And fed it to the hungry fires of courage.*
> *Long after, when the flames had died,*
> *Molten gold gleamed in the ashes.*
> *They gathered it into bruised palms*
> *And handed it to their children*
> *And their children's children forever.*

p. 181 **"We have a divine mandate":** President Gordon B. Hinckley, Prophet of the Church of Jesus Christ of Latter-day Saints.

p. 181 **"There is more faith in honest doubt":** Kathryn Blackett Tempest's notebook, no date.

p. 182 **"All that faith creates or love desires":** Percy Bysshe Shelley, "Prometheus Unbound."

p. 183 **"return to here's hear":** James Joyce, *Finnegan's Wake.*

p. 183 **"I started this group":** Kelli Peterson, quoted in *Salt Lake Tribune,* April 1996.

p. 183　**"It is a divisive issue for the whole society":** Senator Charles Stewart, *Salt Lake Tribune,* February 3, 1996.

p. 184　**"From the Latin Natura is my birth":** Jeanette Winterson, *Art Objects: Essays on Ecstasy and Effrontery,* p. 150.

p. 184　**my community's fear of homosexuality:** "The Gay and Lesbian Political Action Committee of Utah on Friday urged the LDS Church to halt its backing for an initiative that would ban same-sex marriage in California. . . . In a recent letter from top California church leaders, 740,000 members of the The Church of Jesus Christ of Latter-day Saints in that state were encouraged to 'do all you can by donating your means and time to assure a successful vote' on a ballot initiative that would deem only heterosexual marriages as 'valid and recognized.' " "Gays Oppose LDS California Activism," *Salt Lake Tribune,* July 10, 1999.

I think back to El Bosco's image of the man bent over in the Garden; the words of Roland Barthes return to me: "The text is (should be) that uninhibited person who shows his behind to the *Political Father.*" Barthes, *The Pleasure of the Text,* p. 53.

p. 185　**"BYU Bans Four Rodin Works":** *Salt Lake Tribune,* October 27, 1997.

p. 186　**"I am woman, I make love":** Hélène Cixous, *Coming to Writing and Other Essays,* pp. 53–54.

p. 187　**The health of coral depends on both scientists and seers:** Coral reefs are dying throughout the world, due to pollution and the warming of our seas, possibly due to global warming. Traditionally, these concerns have belonged to the realm of scientists and conservationists. There is a recent "greening of religions" and an opening within conservation circles to discuss what an ethical stance on behalf of the Earth might be.

In 1949, Aldo Leopold wrote in *A Sand County Almanac:* "No important change in ethics was ever accomplished without an internal change in our intellectual emphasis, loyalties, affections, and convictions. The proof that conservation has not yet touched these foundations of conduct lies in the fact that philosophy and religion have not yet heard of it. In our attempt to make conservation easy, we have made it trivial" (p. 246). I believe this is changing.

p. 188　**"Man is able, if he wishes":** Federico García Lorca, *Poet in New York,* p. 161.

p. 188　**Mercury, Sulphur, and Salt:** These three powers or principles create the nature of metal or man, a Trinity of Being.

Mercury is known as quicksilver, also "maternal blood," and is associated with the moon and the feminine. It is aligned with the Tree of

Knowledge. "It is the living light which illumines every soul that has ever seen it" (Titus Burckhardt, *Alchemy,* p. 146). Mercury is also associated with the God of Alchemy, Hermes.

Sulphur is associated with the sun and the masculine principle. It is Hellfire and the burning fires of desire, the root of passion. It is aligned with Aries, the ram.

Salt is "the ash that remains over and serves to fix the 'volatile' spirit." It is associated with Venus, goddess of emotions and the heart. It is aligned with the Tree of Life.

The marriage of Sulphur and Quicksilver, Sun and Moon, Masculine and Feminine, is the central symbol of alchemy, known as "The Alchemical Marriage." Spiritual power merges with bodily existence. The cosmic duality ends.

Carl Jung writes in *Psychology and Alchemy:* "However remote alchemy may seem to us, we should not underestimate its cultural importance to the Middle Ages. Today is the child of the Middle Ages and it cannot disown its parents" (p. 311).

One of the clearest books on alchemy is Titus Burckhardt, *Alchemy: Science of the Cosmos, Science of the Soul.* It is considered a classic by many scholars.

p. 190 **"A sensation as pleasurable, tender, horrifying":** Clarice Lispector, *The Hour of the Star,* p. 83.

p. 192 ***El jardín de las delicias* is a fever:** James Joyce describes in *A Portrait of the Artist as a Young Man* what happens when art seizes our souls, "You see I use the word *arrest.*" I believe this was the "aesthetic arrest" I felt when I first saw Bosch's triptych. Stephen, Joyce's protagonist, says beauty ". . . awakens, or ought to awaken, or induces, or ought to induce, an esthetic stasis, an ideal pity or an ideal terror, a stasis called forth, prolonged and at last dissolved by what I call the rhythm of beauty. . . . You apprehend it as one thing. You see it as one whole. You apprehend its wholeness. That is *integritas.*" ("Portrait of the Artist as a Young Man," *The Portable James Joyce,* Penguin Books, New York, 1976, pp. 471–3, 480).

p. 192 **"Philip had begun to live inside his dream":** Garrett Mattingly, *The Armada* (Boston: Houghton Mifflin Co., 1959).

p. 194 **"I would recommend reading Charles de Tolnay's interpretation":** Charles de Tolnay, one of the most respected of Bosch scholars, writes: "With this unusual representation of the universe Bosch introduces into the history of art what is, so far as I know, the first pure landscape. Just as bold as Leonardo in his decision to depict our world without human figures, he differs from the Italian in that he was content to evoke the poetry of enigmatic nature. . . ." De Tolnay, *Hieronymus Bosch,* pp. 30–33.

p. 195 **"I think Fraenger was a lunatic":** Fraenger notes: *naturalia non sunt turpia,* "that which is natural is not shameful"; *sacra sunt naturalia,* "that which is natural is sacred."

p. 196 **"The entire Flemish school is based upon observation":** Peter S. Beagle writes: "But for me, as for most lay viewers, Bosch comes burning out of nowhere, masterless, companionless, slashing like a demon's talon across the rich, placid fleshiness of Flemish art. How could a whirlwind have roots?" Beagle, *The Garden of Earthly Delights,* p. 24.

p. 198 **"There are more than 14,000 volumes here":** Geoffrey Parker, *Philip II,* p. 46.

p. 199 **"live inside the Late Middle Ages":** I recommend two books on this period, *The Waning of the Middle Ages,* by Johan Huizinga, and *A World Lit Only by Fire: The Medieval Mind on the Renaissance Portrait of an Age,* by William Manchester.

p. 200 **"I began to speak to him":** Henry Kamen, *Philip of Spain,* p. 222.

p. 201 **"We must retrace the speaking thread":** Julia Kristeva, *Nations Without Nationalism,* p. 80.

p. 201 **"I cannot think where this will stop":** Hieronymus Bosch freed art from the control of the Counter-Reformation by creating new imagery. Up until that time, paintings had represented reality. With the discovery of the New World, the borderline between fiction and reality opened. Bosch invented new creatures just as new creatures were being discovered in the Americas. He then extended this hybridization of thought and image to religion. Was he a heretic? No and yes. Bosch could get away with his view of Christianity because it was imagined, not real. He chose complete freedom because he had taken poetic license. Imagination can never be controlled, even by the Spanish Inquisition. Bosch creates a window from the Inquisition to the Reformation to the Renaissance. These ideas were explored by the German art scholar Hans Belting at a lecture at the Prado Museum entitled "El jardín de las delicias de El Bosco," on October 28, 1997. Barbara Woods, an art historian, further illuminated these ideas for me in a conversation in Madrid.

p. 203 **"Obra anónima de ciencia hermética":** "Anonymous work of hermetic science, especially talismanic magic and alchemy."

p. 203 **a small Book of Hours:** *The Master of Mary of Burgundy: A Book of Hours* (Oxford: The Bodleian Library; New York: George Braziller, 1970).

p. 206   **the "Council of Blood":** For two excellent sources on the Spanish Inquisition, see Henry Kamen, *The Spanish Inquisition: A Historical Revision;* B. Netanyahu, *The Origins of the Inquisition in Fifteenth-Century Spain.*

p. 209   **"Through the stained glass":** Antonio Machado, "Notes," *Thirty Spanish Poems of Love and Exile,* trans. Kenneth Rexroth, p. 28.

p. 210   **"He'll overtake you":** I was sent the following quotation by a friend in the mail: "Hieronymus Bosch is an orb weaver, a spider who hides in the corner of his web—anyone whose eyes stick to his triptych is forever caught poisoned—wrapped up in silk and slowly sucked into the body of Bosch." *Verdad.*

p. 212   **blood knowledge:** Peter Beagle calls Bosch's triptych full of "underground learning." Beagle, *The Garden of Earthly Delights,* p. 26.

p. 213   **"Firm on our atoll, desert":** Brewster Ghiselin, "Fragments of a Dialogue (dedicated to Eugene England)," *Flame,* p. 21.

p. 214   **I seek the Council of the Kingfisher:** The English alchemist George Ripley (1415–1490) writes: "The philosophers tell the inquirer that birds and fishes bring us the lapis. . . . *Jesus saith, (Ye ask? Who are those that draw us to the kingdom . . . the fowls of the air, and all beasts that are under the earth or upon the earth, and the fishes of the sea? . . .)*" Quoted in Carl G. Jung, *Psychology and Alchemy,* pp. 323–24.

p. 214   **Women Surrounded By a Flight of Birds at Night:** The title of a painting by Joan Miró. Miró believed art was created through a shock, and he was greatly influenced by Hieronymus Bosch. See Gerta Moray, "Miró, Bosch and Fantasy Painting," *Burlington Magazine* 113 (1971): 387–91. Comparisons have been made between Miró's *The Tilled Field* and the left wing of *El jardín de las delicias.* Bosch influences have also been noted in *The Catalan Landscape* by Miró. Miró's repeated motifs of ladders, fountains, and the observing eye have also been linked to Bosch's iconography. The painter's perspective from an aerial view has been seen as another of Bosch's influences on Miró.

Bosch became a hero of the Surrealists, Salvador Dali, among them. Some claimed to see the profile of the Devil in the orange cliffs of the left panel of *El jardín de las delicias,* to the right of the pink fountain. (I think it looks more like the profile of Dali himself.)

Dali is known to have taken the poet García Lorca to the Prado, where they would contemplate and discuss Bosch's masterpieces, particularly the Garden of Earthly Delights. During this period, García Lorca wrote a long poem—never completed—titled *"En el bosque de las toronjas de luna"*—"In the

Forest of the Lunar Grapefruits." He writes, "My garden is the garden of possibilities, the garden of what is not, but could (and at times should) have been,
the garden of theories that passed invisibly by and children who have not
been born. Each word in the poem was a butterfly." Federico García Lorca,
Collected Poems (New York: Farrar, Straus, & Giroux, 1991), pp. 811–12.

The Surrealist painter Remedios Varo (1908–1963), who grew up in
Spain and visited the Prado often, was deeply taken by Bosch's encyclopedic
imagination. Her paintings, like El Bosco's, create a hybrid world of magic
and wonder, using birds and strange vessels as focal points of an earthly
strangeness. Janet A. Kaplan, *Unexpected Journeys: The Art and Life of Remedios
Varo,* p. 193.

p. 214 **The Memory of Birds in Times of Revolution:** The title of a
book by Breyten Breytenbach, the South African poet.

In "An Open Letter to Nelson Mandela, 1991," Breytenbach writes, *"I'd
like you to know that my dissent, even when it is too harsh or unfair, is always meant as a
manifestation of critical loyalty."*

I met Breytenbach in Mexico City in January 1994, as part of El Grupo
de Cien. During a particular conversation on the bus he said to me, *"You
Americans, you have mastered the art of living with the unacceptable."*

p. 214 **"Why should we care what birds may want from us?":** A
line from David Wagoner's poem "The Garden of Earthly Delights (after
the painting by Hieronymus Bosch)," *Through the Forest: New and Selected
Poems* (New York: Atlantic Monthly Press, 1987), p. 203.

p. 215 **"It is no accident women take after birds":** These are the
words of Helénè Cixous, translated by Nancy Kline, in an introduction to
The Tongue Snatchers by Claudine Herrmann, p. ix. Herrmann's book has been
important for me in inspiring courage to speak in my own voice within a
patriarchal society, in helping me to recognize that indeed men and women
speak different languages. She has made me feel less crazy in the world. She
writes: "It strikes me as particularly enriching for the two sexes to try to
learn each other's language, instead of declaring one official language. The
failure of love . . . most often springs from a misunderstanding. Words,
like acts, mean different things to different people, and no one bothers to
explain what seems obvious" (p. 136).

And again, in her biting style: "If feminine thinking has always been
eclipsed, every aspect of virile thinking is emblazoned across the face of the
earth. It is inscribed in things, forms, art, thought, different social systems,
with the unflagging persistence that characterizes children who are sure

of their mother's approval. And isn't that woman's primary function: to approve?" (p. 41).

Finally, in a chapter called "Love and Madness," I love this: "A passionate woman tolerates nothing. She represents a threat to the unimpeded flow of middle-class life. Better to obtain a woman who does not present this major difficulty, who takes you as you are, who gives you what you ask and doesn't make a fuss about the rest" (p. 76).

p. 217 **"It distracts you, history":** David St. John, "River," *Hush* (Baltimore: Johns Hopkins University Press, 1985), p. 48.

p. 220 **"We are not giving you the reproduction":** Umberto Eco, *Travels in Hyperreality,* p. 19. Eco speaks of "the Absolute Fake" that is "the offspring of the unhappy awareness of a present without depth." And in the essay "The Return of the Middle Ages," he writes: "We are dreaming the Middle Ages. . . . The Middle Ages are the root of all our contemporary 'hot' problems, and it is not surprising that we go back to that period every time we ask ourselves about our origin" (p. 65).

p. 220 **the Ballona Wetlands are still here:** This is one of the great stories of urban conservation at the end of the twentieth century, showing how a few impassioned individuals can mobilize community support and intelligently fight large corporate interests. Under the leadership of Marcia Hanscom, the Ballona Wetlands Land Trust has successfully led a public relations campaign against the development of Playa Vista and DreamWorks' involvement in this project, educating the Los Angeles community as well as local politicians to come to the aid of these endangered coastal wetlands.

California Assembly Speaker Antonio Villaraigosa successfully plugged $25 million for acquisition of the wetlands into a $2 billion parks bill that passed both the state senate and the assembly on September 3, 1999. The bill, AB 18, is expected to be signed by Governor Davis and will then be placed on the state ballot in March 2000. With this first step taken by the Speaker, the Ballona Wetlands Land Trust will continue their efforts to encourage U.S. Senators Barbara Boxer and Dianne Feinstein to find the matching funds necessary to complete the public purchase of Ballona, around one thousand acres.

On July 1, 1999, DreamWorks announced its decision to abandon its involvement in the proposed Playa Vista project. The Playa Vista developers had experienced enormous public opposition to their plans to build on and around the last large coastal wetlands in the Los Angeles river basin, and DreamWorks became a target of that opposition in 1995, when it announced its intent to be Playa Vista's anchor tenant. Since that time, Steven Spielberg received over 15,000 postcards, letters, and e-mails from concerned citizens asking him to reconsider his decision to build at Ballona. Even loyal employees of DreamWorks quit over what they considered an issue of conscience. There have been hunger strikes, a boycott of Spielberg's films, production of a PBS documentary called "The Last Stand," a series of community town hall meetings, street theater, numerous rallies and protests, and civil disobedience actions, as well as legal actions taken, all in opposition to DreamWorks' involvement.

p. 221 **I see all the figures below the hedge as mycelium:** It has been reported that scientists who have studied *El jardín de las delicias* have found at least 22 species of slime molds represented in the painting. See article "Hunting Slime Molds" by Adele Conover, *Smithsonian,* March 2001.

p. 221 **"los varios efectos del amor":** "Various Effects of Love," poem by Lope de Vega, a sixteenth-century Spanish writer whose love of God and love of women seemed often in conflict. He was an ordained priest. My thanks to Toby Talbot for this translation:

To be faint-hearted, daring, enraged,
brusque, tender, giving, restrained,
vigorous, mortal, dead, alive,
loyal, disloyal, cowardly, confident. . . .

To believe that heaven can inhabit hell;
to yield life and soul to disillusion;
that is love; whoever has tasted it knows.

p. 222 **I partake of its earthy flesh:** There are those who say Hieronymus Bosch was eating hallucinogenic mushrooms while he was painting *El jardín de las delicias.* This was an especially popular theory during the 1960s, when the poster of the Garden of Earthly Delights served as a popular background for contemplation and meditation while "under the influence."

For a fascinating account of mushrooms and their relationship to alchemy, see William Scott Shelley, *The Elixir: An Alchemical Study of the Ergot Mushrooms* (Notre Dame, Ind.: Cross Roads Books, 1995).

p. 222 **Hieronymus Bosch meets me at every turn:** El Bosco. *El bosque,* the forest. There is a drawing by Bosch titled *The Wood That Sees and Hears,* a picture puzzle that illustrates the Flemish proverb *"The field has eyes, the woods have ears. I will see, be silent, and hear."* It portrays a gnarled dead tree with an owl inside its hollow trunk, similar to the owl inside the pink fountain in Paradise. Perched on the branches are three magpies, who are scolding the owl. The owl appears safe from their mobbing and mockery. Inside the forest of living trees behind the dead tree are a pair of ears. In the meadow in the foreground are seven eyes, open, staring in different directions.

In the library of the Museo del Prado, I stare at the drawing for a long time. What I see is the fierce attention of Hieronymus Bosch. Just as the forest sees and hears, so El Bosco sees and hears. Like the owl who inhabits the dark, even the dark triangular hollow of this tree, El Bosco has developed night vision and observes what the rest of us cannot see.

In another look, I discover a fawn nestled in the exposed roots of the tree. It is almost as though the eyes in the meadow in front of the deer are watching out for its safety.

Owl and deer. The wise one vulnerable to the mockings of the magpies. The artist's plight. He must protect himself, and thereby finds solace in nature, whose perception and watchfulness exceed his own.

Could it be that the way the artist exorcises his or her demons is to paint them, write them? What we expose, we protect. Could it be that by daring to present his vision of the world at the end of the Late Middle Ages, El Bosco protected it? The Church could not kill his imagination, his imagination housed in his body. By giving his viewers enough details to trust, images they were familiar with, he earned the freedom to create new creatures to stretch their belief in what was possible. By giving them just enough of the religious story and iconography to make them feel comfortable, he could then subvert it, turn the accustomed truth upside down, and let them stand on their heads and see the world differently.

p. 222 **a spore print dropped from its gills:** To make a spore print, carefully place the cap of a fresh mushroom on two-tone paper. Place a drop of water on top and cover with a glass bowl. Leave them overnight, and then gently lift off the glass and cap to reveal the spores. Note the colors for identification.

p. 223 **a small circle on their forehead:** The olive oil is consecrated by a special prayer given by a member of the Melchizedek Priesthood for the anointing of the sick in "the household of faith."

p. 223 **Women: Olive Oil May Be an Ally vs. Breast Cancer:** I recommend these citations about the preventive qualities of olive oil in relationship to breast cancer: "Comparison of Monounsaturated Fatty Acids and Carbohydrates," *New England Journal of Medicine* 314, no. 12 (March

1986): 745–48; and "Consumption of Olive Oil and Specific Food Groups in Relation to Breast Cancer Risk in Greece," *Journal of the National Cancer Institute* 87 (January 18, 1995): 110–16.

p. 225   **Tierras Cruzadas:** Paige DeShong has edited an exquisite little book, *Tierra Cruzada,* with Gilberto Lucero, a collaboration between poetry and photography that celebrates *descansos.*

p. 227   **a heart turned upward like a flame:** The image of an inverted flaming heart was drawn by the mystic Jakob Boehme, symbolizing religious devotion and transcendence. Boeme, *XL Questions concerning the Soule, Propounded by Dr. Balthasar Walter. And answered by Jacob Behmen,* trans. John Sparrow (London, 1665).

p. 228   **"The Sagrada Familia was conceived as a great mystical poem":** A phrase used by a guide at the cathedral in Barcelona.

p. 228   **The spirit of Gaudí is alive, ongoing:** The current architect is now Jordi Bonet.

p. 229   **imaginative genius:** For a very different perspective on the Sagrada Familia, see Robert Hughes, *Barcelona,* particularly chap. 8, "The Hermit in the Cave of Making," pp. 464–541. He writes: "on esthetic grounds, one cannot contemplate the progress of this work without a sinking heart. From the costume-jewelry finials of the Façade of the Passion to the sculptures by Josep Subirachs, almost everything that has been added to it in the seventies and eighties is rampant kitsch. . . . It could have been done by the Mormons, not Catholics" (p. 539).

RESTORATION

p. 239   **I return to the Prado, this time with my father:** January 1998.

p. 242   **Obedience:** I received a letter from Professor Rita Pougiales of Evergreen College, May 3, 1999, wherein she expanded my understanding of obedience:

Ivan Illich writes, in "The Educational Enterprise in the Light of the Gospel," that obedience can be another word for trust, not trust in an institutional truth, but trust in an instinctual one.

Modern English has lost the word for this kind of trust. The biblical word for it is obedience. Obedience in the biblical sense means unobstructed listening, unconditional readiness to hear, untrammeled disposition to be surprised by the Other's word. . . . Obedience has nothing to do with what we call obedience today, something which always implies submission, and ever so faintly connotes the relationship between ourselves and our dogs. When I submit my head, my mind, my body, I come to be below the other. When I listen unconditionally, respectfully, courageously with the readiness to take in the other as a radical surprise, I do something else. I bow, bend over towards the total otherness of someone. But I renounce searching for bridges between the other and me, recognizing that a gulf separates us. Leaning into this chasm makes me aware of the depth of my loneliness, and able to bear it in the light of the substantial likeness between the other and myself. All that reaches me is the other in his word, which I accept on faith. But, by the strength of this word, I now can trust myself to walk on the surface without being engulfed by institutional power.

p. 243   **"the heart of the religious experience":** Robert Johnson, *Owning Your Own Shadow* (New York: HarperCollins, 1993), p. 90.

p. 244   **"The Age of the Holy Ghost has begun":** Fraenger, *Hieronymus Bosch,* p. 107. This is an extension of the thinking of Hendrik Niclaes (1502–1581), who founded a *huis der liefde,* or "house of love," where he believed the Age of the Father represented hope; the Age of the Son represented faith, and the Age of the Holy Ghost heralded love.

p. 244   **So this is how we dream the world:** Altamira is located just outside the quaint medieval town of Santillana del Mar. It is harder and harder to gain access to the caves; reservations now may exceed a year in advance, with the understanding that only twenty-five individuals are allowed into the cave per day. Many speculate Altamira's closing is inevitable following the path of Lascaux in France.

These caves were first documented in the 1870s by the prehistory pioneer Marcelino S. De Sautuala, from Santander several kilometers east. He returned in 1879 with his nine-year-old daughter, María, who upon discovery of the remarkable cave paintings said, *"Mira, Papá, ¡bueyes!*—Look, Papa, oxen!"

Carved animals on the cave walls have been dated as far back as 25,000 years. If the drawings are black, they date from 20,000 years ago, and if you see three colors, black, red, and yellow, the date stands around 10,000 years.

There are extraordinary caves throughout northern Spain with remarkable drawings that are less well known than Altamira's, but equally inspiring.

p. 255   **a friend helps me translate:** While staying in Madrid, I was fortunate to be able to rent a room from a remarkable and gracious woman,

Gillian Watling Ceballos, who writes for the Spanish magazine *Guidepost*. She provided enormous help in understanding Spanish culture. Her daughter, Leonor Watling Ceballos, was most helpful in translating long, complicated documents, particularly about art history, restoration, and the history of the Museo del Prado.

By coincidence, Elí, who is an actress, was called to audition for a film titled *La hora de los valientes,* directed by Antonio Mercero. It is about a security guard in the Prado during the Spanish Civil War who, as the museum is being bombed, decides at the last minute to rescue a painting, a self-portrait of Goya, to protect it from harm. Elí was reading for the role of his wife, who must help him hide the painting. Elí got the part. She said that after all she had been reading about the conservator Seisdedos's love of El Bosco and Fra Angelico, and about how art can heal the soul, her heart was opened to a deeper level of feeling. The film met with great success in Spain, and Leonor Watling won the prestigious San Jordi Award in 1999 for her performance.

There is another extraordinary story to be told that is not fiction. During the Spanish Civil War, many individuals associated with the Comite Internacional (an international committee of museum curators, art historians, etc.) were concerned about the masterpieces in the Prado Museum as Madrid was being bombed by General Franco and his army. A plan was set into motion to remove 525 paintings from the Prado and send them to Valencia. Under cover of darkness, seventy-one trucks were employed to dispatch these priceless works of art.

F. J. Sánchez Canton writes, "Between 1931 and 1936, I had the honour and the heavy responsibility of duties as both deputy director and acting director of the Prado." (Afterwards the Spanish government appointed Pablo Picasso as director of the Prado.)

Sánchez Canton explains: "At the beginning of November 1936, orders were received to forward the works of art to Valencia. I was most reluctant to do so. Transport and the possibility of eventual evacuation abroad would certainly expose these items to more risk than retaining them in Madrid. . . . I therefore proceeded as slowly as possible in giving instructions for the dispatch of the pictures, hoping that a cessation of the siege of the capital would soon render it unnecessary to face the hazards of removal. Five hundred and twenty-five paintings were eventually sent, together with some carefully selected Goya drawings and the jewels of the 'Dauphin's Treasure.' "

From the Prado, the paintings were safely transported to Valencia, where they stayed at Torres de Serrano until April 1938. At that time the paintings were moved to Figueras, where they were stored in a silver-mine shaft at La Vajol, some 100 meters deep. They stayed there until February 1939, when they were moved north through Cataluña to the French frontier under dangerous circumstances—faulty vehicles, a huge human exodus, mountainous terrain, bombings—and on to Switzerland, where they were met at the train station at Ceret on February 12, 1939. When they reached Geneva on February 14, the paintings were greeted as ambassadors against fascism and prepared for an extraordinary exhibition at the Palacio de las Naciones de Ginebra at the Geneva Expo '39 from June to August 1939.

In the bowels of the Prado, I found a copy of the exhibition catalog, *Ville de Génève, Les Chefs-d'oeuvre du Musée du Prado, Exposition, Musée d'art et d'Histoire—Génève, Juin–Aout, 1939*. I wanted to see if *El jardín de las delicias* had made this perilous journey as one of the 525 refugee paintings. As I ran my finger down the inventory of paintings, it read like a Who's Who in the annals of world art: thirty-four canvases by Velázquez, including *Las Meninas;* thirty-eight paintings by Goya, *Shootings of May 3, 1808* among them; twenty-five paintings by El Greco; paintings by Morales, Murillo, Ribera, Rubens, Zurbarán, Tintoretto; Titian, Van der Wyden, Dürer, and Brueghel, among others. Finally on the list I located El Bosco: *The Haywain, The Adoration of the Magi,* and *The Temptation of Saint Anthony.*

El jardín de las delicias was not among the travelers. Having just been restored by Seisdedos, the triptych remained safe inside the Prado. Four centuries later, Philip II was still watching over "The Strawberry."

The Geneva exhibition closed early as the international atmosphere darkened. The paintings were returned to Madrid by train, carried "on roundabout routes, with all lights in the coaches extinguished."

On July 7, 1939, the Prado reopened. It had been closed since August 30, 1936. Ironically, General Franco, now in power, signed the paintings back into the custody of Spain.

For detailed accounts, see "The Revolution of 1936" in Sánchez Canton's history *The Prado* (London: Thames & Hudson, 1959); and *El Museo del Prado y la Guerra Civil,* by Arturo Colorado Castellary (Madrid: Museo del Prado, 1991).

My account was amplified by talking to various curators in the Prado who did not wish to be identified. Many of the old-timers are still unhappy that the paintings were removed at such risk. For details I may have missed in translation and for any errors, I apologize.

p. 262 **apple orchards were planted by latter-day pioneers:** When we moved into this valley, I was met by two women, Hertha Wakefield and Joanna Dalton. They brought me apples. Joanna, a Mormon woman, moved here over twenty years ago with her husband and family. She knows my mother's family from Provo, Utah, and has raised eighteen children. "Wherever I move, I plant an apple orchard." This autumn she canned one thousand quarts of apples.

"May I see your hands?" I asked.

I recognized them as the pioneering hands of my ancestors.

p. 262 **Nine months later, I return to Madrid:** January 1999. What I note is the placental quality of the vessels; restoration has revived the blood of the triptych. I also notice a small red bar where a pair of cherries once rested below the Red Coral Tent. When I see Rocío Dávila, she says that they learned many things through the restoration. The cherries were originally a broken piece of red coral. The coral has been restored.

Rocío also says that some of the gestures were incorrect, a result of extreme deterioration where past restorers did the best they could to reinstate El Bosco's intention. For example, where the arms of a woman might have been folded, they are now raised; where hands were hidden, they now rest on top of the blue shell where a woman leans toward a man who feeds her a cherry. Restoration is a change in perception. I can now see bodies submerged, amphibious, in the waters of *El jardín de las delicias.*

p. 264 **We can have visions:** In an essay entitled "A Poet's View," Denise Levertov calls the imagination "the chief of human faculties. It must be therefore by the exercise of that faculty that one moves toward faith, and possibly by its failure that one rejects it as delusion. . . . Where Wallace Stevens says, 'God and the imagination are one,' I would say the imagination, which synergizes intellect, emotion and instinct, is the perceptive organ through which it is possible, though not inevitable, to experience God." ("Denise Levertov: A Memoir and Appreciation," Murray Bodo, *Image—A Journal of the Arts & Religion,* Summer 2000, Number 27, p. 88).

p. 264 **"We believe all things":** Joseph Smith, *The Thirteenth Article of Faith.* The passage reads in full: "We believe in being honest, true, chaste, benevolent, virtuous, and in doing good to all men; indeed, we may say that we follow the admonition of Paul—We believe all things, we hope all things, we have endured many things, and hope to be able to endure all things. If there is anything virtuous, lovely, or of good report or praiseworthy, we seek after these things."

p. 265 **What is the wound?:** James Hillman writes, "Below the ecological crisis lies the deeper crisis of love, that our love has left the world." Hillman, "The Practice of Beauty," *Uncontrollable Beauty* (New York: Allworth Press, 1998), p. 264. To heal "the wound" requires reflection, a return of our love, a restoration of our affection for the world we are a part of.

p. 266 **I am the traveler returning home:** The complete triptych *El jardín de las delicias* was restored in full by the Dávila sisters and returned in September 1999 to the Museo del Prado, where it now hangs. See *La Razón* 2, no. 307 (September 10, 1999).

Afterword: I had to return to Madrid one last time to see *El jardín de las delicias* restored in its entirety.

From my journal:

7 marzo 2000

El jardín de las delicias has moved. No longer in Gallery LVIIa, it now resides in Gallery LVIa. Restored, completely restored, all three panels are rejoined. The triptych is no longer hanging, suspended, but resting, supported on a solid base where it can now be seen as the altarpiece that it is, vibrant and alive. Somehow, it feels grander, calmer, more secure, having been released from the weight of time, the water damage and grime. There is a new clarity. Details lost, now emerge. Translucent. Transcendent. The Davila sisters have worked their magic by listening to what the painting desired.

Today, alone in the Prado, I stand before this triptych that has held me captive for seven years and feel a peace not known to me before. Integration: Paradise. Hell. Earthly Delights. All states are vibrating simultaneously within me, within us, anyone who dares to enter the terrifying, tantalizing, heart-throbbing landscape of Hieronymus Bosch.

El jardín de las delicias has moved. I have moved. We are transformed and transported through love.

I see the woman with wings lifted by a cherry, the image that called to me when I first saw the triptych. Now, my eye catches something new, something I have not seen before, there—on top of the cherry stands a white egret, revealed through restoration.

In my life and Art I feel a pilgrim.

—Cecil Collins

Adler, Gerhard. *The Living Symbol: A Case Study in the Process of Individuation.* New York: Pantheon Books, 1961.

Auden, W. H. *The Prolific and the Devourer.* Hopewell, N.J.: Ecco Press, 1976.

Bachelard, Gaston. *The Poetics of Reverie.* Boston: Beacon Press, 1971.

————. *The Poetics of Space.* Boston: Beacon Press, 1958.

————. *The Psychoanalysis of Fire.* Boston: Beacon Press, 1964.

Baldass, Ludwig von. *Hieronymus Bosch.* Vienna: A. Schroll & Co., 1943.

Barthes, Roland. *The Pleasure of the Text.* Translated by Richard Miller. New York: Hill & Wang, 1975.

Bataille, Georges. *Eroticism: Death and Sensuality.* Translated by Mary Dalwood. San Francisco: City Lights Books, 1986.

————. The *Impossible.* Translated by Robert Hurley. San Francisco: City Lights Books, 1991.

————. *Story of the Eye.* Translated by Joachim Neugroschel. San Francisco: City Lights Books, 1967.

————. *Theory of Religion.* Translated by Robert Hurley. New York: Zone Books, 1992.

Baudelaire, Charles. *The Flowers of Evil and Paris Spleen.* Translated by William H. Crosby. Brockport, N.Y.: BOA Editions, 1991.

Baudrillard, Jean. *The Transparency of Evil: Essays on Extreme Phenomena.* London: Verso, 1993.

Bax, Dirk. *Hieronymus Bosch: His Picture-writing Deciphered.* Rotterdam: Abner Scram, 1979.

————. *Hieronymus Bosch and Lucas Cranach: Two Last Judgment Triptychs: Description and Exposition.* Amsterdam: North-Holland Publishing Co., 1983.

Beagle, Peter S. *The Garden of Earthly Delights.* New York: Viking Press, 1982.

Beckley, Bill, and David Shapiro, eds. *Uncontrollable Beauty: Toward a New Aesthetics.* New York: Ashworth Press, 1998.

Beegel, Susan F. *Hemingway's Neglected Short Fiction.* Cambridge: Cambridge University Press, 1998.

Benesch, Otto. "Hieronymus Bosch and the Thinking of the Late Middle Ages," *Konsthistorisk Tidskrift* 26 (1957): 21ff.

Bercovitch, Sacvan. *The Puritan Origins of the American Self.* New Haven: Yale University Press, 1975.

Berger, John. *And Our Faces, My Heart, Brief as Photos.* New York: Vintage International, 1984.

———. *Art and Revolution.* New York: Vintage Books, 1997.

———. *Photocopies: Stories.* New York: Pantheon Books, 1996.

———. *The Sense of Sight.* New York: Vintage Books, 1985.

———. *Ways of Seeing.* London: Penguin Books, 1972.

Bergera, Gary James, ed. *Line Upon Line: Essays on Mormon Doctrine.* Salt Lake City: Signature Books, 1989.

Bergman, Madeleine. *Hieronymus Bosch and Alchemy: A Study of the St. Anthony Triptych.* Stockholm: Almqvist and Wiksell International, 1979.

Bertine, Eleanor. *Close Relationships: Family, Friendship, Marriage.* Toronto: Inner City Books, 1992.

Blake, William. *Songs of Innocence and of Experience.* New York: Orion Press, 1967.

Blanch, Santiago Alcolea. *The Prado.* New York: Harry N. Abrams, 1991.

Blinkoff, Jodi. *The Avila of Saint Teresa: Religious Reform in a Sixteenth-Century City.* Ithaca, N.Y.: Cornell University Press, 1989.

Bloom, Harold. *The American Religion: The Emergence of the Post-Christian Nation.* New York: Simon & Schuster, 1992.

———. *Omens of Millennium.* New York: Riverhead Books, 1996.

Bonnefoy, Yves. *The Lure and the Truth of Painting: Selected Essays on Art.* Edited by Richard Stamelman. Chicago: University of Chicago Press, 1973.

Borges, Jorge Luis. *Ficciones.* Edited by Anthony Kerrigan. New York: Grove Press, 1962.

———. *Labyrinths: Selected Stories and Other Writings.* Edited by Donald A. Yates and James E. Irby. New York: Modern Library, 1983.

Bosch, Hieronymus. *The Complete Drawings of Hieronymus Bosch.* London: Academy Editions, 1973.

Bosing, Walter. *The Complete Paintings: Bosch.* London: Benedict Taschen, 1994.

Breytenbach, Breyten. *The Memory of Birds in Times of Revolution.* New York: Harcourt, Brace & Co., 1996.

Brodsky, Joseph. *Watermark.* New York: Noonday Press, 1992.

Brooke, John L. *The Refiner's Fire: The Making of Mormon Cosmology, 1644–1944.* Cambridge: Cambridge University Press, 1996.

Brown, Norman O. *Love's Body.* Berkeley: University of California Press, 1966.

Bryant, Barry. *The Wheel of Time.* San Francisco: HarperSanFrancisco, 1992.

Burkhardt, Titus. *Alchemy: Science of the Cosmos, Science of the Soul.* London: Stuart & Watkins, 1967.

Burroughs, William S. *My Education: A Book of Dreams.* New York: Viking Press, 1995.

Cahan, Claudia Lyn, and Catherine Reilly. *Bosch, Brueghel, and the Northern Renaissance.* New York: Avenel Books, 1979.

Calvino, Italo. *Six Memos for the Next Millennium.* Cambridge: Harvard University Press, 1988.

Campbell, Joseph. *The Inner Reaches of Outer Space: Metaphor as Myth and Religion.* New York: Alfred von der Marck Editions, 1986.

Canaday, John. *Metropolitan Seminars in Art.* New York: Metropolitan Museum of Art, 1959.

Carandel, Josep Maria. *El Temple de la Sagrada Familia: Barcelona.* Sant Lluís: Triangle Postals, 1997.

Carotenuto, Aldo. *Eros and Pathos: Shades of Love and Suffering.* Toronto: Inner City Books, 1989.

Carr, Dawson W., and Mark Leonard. *Looking at Paintings: A Guide to Technical Terms.* Malibu, Calif.: J. Paul Getty Museum, 1992.

Carr-Gomm, Sarah. *The Dictionary of Symbols in Western Art.* New York: Facts on File, 1995.

Carson, Anne. *Plainwater.* New York. Alfred A. Knopf, 1995.

Cela, Camilo José. *Journey to the Alcarria.* Translated by Frances M. Lopez-Morillas. Cambridge: Granta Books, 1990.

Checa, Fernando. *Felipe II: Mecenas de las Artes.* Madrid: Nerea, 1992.

Cixous, Helene. *Coming to Writing and Other Essays.* Edited by Deborah Jensen. Cambridge: Harvard University Press, 1991.

———. *Newly Born Woman.* Minneapolis: University of Minnesota Press, 1975.

———. *Rootprints: Memory and Life Writing.* London: Routledge, 1997.

———. *Three Steps of the Ladder of Writing.* New York: Columbia University Press, 1993.

Clark, Kenneth. *What Is a Masterpiece?* New York: Thames & Hudson, 1979.

Collings, Matthew. *Blimey! From Bohemia to Britpop: The London Artworld from Francis Bacon to Damien Hirst.* Cambridge: 21 Publishing, 1997.

Colorado-Castellary, Arturo. *El Museo del Prado y la Guerra Civil.* Madrid: Museo del Prado, 1991.

Comley, Nancy R., and Robert Scholes. *Hemingway's Genders.* New Haven: Yale University Press, 1994.

Cronon, William, ed. *Uncommon Ground: Toward Reinventing Nature.* New York: W. W. Norton & Co., 1995.

Crosby, Alfred W. *Ecological Imperialism: The Biological Expansion of Europe 900–1900.* Cambridge: Cambridge University Press, 1986.

Crow, John A. *Spain: The Root and the Flower: An Interpretation of Spain and the Spanish People.* Berkeley: University of California Press, 1963.

Dante Alighieri. *The Divine Comedy; or, Vision of Hell, Purgatory, and Paradise.* Translated by Henry Francis Cary. New York: A. L. Burt, 1890.

DeShong, Paige, and Gilberto Lucero, eds. *Tierra Cruzada: Collaborative Exhibit of Poetry and Photography.* Las Cruces, N.M.: Blue Guitar Press, 1998.

De Tolnay, Charles. *Hieronymus Bosch.* New York: Reynal & Co., 1966.

Dewey, John. *Art as Experience.* New York: Perigee Books, 1980.

Dickinson, Emily. *Final Harvest: Emily Dickinson's Poems.* Edited by Thomas H. Johnson. Boston: Little, Brown, 1961.

Dixon, Laurinda S. *Alchemical Imagery in Bosch's Garden of Delights.* Ann Arbor, Mich.: UMI Research Press. 1981.

Domínguez Barbera, Martín. *Las Fallas.* Valencia: Ajuntament de Valencia, 1982.

Douglas, Mary. *Natural Symbols: Explorations in Cosmology.* New York: Pantheon Books, 1982.

Eco, Umberto. *Art and Beauty in the Middle Ages.* New Haven: Yale University Press, 1986.

———. *Travels in Hyper-reality: Essays by Umberto Eco.* Translated by William Weaver. New York: Harcourt Brace Jovanovich, 1973.

Evans, John Henry. *Joseph Smith: An American Prophet.* Salt Lake City: Deseret Book Co., 1989. Reprint edition. New York: MacMillan Co., 1933.

Fabricius, Johannes. *Alchemy: The Medieval Alchemists and Their Royal Art.* London: Diamond Books, 1994.

Ferguson, George. *Signs and Symbols of Christian Art.* London: Oxford University Press, 1954.

Fisher, Sally. *The Square Halo and Other Mysteries of Western Art: Images and the Stories That Inspired Them.* New York: Harry N. Abrams, 1995.

Flegg, Jim. *Field Guide to the Birds of Britain and Europe.* Ithaca, N.Y.: Cornell University Press, 1990.

Fontana, Bernard L. *Entrada: The Legacy of Spain and Mexico in the United States.* Tucson, Ariz.: Southwest Parks and Monuments Association, 1994.

Foucault, Michel. *Religion and Culture.* Edited by Jeremy R. Carrette. New York: Routledge, 1999.

Fowles, John. *The Collector.* Reprint edition. Boston: Little, Brown, 1997.

Fox, Matthew. *Creation Spirituality.* San Francisco: HarperCollins, 1991.

Fraenger, Wilhelm. *Hieronymus Bosch.* Amsterdam: G & B Publishing Group, 1994.

———. *The Millennium of Hieronymus Bosch: Outlines of a New Interpretation.* New York: Hacker Art Books, 1976.

Frère, Jean-Claude. *Early Flemish Paintings.* Paris: Terrail, 1997.

Fuentes, Carlos. *The Buried Mirror: Reflections of Spain and the New World.* Boston: Houghton Mifflin Co., 1992.

———. *Terra Nostra.* New York: New York Press, 1976.

Gablik, Suzi. *The Reenchantment of Art.* New York: Thames & Hudson, 1991.

Galeano, Eduardo. *The Book of Embraces.* New York: W. W. Norton & Co., 1989.

García Guinea, Miguel Ángel. *Altamira and Other Cantabrian Caves.* Madrid: Silex Ediciones, 1979.

García Lorca, Federico. *Barbarous Nights: Legends and Plays for the Little Theater.* Translated by Christopher Sawyer-Laucanno. San Francisco: City Lights Books, 1991.

———. *Bilingual Poems.* Edited by Christopher Maurer. New York: Farrar, Straus & Giroux, 1989.

———. *Deep Song and Other Prose.* Translated by Christopher Maurer. New York: New Directions, 1975.

———. *Gypsy Ballads and Songs.* Translated by David K. Loughton. Hanover, N.H.: Ediciones del Norte, 1994.

———. *Poet in New York.* Translated by Greg Simon and Steven F. White. London: Penguin Books, 1990.

———. *Three Plays.* Translated by Michael Dewell and Caren Zapata. London: Penguin Books, 1992.

Ghiselin, Brewster, ed. *The Creative Process: A Revealing Study of Genius at Work.* Berkeley, Calif.: Mentor Books, 1955.

———. *Flame.* Salt Lake City: University of Utah Press, 1991.

Gibson, Walter. *Hieronymus Bosch.* London: Thames & Hudson, 1973.

———. *Hieronymus Bosch: An Annotated Bibliography.* Boston: G. K. Hall, 1983.

Girard, René. *Violence and the Sacred*. Translated by Patrick Gregory. Baltimore: Johns Hopkins University Press, 1972.

Gombrich, E. H. *Art and Illusion*. Princeton: Princeton University Press, 1960.

Gonzales-Crussi, F. *On the Nature of Things Erotic*. New York: Harcourt Brace Jovanovich, 1988.

Grunsfeld, Fredric V. *Wild Spain: The Sierra Club Natural Traveller*. San Francisco: Sierra Club Books, 1994.

Guilland, Jacqueline and Maurice. *Hieronymus Bosch: The Garden of Earthly Delights*. New York: Clarkson N. Potter, 1989.

Gunton, Colin. *The One, the Three, and the Many*. New York: Cambridge University Press, 1993.

Hand, J. O., and M. Wolff. *Early Netherlandish Painting*. Cambridge: Cambridge University Press. 1986.

Harris, Lynda. *The Secret Heresy of Hieronymus Bosch*. Edinburgh: Floris Books, 1995.

H.D. *Notes on Thoughts and Vision*. San Francisco: City Lights Books, 1982.

Hemingway, Ernest. *Death in the Afternoon*. New York: Charles Scribner's Sons, 1932.

———. *The Garden of Eden*. New York: Charles Scribner's Sons. 1986.

———. *The Short Stories*. New York: Charles Scribner's Sons. 1995.

———. *The Sun Also Rises*. New York: Charles Scribner's Sons, 1926.

Herrmann, Claudine. *The Tongue Snatchers*. Lincoln: University of Nebraska Press, 1989.

Hess, Thomas, ed. *The Grand Eccentrics*. Art News Annual 32. New York: Macmillan Co., 1966.

Hickey, Dave. *The Invisible Dragon: Four Essays on Beauty*. Los Angeles: Art Issues Press, 1993.

Highet, Gilbert. "The Mad World of Hieronymus Bosch." *American Heritage* 12, no. 2 (Spring 1970): 66–80.

Hillman, James. *Insearch: Psychology and Religion*. Woodstock, Conn.: Spring Publications, 1994.

———. *The Thought of the Heart and the Soul of the World*. Dallas, Texas: Spring Publications, 1994.

Hinckley, Gordon B. *Teachings of Gordon B. Hinckley*. Salt Lake City: Deseret Book Co., 1997.

Hirst, Damien. *I Want to Spend the Rest of My Life Everywhere, with Everyone, One to One, Always, Forever, Now*. London: Booth-Clibborn Editions, 1997.

hooks, bell. *Art on My Mind: Visual Politics.* New York: New Press, 1995.

Hughes, Robert. *Barcelona.* New York: Vintage Books, 1992.

Huizinga, Johan. *Homo Ludens: A Study of the Play Element in Culture.* Boston: Beacon Press, 1950.

——. *The Waning of the Middle Ages.* New York: St. Martin's Press, 1949.

Hunt, Lynn, ed. *Eroticism and the Body Politic.* Baltimore: Johns Hopkins University Press, 1991.

Hyde, Lewis. *Trickster Makes This World: Mischief, Myth, and Art.* New York: Farrar, Straus & Giroux, 1998.

Hymns: The Church of Jesus Christ of Latter-day Saints. Salt Lake City: Deseret Book Co., 1948.

Irigaray, Luce. *Elemental Passions.* Translated by Joanna Collie and Judith Still. New York: Routledge, 1982.

Jacobi, Jolande. *Complex/Archetype/Symbol in the Psychology of C. G. Jung.* Princeton: Princeton University Press, 1959.

Jacobsen, Daniel. "Martha Clarke's Imaginary Garden." *Ballet Review* 12, no. 4 (Winter 1985): 9–14.

Joyce, James. *A Portrait of the Artist as a Young Man.* New York: Penguin, 1993.

——. *Ulysses.* New York: Vintage, 1990.

Juan de la Cruz, San. *The Poems of Saint John of the Cross.* Translated by Willis Barnstone. New York: New Directions, 1968.

——. *The Poems of Saint John of the Cross.* Translated by John Frederick Nims. Chicago: University of Chicago Press, 1959.

Jung, Carl Gustav. *Collected Works.* Edited by Sir Herbert Read, Michael Fordham, and Gerhard Adler. Translated by R. F. C. Hull. Bollingen Series no. 20. New York: Bollingen Foundation (distributed by Pantheon Books), 1953–.

   Civilization in Transition: Including "Flying Saucers" and "The Undiscovered Self." Volume 10. 1964.

   Psychology and Religion: East and West. Volume 11. 1958.

   Psychology and Alchemy. Volume 12. 1953.

   Alchemical Studies. Volume 13. 1967.

   Mysterium Conjunctionis. Volume 10. 1963.

   The Spirit in Man, Art, and Literature. Volume 15. 1966.

——. *Psychology and Religion.* New Haven: Yale University Press, 1938.

Kamen, Henry. *Philip of Spain.* New Haven: Yale University Press, 1997.

——. *The Spanish Inquisition: A Historical Revision.* New Haven: Yale University Press, 1997.

Kandinsky, Wassily. *Concerning the Spiritual in Art.* Translated by M. T. H. Sadler. New York: Dover Publications, 1977.

Kaplan, Janet A. *Unexpected Journeys: The Art and Life of Remedios Varo.* New York: Abbeville Press, 1988.

Kripke, Saul A. *Wittgenstein on Rules and Private Language: An Elemental Exposition.* Cambridge: Harvard University Press, 1982.

Krishnamurti, J. *Commentaries on Living.* Edited by D. Rajagopal. New York: Harper & Brothers, 1960.

———. *You Are The World.* New York: Harper & Row, 1972.

Kristeva, Julia. *Nations Without Nationalism.* New York: Columbia University Press, 1993.

Kundera, Milan. *The Art of the Novel.* Translated by Linda Asher. New York: HarperCollins, 1989.

Larsen, Erik. *Bosch: The Complete Paintings by the Visionary Master.* New York: Smithmark, 1998.

Lee, Laurie. *A Moment of War: A Memoir of the Spanish Civil War.* New York: New Press, 1991.

Lefald, Robert Allan. *Hemingway's Search for the Sacred: A Study of the Rituals of a Twentieth-Century Adam.* Minneapolis: University of Minnesota Press, 1976.

Leopold, Aldo. *A Sand County Almanac.* New York: Oxford University Press, 1949.

Linfert, Carl, ed. *Hieronymus Bosch.* Translated by Robert Erich Wolf. New York: Harry N. Abrams, 1989.

———. *Hieronymus Bosch: The Paintings.* New York: Phaidon, 1959.

Lippard, Lucy R. *The Lure of the Local: Senses of Place in a Multicentered Society.* New York: New Press, 1997.

———. *Overlay: Contemporary Art and the Art of Prehistory.* New York: Pantheon Books, 1983.

Lispector, Clarice. *An Apprenticeship; or, The Book of Delights.* Translated by Richard A. Mazzarra and Lorri A. Parris. Austin: University of Texas Press, 1969.

———. *The Hour of the Star.* New York: New Directions, 1977.

———. *Selected Crónicas.* Translated by Giovanni Pontiero. New York: New Directions, 1992.

Luaces, Joaquín Yarza. *El jardín de las delicias.* Madrid: TF Editores, 1998.

Luther, Martin. *Martin Luther: Selections from His Writings.* Edited by John Dillenberger. Garden City, N.Y.: Anchor Books, 1961.

MacHarg, John Brainerd. *Visual Representatives of the Trinity.* Cooperstown, N.Y.: Arthur Crist Publishing, 1917.

Madsen, Thomas G. *Eternal Man*. Salt Lake City: Deseret Book Co., 1966.

Manchester, William. *A World Lit Only by Fire: The Medieval Mind on the Renaissance Portrait of an Age*. Boston: Little, Brown, 1993.

Margulis, Lynn, and Dorian Sagan. *Mystery Dance: On the Evolution of Human Sexuality*. New York: Summit Books, 1991.

Marijnissen, Roger H. *Hieronymus Bosch: The Complete Works*. Antwerp: 1987.

Maritain, Jacques. *Creative Intuition in Art and Poetry*. New York: Pantheon Books, 1952.

Martin, Gregory. *Hieronymus Bosch*. New York: St. Martin's Press, 1979.

Maso, Carole. *Ava*. Normal, Ill.: Dalkey Archive Press, 1993.

McConkie, Bruce R. *Mormon Doctrine*. Salt Lake City: Bookcraft, 1966.

Medwick, Cathleen. *Teresa of Avila: The Progress of a Soul*. New York: Alfred A. Knopf, 1999.

Merwin, W. S. *From the Spanish Morning: Translations of Spanish Ballads, Eufemia by Lope de Rueda and Lazarillo de Tormes*. New York: Atheneum, 1985.

Miller, Henry. *Big Sur and the Oranges of Hieronymus Bosch*. New York: New Directions, 1957.

Mitchell, Stephen. *Genesis: A New Translation of the Classical Biblical Stories*. New York: HarperCollins, 1996.

Nabokov, Vladimir. *Nabokov's Butterflies—Unpublished and Uncollected Writings*. Edited by Brian Boyd and Robert Michael Pyle. Boston: Beacon Press, 2000.

Nelson, Robert S., and Richard Shiff, eds. *Critical Terms for Art History*. Chicago: University of Chicago Press, 1996.

Neruda, Pablo. *Spain in the Heart: Hymns to the Glories of the People*. Translated by Richard Schaaf. Washington, D.C.: Azul Editions, 1937.

Netanyahu, B. *The Origins of the Inquisition in Fifteenth-Century Spain*. New York: Random House, 1995.

Neumann, Erich. *Art and the Creative Unconscious*. New York: Harper Torchbooks, 1959.

Nooteboom, Cees. *Roads to Santiago*. Translated by Ina Rilke. New York: Harcourt Brace & Co., 1992.

Odent, Michael. *Water and Sexuality*. London: Arkana Publishing, 1990.

Orwell, George. *Homage to Catalonia*. London: Penguin Books, 1989.

Ortega y Gasset, José. *Invertebrate Spain*. Translated by Mildred Adams. New York: Howard Fertig, 1937.

———. *Revolt of the Masses*. New York: W. W. Norton & Co., 1930.

Pagels, Elaine. *The Origin of Satan*. New York: Vintage Books, 1995.

Papasogli, Giorgio. *Santa Teresa de Avila*. Boston: St. Paul Books and Media, 1990.

Paracelsus. *Paracelsus: Selected Writings*. Edited by Jolande Jacobi. Princeton: Princeton University Press, 1959.

Parker, Geoffrey. *The Grand Strategy of Philip II*. New Haven: Yale University Press, 1998.

———. *Philip II*. Chicago: Open Court, 1995.

Patchen, Kenneth. *Doubleheader: Hurrah for Anything and Poemscapes*. New York: New Directions, 1957.

Paz, Octavio. *Conjunctions and Disjunctions*. New York: Arcade Publishing, 1991.

———. *Convergences: Essays on Art and Literature*. Translated by Helen Lane. New York: Harcourt, Brace & Co., 1987.

———. *The Double Flame: Love and Eroticism*. Translated by Helen Lane. New York: Harcourt Brace & Co., 1995.

———. *An Erotic Beyond: Sade*. New York: Translated by Eliot Weinberger. New York: Harcourt, Brace & Co., 1998.

———. *One Word to the Other*. Fort Worth, Texas: Latitudes Press. 1992.

———. *The Other Voice: Essays on Modern Poetry*. Translated by Helen Lane. New York: Harcourt Brace Jovanovich, 1992.

———. *Sor Juana; or, The Traps of Faith*. Translated by Margaret S. Peden. New York: Cambridge: Harvard University Press, 1988.

Peaslee, Richard. *The Garden of Earthly Delights*. Ocean, N. J.: Musical Heritage Society, 1987.

Pinnock, Hugh W. *Finding Biblical Hebrew and Other Ancient Literary Forms in the Book of Mormon*. Provo, Utah: Foundation for Ancient Research and Mormon Studies, 1999.

Pinsky, Robert. *An Explanation of America*. Princeton: Princeton University Press, 1979.

poe(li)tical object: Experimental Poetry in Spain. Madrid: Calcografía Nacional, 1989.

Poniatowsky, Elena. *Dear Diego*. Translated by Katherine Silver. New York: Pantheon Books, 1986.

Quinn, D. Michael. *Early Mormonism and the Magic World View*. Salt Lake City: Signature Books, 1987.

———. *The Mormon Hierarchy: Origins of Power*. Salt Lake City: Signature Books, 1994.

Razzell, Arthur G. *Three and the Shape of Three*. Garden City, N.Y.: Doubleday & Co., 1964.

Reid, Alastair. *An Alastair Reid Reader: Selected Prose and Poetry*. Hanover, N.H.: University Press of New England, 1995.

Rexroth, Kenneth, ed. and trans. *Thirty Spanish Poems of Love and Exile*. The Pocket Poets Series, no. 2. San Francisco: City Lights Books, 1955.

Reynolds, Michael. *Hemingway: The 1930's*. New York: W. W. Norton & Co., 1997.

Robinson, Marilynne. *The Death of Adam*. Boston: Houghton Mifflin Co., 1998.

Roob, Alexander. *Alchemy and Mysticism*. Cologne: Taschen, 1997.

Rosenberg, David. *The Lost Book of Paradise: Adam and Eve in the Garden of Eden*. New York: Hyperion, 1993.

———. *A Poet's Bible: Rediscovering the Voices of the Original Text*. New York: Hyperion, 1991.

Sánchez-Canton, F. J. *The Prado*. London: Thames & Hudson, 1959.

Saraydarian, Torkom. *The Triangles of Fire*. Agoura, Calif.: Aquarian Educational Group, 1977.

Sargent, Walter. *The Enjoyment and Use of Color*. New York: Dover Publications, 1964.

Schama, Simon. *The Embarrassment of Riches: An Interpretation of Dutch Culture in the Golden Age*. New York: Vintage Books, 1997.

———. *Landscape and Memory*. New York: Alfred A. Knopf, 1995.

Schwartz, Gary. *Hieronymus Bosch*. New York: Harry N. Abrams, 1997.

Shapiro, Gary. *Earthwards: Robert Smithson and Art after Babel*. Berkeley: University of California Press, 1995.

Singer, June. *Androgyny: Toward a New Sexuality*. Garden City, N.Y.: Anchor Press/Doubleday. 1976.

Slade, Carole. *Saint Teresa of Avila: Author of a Heroic Life*. Berkeley: University of California Press, 1995.

Smith, Joseph Fielding. *Teachings of the Prophet Joseph Smith*. Salt Lake City: Deseret Book Co., 1977.

Smith, Paul, and Susan F. Beegel. *New Essays on Hemingway's Short Fiction*. Cambridge: Cambridge University Press, 1998.

Smucker, Samuel M. *The Religious, Social and Political History of the Mormons or Latter-day Saints from Their Origins to the Present Time*. New York: Miller Orton & Co., 1857.

Snyder, James. *Hieronymus Bosch: The Man and His Paintings*. New York: Excalibur Books, 1977.

———, ed. *Bosch in Perspective*. Englewood Cliffs, N.J.: Prentice-Hall, 1973.

Spychalska-Boczkowska, Anna. *Hieronnim Bosch: Astrologiczna Symbolika Jego Dziel*. Wroclaw: Zaklad Narodowy im. Ossolianskich, 1977.

———. *Tryumf Luny i Wenus: Pasya Hieronyma Bosch*. Krakow: Wydawn, 1980.

Stein, Gertrude. *Bee Time Vine and Other Pieces: 1913–1927.* New Haven: Yale University Press, 1953.

Steiner, Wendy. *The Scandal of Pleasure: Art in the Age of Fundamentalism.* Chicago: University of Chicago Press, 1995.

Steyn, Juliet, and John Gange, eds. *Act 2: Beautiful Translations.* London: Pluto Press, 1996.

Stockton, Kathryn Bond. *God Between their Lips: Desire Between Women in Irigaray, Brontë, and Eliot.* Stanford, Calif.: Stanford University Press, 1994.

Strand, T. A. *Tri-ism: The Theory of the Trinity in Nature, Man, and His Works.* New York: Exposition Press, 1958.

Taki, Mariko Umeoka. *Encuentro con El Bosco.* Madrid: Círculo de Belles Artistes, 1997.

Talmage, James E. *A Study of the Articles of Faith.* Salt Lake City: Church of Jesus Christ of Latter-Day Saints, 1925.

————. *The Essential James E. Talmage.* Edited by James P. Harris. Salt Lake City: Signature Books, 1997.

Teresa de Ávila, Santa. *Saint Teresa of Ávila: Collected Works.* Vols. 1 and 3. Translated by Kieran Kavanaugh and Otilio Rodríguez. Washington, D.C.: ICS Publications, 1976, 1985.

————. *The Complete Poetry of Saint Teresa of Ávila: A Bilingual Edition.* Edited by Eric W. Vogt. New Orleans: University Press of the South, 1996.

————. *The Interior Castle.* Translated by E. Allison Peers. New York: Image Books, 1961.

————. *The Interior Castle.* Translated by John Venard. Sydney: E. J. Dwyer, 1985.

————. *The Life of Saint Teresa of Ávila by Herself.* Translated by J. M. Cohen. London;: Penguin Books, 1957.

————. *Teresa of Ávila: Mystical Writings.* Edited by Tessa Bielecki. New York: Crossroads, 1994.

Toscano, Paul James. *The Sanctity of Dissent.* Salt Lake City: Signature Books, 1994.

Tuttle, Virginia. *Lilith in Bosch's Garden of Earthly Delights.* Simolins. 1985.

Van Doornik, N. G. M. *The Triptych of the Kingdom.* Westminster, Md.: Newman Press, 1954.

Ventura, Michael. *Shadow Dancing in the USA.* Los Angeles: Jeremy P. Tarcher, 1985.

Von Franz, Marie-Louise. *Alchemy: An Introduction to the Symbolism and the Psychology.* Toronto: Inner City Books, 1980.

————. *Creation Myths.* New York: Spring Publications, 1975.

————. *On Divination and Synchronicity: The Psychology of Meaningful Chance.* Toronto: Inner City Books, 1980.

————, ed. *Aurora Consurgens: A Document Attributed to Thomas Aquinas on the Problems of Opposites in Alchemy.* Translated by R. F. Hull and A. S. Glover. Princeton: Princeton University Press, 1966.

Von Goethe, Johann Wolfgang. *Theory of Colors.* Translated by Charles Lock Eastlake. London: John Murray, 1840. Reprint. Cambridge, Mass.: MIT Press, 1970.

Warner, Marina. *The Inner Eye: Art Beyond the Visible.* Manchester: Cornerhouse Publications, 1996.

Weil, Simone. *Waiting for God.* New York: Harper & Row, 1951.

Weiss, John, ed. *Venus, Jupiter and Mars: The Photographs of Frederick Sommer.* Wilmington: Delaware Art Museum, 1980.

Welch, John. *Spiritual Pilgrims: Carl Jung and Teresa of Avila.* New York: Paulist Press, 1982.

Willard, Nancy. *Pish, Posh, Said Hieronymus Bosch.* San Diego: Harcourt Brace Jovanovich, 1991.

Winterson, Jeanette. *Art Objects: Essays on Ecstasy and Effrontery.* New York: Alfred A. Knopf, 1996.

Wittig, Monique. *Les Guerillères.* Translated by David Le Vay. Boston: Beacon Press, 1969.

Wood, Wilford C. *Joseph Smith Begins His Work.* Vol. 2. U.S.A.: Author Books, 1962.

Woodman, Marion. *Conscious Femininity: Interviews with Marion Woodman.* Studies in Jungian Psychology by Jungian Analysts, no. 58. Toronto: Inner City Books, 1993.

Woolf, Virginia. *The Waves.* New York: Harcourt, Brace & World, 1931.

A C K N O W L E D G M E N T S

Over the course of seven years in exploring the landscape of Hieronymus Bosch, there have been many individuals who have contributed to my
understanding and who have offered their support.

The Spanish writer Camilo José Cela believes "the traveler reflects on
love." Consider these acknowledgments exactly that.

Dan Frank, my editor, is an alchemist. Every sentence has moved
through his imagination as well as mine. He saw the core of this book and
waited patiently while I took my own circuitous route. I am blessed by his
care and collaboration, this man who so elegantly favors indirection.

Carl Brandt, my agent, made a trip to Salt Lake City, knocked on
my door, and made me articulate what I was afraid to say, that this book
was about faith. While I wavered, he did not. I cherish the depth of our
friendship.

Dan Tempest, my brother, has been a deep source of inspiration and my
guide through various disciplines of philosophy. Our conversations, dark
and light, have been a golden strand that I have followed through this maze.

Lyn Dalebout has been the midwife to these words. Her wisdom, compassion, courage, and friendship have been my fountain of water in the
desert.

Charles Wilkinson drew me a larger map of the American West and then
wrote the word "temperance" in the center and circled it in red. That map
accompanied me in Spain.

Barry Lopez has traveled the distance with me and for that I am grateful,
and for his love and friendship.

Linda Asher, Laurie Graham, Florence Krall Shepard, and Lynne Tempest all read the manuscript in various incarnations. Their tough, insightful,
candid edits always inspired me to go farther and deeper. Sisters.

Callie Romney Tempest provided tremendous assistance in developing
the bibliography. Time together is my great pleasure.

331

Roberto Díaz was translator *extraordinaire*. His sensitivity to the nuance of words and the Spanish language has been a gift.

Altie Karper, Jennifer Weh, Sid Albert, Ron Smith, Sophie Cottrell, Suzanne Williams, Claudine O'Hearn, Nancy Gilbert, Archie Ferguson, and especially Jeanne Morton, all at Pantheon Books, have provided enormous support in the production of this book. I value each of their strengths, alongside the good works of Marianne Merola at Brandt & Brandt Literary Agency.

Art Winslow of *The Nation* provided editorial savvy on the essay about Damien Hirst. David Applebaum of *Parabola* provided care on the essay about my grandfather and his radio.

Katharine Metcalf Nelson has been my mentor through art history, showing me the consilience which exists between painting and landscape.

Professor Sheila Muller at the University of Utah let me audit her class "Northern Renaissance Art: Bosch and Bruegel." It was the beginning of my journey.

I have had many traveling companions: Anne and John Milliken, Chris Noble, Sandra Lopez, Doug Peacock, Deb Clow, Jack Turner, Laura Simms, Dave Nimkin, Jan Sloan, Mary O'Brien, Antonio Bolle, Jeff Foott, Martha Young Moench, Dru Brewer, Glen Lathrop, Kim Barton, Mark Strand, Betsy Burton, Sydney Bullen, Annie Bloom, Trent Alvey, Dennis Sizemore, Rick Bass, Judith Freeman, Antonio Hernandez, Denise Chavez, Leslie Ryan, Bill Anderson, Sarah Rushforth, Julie Mack, Mike Matz, Scott Groene, Cindy Shogan, Tom Price, Amy Irvine, Bert Fingerhut, Annick Smith, Bill Kittredge, Mary Frank, Leo Treitler, Aaron Asher, John Elder, Scott Slovic, Steve Tatum, Meg Brady, John Tallmadge, John Dipompio, Cort Conley, Keats Conley, Dave, Rainie, and Blair Fross, Bonnie Kreps, Nancy Shea, Charlie Craighead, Renée Askins, Tom Rush, Mickey Houlihan, Rachel Bagby, Rita Dove, Fred Viebahn, Satish Kumar, Jordi Pigem, John Goldthorpe, Barrie Staniford, Hayden Mathews, Michael Collier, Ed Hirsch, Mark Cox, Michael White, Phoebe Milliken, Susan Mary Alsop, Arthur Patten, Bill McKibben, Sue Halpern, Ross Gelbspan, Vijaya Najarajan, Lee Swenson, Carl Anthony, John deGraff, Kathleen Hart, Chris Merrill, W. S. Merwin, Mark Doty, and Peter Matthiessen. All of them have contributed to the evolution of this book.

Ken Brecher and Rebecca Rickman contributed to my understanding of art and the creative process. Their imaginations have been beacons, showing me what is possible.

Carole Maso inspired me to be a student again. Her conceptual guidance in the early stages of the manuscript was inspiriting.

Acknowledgments

Bob Pyle tipped me off to Vladimir Nabokov's obsession with butterflies depicted in art, directing me to *Nabokov's Butterflies—Unpublished and Uncollected Writings,* which he edited with Brian Boyd, in helping me identify various species inside the triptych.

Bob Hass, Dick Shelton, and Jorie Graham gave me their gifts of faith and generosity.

Without the help of the Lannan Foundation, Patrick Lannan and Jeannie Kim; the John Simon Guggenheim Memorial Foundation, Joel Conarroe; and the Hemingway Foundation, the wit and wisdom of Susan Beegel and the enduring help and insight of Stephen Plotkin at the John F. Kennedy Library where the Hemingway Collection is stored; I would not have been able to follow my passion to Spain. They have my heartfelt gratitude for their belief in these ideas. I also want to acknowledge the inspiration and support of the Orion Society, who continue to honor the correspondence between language and landscape. Marion Gilliam, Laurie Lane-Zucker, and Chip Blake are family.

The Sundance Institute, the Playwright Lab in particular, changed my approach to writing. Through the brilliance of Robert Blacker as a dramaturge, I heard a different voice. Philip Himberg, Beth Nathanson, Craig Lucas, Moises Kaufman, Molly Smith, Dael Orlandersmith, Lisa Peterson, and especially Elizabeth Marvel became mentors. I owe a debt of gratitude to all who participated in the lab in the summer of 1999.

And I want to acknowledge the vision and creative intelligence of Robert Redford. The risks he takes artistically as well as politically benefit all of us.

The scholarship of D. Michael Quinn, Paul Toscano, William Mulder, John L. Brooke, John Henry Evans, Gary James Bergera, and Harold Bloom regarding Mormon theology has been enormously helpful and full of insights. I am in their debt.

The Association of Mormon Arts and Letters has been a force for good. I want to thank them for the risks they take in their discussion of literature and theology at once.

Also, Bill Smart, Eugene England, Clayton White, Nancy and Sam Rushforth, Maxine Hanks, Lavina Fielding Anderson, Ellen Fagg, Emma Lou Thayne, Marilyn Arnold, and Elder Hugh W. Pinnock have provided depth and understanding to my sense of Mormonism. Paul Gorman, Susan Armer, and the Right Reverend Carolyn Tanner Irish provided me with spiritual support.

Betty and Homero Aridjis, through their extraordinary creation of El Grupo de Cien, have mobilized a global community of artists, philosophers, scientists, and ethicists to consider how we might behave with compassion toward the Earth. For their fire, I thank them.

Susan Griffin gave me a nudge toward the truth on a drive from Berkeley to San Francisco. Her mind and heart are formidable.

The Mesa Refuge, through the generosity of Peter Barnes and Ann Dowley, provided me with shelter: David and Lorna Petersen in Jackson Hole, Wyoming; Rex Williams in St. George, Utah; and Anne and John Milliken on Little Tree Road. As neighbors, Anne and John have created a sense of kinship that has become a sustaining grace where honesty dwells.

Natalie Taylor provided a continual circle of warmth in Salt Lake City.

In Spain, the doors opened when Fran Dillon and I had a late-night dinner at Castellana 8 in Madrid. It was hot and the cicadas were singing. She shared her community with me and made Spain feel like an artistic sanctuary. I appreciate her radiance and savvy, along with her husband, Don Dillon.

Gillian Watling Ceballos and her daughter, Leonor Watling Ceballos, became my dearest friends and sisters. My time in their home was my true Spanish education. For their love and joy, I wish them fields of poppies in the countryside. It is through their eyes I came to see what *duende* might mean. *Brazos alrededor de ti.*

Marte Casares Bidasoro taught me about the political and artistic power of what it means to be Basque. Her strength of character and friendship allowed me to see Spanish culture from another point of view that widened my reach.

Mariko Umeoka Taki altered how I looked at El Bosco. Her courage and persistence in following the path of originality through discipline were most inspiring. I appreciate all she shared with me and the personal nature of her quest. Her friendship has become a compass point for me.

Barbara Woods, Cassandra Constant, and Mil Lubroth, members of the artistic community in Madrid, shared their astute perceptions with me.

Ricardo Berriobena López introduced me to his art and took me on a walk through Madrid where walls disappeared and interior Spain was exposed.

Señora Elena Diz Cabos, my language teacher at Eurocentres, was remarkably good-humored and patient as I struggled.

Señora Pacquita Canada and her entire family—her husband, Antonio, their son and daughter-in-law, Antonio and Pepa, their sons, Alejandro, and Juani and Alberto, all were most gracious in allowing me to live with them while I was attending language school. I fell in love with the Barrio de San Isidro because of them.

Ricardo Roucero Díaz, a friend from the Hotel Reyes Católicos, shared the streets of Madrid with Brooke and me when we first arrived. He would not allow us to be timid.

At the Museo del Prado, my largest debt of gratitude goes to Theresa Dávila Álvarez and Rocío Dávila Álvarez, for their openness in sharing the restoration of *El jardín de las delicias* with me. They exposed me to both the professional rigor and the emotional commitment that must exist between the conservator and the work of art. In their studio, I touched the sacred.

Rocío Arnaez, a curator in the Biblioteca del Prado, was my angel. Her compassion and care provided me with access to all the records and written material surrounding *El jardín de las delicias*. Without her, I would still be sitting in front of the painting wondering what I was seeing.

Juan Manuel Maquieria Davesa, *guía patrimonio nacional,* brought the elegance and complexity of Spanish art to my father and me and our friends. I thank him for the enthusiasm and knowledge he shares with the public.

Sofía Rodríquez Bernís and Fernando Chica were powerful examples of the kind of leadership that exists within the Museo del Prado.

And perhaps most importantly, I want to acknowledge the first guide I met in the Prado, who became a very dear friend: Faustino Calvo, a Spanish gentleman in his seventies. Winter, 1993. It was he who said before El Bosco, "I am drunk with colors, *señora*." He then rolled up his newspaper and invited me to look through his "magic lens." Through the circular frame, he taught me how to isolate images, removing distractions to see more fully what was there. "Focus. Isolate. Feel. Don't be afraid to transfer your soul to art."

On another day, Tino walked me through the Prado until we found ourselves in the gallery where El Greco's paintings hung. He said simply, "Genius is breaking all the rules."

He sent me to Toledo in search of silence.

He read me his poetry out loud.

He dared me to follow my obsession with Bosch.

And the last time I saw him, he said, as we were discussing Goya, "Passion. Passion. Passion. I hope you know this at your age. If you do not, then give up your studies and live."

To our new community in Grand County, I offer my special thanks to Eleanor and Bill Hedden and their beautiful daughters, Chloe and Sarah; Ed Derderian and Annie Goodenough; Alice and Ken Drogin and their daughter, Nicole; Laura Kamala; Chris Coffey; Adele Alsop; Dave Erley; Bernice Nootenbaum; the family of Mynoa and Alan Williams, their daughters Sherlene and Amy; Richard and Jolene Williams; Catherine Howells and Mef Fisher, Miso; Susan Ulery; Mary and Russell Williams; our branch president, Ron Drake; Joanna Dalton; Hertha Wakefield; Tom Rees; Sandy and Mike Tortenelli; Kitty Calhoun; José Knighton; Diane Fouts; Vijali Hamilton; Catherine Shank; Jane and Ken Sleight; Andy Nettell; Jeanne Smith; Julie Fox; and Lisa Roman; also Michael Barrett and Leslie Tomkins.

Michaelene Pendleton has been my saving grace. Her intelligence and good humor, alongside her sound judgment, have been an anchor for me.

My family is the turquoise stone I carry with me.

My father, John Tempest, has been an extraordinary traveling companion and friend. In our differences, we find our pleasures in a world that keeps expanding. I appreciate his keen intellect and willingness to be exposed to new things. He has my enduring love and respect. I honor his growth. Growing up, it was his example of integrity and humility that let me know the difference between a spiritual life and a religious one.

Ann and Steve Tempest and their daughters, Callie, Sara, and Diane, are the nucleus of our family. In so many ways, my happiness revolves around them. Such complete joy. Their unconditional love and support create a grounding I would be lost without.

I appreciate Hank Tempest and his wife, Marlénè Lambert-Tempest, for the spiritual path they have shared with us. It has made an extraordinary difference.

Thalo Porter and Dan Tempest were married on October 1, 1999, creating an occasion for all of us to celebrate their love. A day of thanksgiving.

My uncle Richard Tempest has been a beloved example of a man who cherishes the Church of Jesus Christ of Latter-day Saints. My love for him and my aunt Ruth is a tender one. Also, my affection to Diane and Don Dixon. I cannot imagine growing up in a safer embrace of extended family. To all my cousins, *mi casa es tu casa.*

Rex Williams, Brooke's father, has been a tremendous source of strength and stability. A man of spirit who has spent his life in the service of the Church of Jesus Christ of Latter-day Saints, he has been kind enough to provide invaluable notations and scriptorial references for this book. His love and tolerance of Brooke's and my beliefs have been a testament of trust. His wife, Shirley, has also provided great care.

Becky and David Thomas and their children, Nate, Abby, and Libby, have provided refuge for us repeatedly. And it was Becky who exposed me to another Bosch, Harry Bosch, through the mysteries of Michael Connelly.

Acknowledgments

And this acknowledgment is the one that matters most: Brooke Williams. He allowed a third presence into our home, Hieronymus Bosch, as we set a place for him around our dinner table each night. For the days, weeks, months we shared in Spain together, none were as emblematic as the long nights in Cádiz during Carnival where we walked along the beach after taking off our masks, and gathered shells. Pilgrims. This life. Together.

Retornos del amor en los vívidos paisajes.

Now, home in the desert. I thank this land.

And to El Bosco . . . *gracias por las invisibles cosas del mundo. Verde viento.*